This Far and No More

This Far and No More

A TRUE STORY

Andrew H. Malcolm

Times BOOKS

Copyright © 1987 by Unlimited Words, Ltd.

All rights reserved under International and Pan-American
Copyright Conventions. Published in the United States by Times Books,
a division of Random House, Inc., New York, and simultaneously
in Canada by Random House of Canada Limited, Toronto.
Grateful acknowledgment to reprint excerpts from the poem
"East Coker" from *Four Quartets* by T. S. Eliot is made to Harcourt
Brace Jovanovich, Inc., and Faber and Faber Limited. Copyright 1936 by
Harcourt Brace Jovanovich, Inc.; copyright © 1963, 1964 by T. S. Eliot.
Rights outside of the United States administered by Faber and Faber Limited.
Reprinted by permission of the publishers.
Library of Congress Cataloging-in-Publication Data
Malcolm, Andrew H., 1943–
This far and no more.
1. Amyotrophic lateral sclerosis—Patients—United States—Biography.
2. Right to die.
3. Amyotrophic lateral sclerosis—Patients—Family relationships.
4. Amyotrophic lateral sclerosis—Patients—Socioeconomic status.
I. Title.
[DNLM: 1. Amyotrophic Lateral Sclerosis—popular works.
2. Attitude to Death—popular works.
3. Ethics, Medical—popular works.
4. Euthanasia—popular works. WE 550 M243t]
RC406.A24M32 1987   362.1'9683 [B]   86-23071
ISBN 0-8129-1606-9
Manufactured in the United States of America
9 8 7 6 5 4 3 2
First Edition
Book design: Elissa Ichiyasu

To Con, who's been there and now, thankfully, is here

Foreword

One morning in 1984 I was struck by a short news service item in *The New York Times* about an elderly man in Texas who had walked into his wife's hospital room for his daily visit. The woman was long suffering from the senile debilitations of advanced Alzheimer's disease and no longer recognized her spouse. The man shot his wife in the heart that morning and then turned the gun on himself. I thought what an awful twisted predicament to be in, to think that one's love could best be expressed by killing a spouse.

A few weeks later I telephoned that hospital to get some more details. I told the hospital spokesman that I wanted to know more about the man who had walked into their institution and killed his wife. And the spokesman replied, "Which one?"

That chilling moment, the sudden realization that this was not the isolated, freakish happening it seemed, launched me on a long period of research, reporting, and writing back and forth across the country in the ensuing months and years. It turned out that this phenomenon and other related predicaments actually were very common. In a lengthy series of articles in *The New York Times* we sought to explore the developing right-to-die issue and the new kinds of painful dilemmas that patients, their families, and doctors face every day and night.

Rapidly advancing medical technology applied by dedicated and highly skilled health professionals has saved many lives, given individuals priceless extra moments, days, weeks, even years of meaningful life. But, it seemed, there was another side to this tale. Now that doctors, nurses, and technicians could do more, they had to decide when not to. In the days past when little or nothing could be done for a dying patient, it may have been far from agreeable, but simply providing comfort presented no moral or ethical problem. It was all one could do. Today, it is, however, quite something else simply to provide comfort for a dying human when standing right next to that person's bed is a machine that can prolong that life.

Can a doctor, a nurse, a relative, an institution allow a life-threatening disease or condition to continue its natural course because they wouldn't be prolonging a life anymore, but prolonging a death? Should a man dying of painful bone cancer be kept going as long as medically and mechanically possible simply because the technology exists to do this? Should a patient be treated for pneumonia and respiratory failure now so that he can surely die of an underlying disease next year? When do the valiant efforts to preserve the life of a grossly premature infant with inadequate lungs become instead a grotesque and inconsiderate prolongation of suffering? How does society protect its values as well as the civil rights of patients to control their medical treatment when the exercise of those rights also affects the professional and personal ethics of many others? "It was," one elderly woman said, "so much easier when God made all the decisions."

All parties to these painful predicaments are being forced to make these decisions every hour of every day in this country, and many others around the world are beginning to face the same problem, too. In a society that has yet to reach a consensus on when life begins, perhaps one shouldn't be surprised by our lack of agreement in defining when life ends.

Yet family after family makes these choices without much of a legal or moral framework for guidance. It is the same for doctors, who may or may not have taken the elective course on ethics in medical school.

In our litigious society these doctors also face the frightening prospects of career-stopping lawsuits for any perceived misstep.

Americans don't like to talk about death, let alone consider or even plan for it. The proof lies in the lack of properly prepared wills, the euphemisms we use—she passed away; he's gone—and the fact that a majority of Americans used to die at home but now 80 percent of them die in institutions. We have systematically arranged society so that the living can be separated from death in as many ways as possible, through hospitals, nursing homes, hospices, and undertakers. Even our cemeteries are out of sight, on the edge of town. And so case after case, family after family sits in small hospital visiting rooms, isolated and convinced that they are the first ever to have to travel this route of painful decisions. And feeling just as convinced that they must never discuss this matter with anyone outside those walls.

As a naïve young man blissfully and blessedly ignorant of physical limitations, I had long assumed that everyone outside of a war zone would want every life preserved for as long as possible. For heaven's sake, why not? Then one day my father, who was not in good health to begin with, underwent a complicated operation to correct a life-threatening condition. It was an operation that, familiarly, helped begin a series of other painful complications. Months later, in his bedroom breathing oxygen from a bedside tank, he started to recount what it was like to have tubes down his throat, in his arms, up his nose, and in other orifices. He spoke of the strangers who worked on him, of their strange, intimidating language, and of the operating room, that place so alien, sterile, and strange for those who don't live in it at least eight hours a day. My father didn't finish his detailed description. It was somehow too painful, even many months afterward. He just summed it up: "If I had it to do all over again," he said, "I never would go through that."

I was shocked then. Five days after this conversation he died, peacefully in his bed, in his home, without a stranger in sight. Fortunately, no one found his body until it was obviously too late to restart his heart.

I found deeply fascinating these experiences and the myriad efforts by our rapidly aging society to fashion appropriate guidelines on death and dying, privately and publicly, through legislation, court decisions, public debate and education, professional literature, and especially quiet negotiation.

As Chicago bureau chief for the *Times*, I spent several months negotiating with friends, family lawyers, friends of friends, and some groups who could provide access to families who would discuss their decisions on a relative's death. Some of these families had fallen apart under the pressures and the oppressive guilt because they thought they, and not the underlying disease, had killed their loved one. Many still could not talk about it. Typically, a wife would, but a husband would not.

And then I found the Bauers. That is not their name. All personal names in this book have been changed or deleted, as have some dates and details, to protect the family's identity and privacy. This true story of an ordinary family and its financial and emotional destruction by disease and a well-meaning health care system is an extraordinary and revealing three-year saga of pain, courage, fear, and simple stamina. It is one of the most timely and compelling human stories I have encountered in more than two decades of professional reporting and writing.

The material for this book was gathered from Emily Bauer's unusual diary and through scores of interviews during countless hours over the course of more than a year with many family members, doctors, nurses, technicians, consultants, hospital administrators, attorneys, and numerous other authorities not connected to this case.

They all agreed to talk in the belief that broadened public debate on these issues was necessary and in the hope that many other families, patients, and health care professionals would learn through these experiences and insights how better to cope with the agonizing decisions that accompany marvelous advances.

I share that belief and, especially, that hope.

Andrew H. Malcolm
The Yaak, Montana
August 1986

Acknowledgments

I should like to thank many people for their thoughtful help, direct and indirect, on a project of this scale. Only some of them can be listed here. But they include Arthur Ochs Sulzberger, A. M. Rosenthal, Seymour Topping, Arthur Gelb, and David R. Jones, all of *The New York Times*, whose commitment to excellence and investments in news coverage of vital social subjects enabled me to do the original research on this subject and to first write about it in that newspaper. I should also like to thank Irv Horowitz and Rusty King for their determination and sensitivities in editing. Also Jon Segal and Julian Bach and my friend Sara Hennings.

The three major "right-to-die" groups generously provided much information, background, and guidance during my research. These include the Society for the Right to Die, in New York City, and the Hemlock Society, in Los Angeles. Of very special help on this project was Concern for Dying at 250 West 57th Street, New York, New York 10107, which provides the public with information on the subject of death and dying, and which provided me with unlimited access to their files and experience.

Acknowledgments

All the members of the Bauer family and their friends were exceptionally generous with their time and patience during the countless long hours of interviews and reinterviews as I sought to reconstruct this painful time in their lives. This group includes the doctors and nurses who also shared their continuing experiences with the treatment of terminally ill patients. Sadly, their names must remain confidential.

But I would like to thank publicly Dr. Jack Antel, Pat Heidekamp, Lissa Schwartz, and the other workers and many patients of the University of Chicago Motor-Neuron Disease Center. They had nothing to do with the Bauer case, but gave me invaluable insights into amyotrophic lateral sclerosis (ALS), its treatments, and the experience of this disease. The ALS Association, at 15300 Ventura Boulevard, Suite 315, Sherman Oaks, California 91403, also provided very helpful material to me, as it does to the public at large.

The teachings of some very important people in my life—Arthur G. Hughes, Ben Baldwin, and Fred Whiting, most specifically—have become so much an integral part of me that I can no longer identify the specific lessons. But their presence is there, and deeply appreciated.

My family—Connie, Christopher, Spencer, and Emily—has been very patient during my frequent work absences, whether out of town or in the basement. (Kids, the radios can now be turned back up.) My wife, Connie, has been both an inspiration and an editor, which can be an unusual combination. Her enthusiasm, interest, insight, knowledge of grammar, and unflagging personal and professional support and encouragement at both ordinary and crucial times have added more than words can say to this book and my life.

I would also like to express my appreciation for guidance, good times, a breadth of experience, and so much more to my mother, Beatrice, and my father, Ralph, who got his wish.

A.H.M.

This Far and No More

I t started with a stumble.

Without thinking, a happy Emily Bauer nimbly jumped from the taxi into the busy street and went to step up on the dirty curb. Her right foot caught on the raised cement, and she quickly pitched forward onto the wet pavement. It was really more embarrassing—Emily hated to look awkward—than it was damaging, since she dropped her packages all over, breaking the fall. For a moment, she paused there amid the passersby, checking for breakage elsewhere. She ran down a mental checklist of her body, the way pregnant women quickly learn to do after unexpected events, making sure that everything is still in place and operating or, more important, growing properly. And perhaps giving their increasingly large belly a soft pat.

Then she got up and went about her business on another busy day in the busy life of a modern urban working mother. Emily was a naturally active person, one of those people who always seems to be going somewhere or just returning, always doing, always on the move. Unless it was late evening, when she might be found sitting quietly on the sofa with her husband, a glass of white wine in her hand. Even then, her organized mind was still on the go, reviewing her dying day and dividing the next into energetic, productive segments.

Emily mentioned the fall to her husband, Bob, that evening while she set the table for dinner and he fed the baby. Had it been nearly two years already since Allison had popped into their lives? It was somewhat puzzling to Emily that her foot hadn't quite cleared the curb. She knew unconsciously how high it was; she'd walked by there hundreds of times on the way to and from her apartment-office. Emily couldn't think of herself as clumsy.

Emily and Bob decided after the briefest discussion that the fall was associated with the pregnancy, maybe a pinched nerve or something. It was probably one of those unexplained events that just seem to happen when the body gets bigger yet the mind still thinks it is controlling a more active, thinner self. Maybe the couple was just too aware. They were, after all, monitoring this pregnancy especially closely.

Emily was about to celebrate, or at least observe, her birthday, the Big Four-Oh. She had done her research thoroughly; she always did. She knew that for unknown reasons, which all those male doctors were taking their sweet time uncovering, complications are far more likely to develop in older pregnant women, especially older pregnant mothers, which Emily had become with Allison's birth.

Emily had a sense of urgency about this second pregnancy, as if time was running out. At her age it was, in at least one obvious way. Like many American women in the last two decades of the twentieth century, Emily had set aside traditional ideas of life's normal progression involving family, children, and then, perhaps, a part-time career. Instead, she fully focused the first fifteen years of adulthood on a graduate education and a busy career and city social life, figuring that family and children could come later; there was plenty of time for that kind of guaranteed happiness.

Her parents, sometimes to their own regret, gave Emily much of that independence, and her network of fiercely cultivated female friends reinforced one another's beliefs and helped squelch the fears. Emily wasn't about to give up any of that independence, except grudgingly in the smallest of pieces. When Emily Bauer went down in the confrontations she did not avoid, she went down swinging, whether it was at a faculty meeting or in the living room.

Approaching her mid-thirties after a brief marriage (with no children, of course) and a longer stretch in a circle of sophisticated singles, Emily had begun to sense that the biological clock was ticking. She and Bob had happened to meet then. Well, actually, on that sunny weekend afternoon in May when it all began in a police bicycle registration line, there was no chance to the encounter whatsoever. She had made damned sure she met that tall fellow with the gentle eyes and the soft beard. Later, she would recall knowing at that instant that this bear of a man would be the father of her children. She had let him see her looking at him that afternoon. Also a veteran of a broken marriage and the intricate protocols and routines of the urban singles scene, Bob had seen her looking at him. And she saw him seeing her looking at him. By the time the two wary strangers had inched to the front of the line, the guy hadn't made a move. Nothing. In a moment this handsome hunk was going to hop on his bike and ride into the sunset, not even leaving a phone number behind. Well, Emily wasn't going to let this one slip away. So the determined thirty-four-year-old woman decided to make the first move.

"Hi!" she said enthusiastically, looking up with that bright smile she knew had enchanted so many over the years.

"Hello," the forty-year-old man replied warmly with a smile partially hidden by his bushy beard. Later he would recall thinking it was a good thing this sexy, energetic woman with the incredible smile and bright eyes had initiated their meeting because he certainly never would have. There would come another sunny Saturday when Bob would bitterly resent Emily's dogged determination. And some lonely times in the dark when he wished their weekend bicycle paths had never crossed.

That first day, though, was carefree, as first encounters go, their individual lonelinesses melting for a time. Neither man nor woman did anything irretrievably stupid. They rode along together, side-by-side, for a couple of hours talking about bikes and the city and the museums that they both said fascinated them. Emily was glad she had worn shorts, and so too, looking sideways now and then, was Bob.

Emily had always been very proud of her body, and as a younger woman chose to wear her sweaters open one button lower than some thought appropriate for a minister's daughter, even in California. She also was especially conscious of her legs, which she oiled and stretched and exercised regularly. Emily had always taken her healthy legs for granted as mere extensions of her active mind, doing what she told them to do when she told them and taking her wherever curiosity and a busy schedule required. She knew those same limbs drew admiring looks from men at times. That was important to her.

Bob asked Emily back to his apartment for dinner that day, an invitation she quickly accepted without coyness. They talked long into the evening about movies, their tastes, and their careers (she was a psychologist, and he was a documentary filmmaker). Their conversations were so free back then, unencumbered by any awareness of the other's sensitivities, politics, or proclivities. Emily was eager for new ideas, although doing new things was more exciting. Bob had stimulating ideas, but he would have liked to be doing more. The film business, however, was a very tough one, just as his father had warned during their many arguments. Although Bob worked very hard, loved every minute, and didn't feel the need to be rich, some more money would have saved an awful lot of hassles. Consistent financial success consistently seemed to elude Bob's gentle grasp.

Now, on this chilly, wet evening early in 1980, four years into their marriage, Emily and Bob were sitting in their tiny apartment with a baby in the bedroom and another just five months away. Emily's knee hurt from the fall, but she wanted to talk about the pregnancy. Its emotions, sensations, and fears were coming to dominate her life every moment, igniting strange motherly instincts that made her other career sometimes seem almost trivial. Although, of course, it wasn't; it was very important and significant, and the money kept them comfortably middle-class, and Bob didn't seem threatened by that. Emily's professional work and her income were also important badges of achievement and worth in a world of changing values for a female born at a time when a married woman's place was not in the workplace.

Emily's second pregnancy had been a point of some real tension between them recently, for while Bob had agreed in theory to another

6

child, the discussion had been general. Surely, though, he must have realized it had to be sometime pretty soon—even men had to know that. Emily, in one of her ultra-assertive moods, simply decided one day that it was time for the second child. No time to fiddle with coaxing a possibly recalcitrant husband who already had a child, a teenage boy from his previous marriage. Without announcement one day the previous summer, Emily had just stopped taking the pill and, voilà, she'd gotten pregnant. Between her teaching job and her therapy patients, she was, after all, making the most money of the two of them; she'd made it on her own for many years, too. Financing another family member and the hired hands to help at times chosen by her could never be a problem. During their talks Bob could have said, "No more children!" Or he at least could have asked if Emily was planning to get pregnant, but he hadn't. Of course, she hadn't really asked him point blank either—"How about right now?" But she was sure Bob would come around eventually. He was so agreeable when she grew firm about her desires. Emily did so like little babies, so helpless and automatically loving of their mother. They stared up with wondering eyes and released uncontrolled gurgles, at both ends. When they got a little older, Emily was discovering, babies—at least, hers—began developing determined minds of their own, just like their mother's.

The Bauers were thoroughly enjoying life. They were comfortable, happy, and, most important of all, healthy. They even had two homes, or rather, residences. There was Emily's tiny apartment in the city, a one-bedroom cubbyhole carried over from her single life, and a beautifully ramshackle old house in the country. Friends who spent enjoyable weekend afternoons touring rural properties for sale had taken the Bauers with them one Sunday. Two minutes after seeing that place for the first time, Emily and Bob looked at each other and simultaneously said, "Let's buy it!"

That was not easy, since, at the time, they were not married, and banks and other creditors were not yet accustomed to women without a husband or a helluva alimony payment asking to borrow money to buy a rundown house for $38,000. This, however, was just the kind of challenge Emily loved to overcome. Some years before hadn't she finished her bachelor's degree while working? Hadn't she then convinced that stern-looking committee of university professors, males every single one of them, that a former secretary like herself, even one with a warm smile and expressive eyes, was dedicated enough to survive several years of grueling graduate studies? Emily took on the finance challenge.

First, she called her parents. Her father was a retired minister who throughout an itinerant career would bury himself in his basement study to scribble out Sunday's sermon with all the appropriate detailed Biblical references. This seemed to take several days every week. He wasn't around for other longer times, either. During most of World War II he'd gone wherever God had sent him to help the troops; God hadn't sent him home very often.

Emily remembered many things from her childhood, like that sunny morning she stood out in the yard overlooking Pearl Harbor and asked her mother why all those black puffs of smoke would appear so suddenly near the airplanes diving about. She remembered the smelly, suffocating rubber gas masks all school children had to wear during air raid drills. They were so tight and confining. She loved puzzles in that school, studying them closely, planning her attack, and barreling in armed with a steely determination and a disregard for others of less tempered character. Nothing would defeat her. Emily recalled a doctor once telling her that she must always exercise, exercise, exercise to burn off some of this intense energy her character generated. One day the little girl, about to be disciplined for disregarding others, turned to her mother in tears and asked, "Why do I act this way?"

Emily also vividly remembered the sense of tingling and mounting anticipation that lasted for months before each of her father's triumphant returns from strange places. Somehow, though, even after years of trying, she couldn't remember anything that happened during her father's visits. The waiting, though, was delicious.

Emily did notice that her father had an abiding aversion to any confrontations, unless they concerned significant social issues such as segregation. Those he could get outraged about. If Emily misbehaved at the dinner table, it was her mother who sent the child to her room. The father would be silent, thinking that scolding soured the food and the same lesson could be taught by talking.

8

For one of Emily's early birthdays, the minister got his daughter a special gift. He had remembered the joys of driving one of those metal pedal cars around the sidewalks of his childhood. The little cars were hard to come by during the war, but he had found one and made a proud presentation to Emily. She cried and kicked it; she had wanted a bicycle. Emily's father did the one thing he could think of doing: He bought her a bike, too.

When Emily called her parents to seek help financing the house, she thought her mother sounded strange, a little slower to grasp things and more than a little forgetful. Worse yet, there was an evident strain between her mother and father. In fact, after all these years, they were getting a divorce. Join the crowd, Emily thought. Then she realized the financial implications of this split: Two senior-citizen households supported by one pension; they could not help with her rundown dream house. And was Emily absolutely certain she wanted to buy a house so soon with this bearded fellow, marvelous man though he no doubt was?

Emily turned for financial help to her younger brother, Bryan. Though they were several years apart in age, their relationship had changed often through time. There was an early era with older sister tyrannizing younger brother. Emily learned that if she ate her ice cream cone quickly enough, little Bryan's would only be half gone and she could take it, too, if her mother wasn't around. One time, however, she pushed this routine a little too hard. Having broken a neighbor's plaster birdbath by spinning the top until it fell on the ground, Emily announced to household authorities that little Bryan had done it. This was not generally believed. When an eyewitness identified Emily as the real perpetrator, Emily's mother spanked her daughter's bottom hard. This physical punishment was in direct opposition to the philosophy of Emily's father. The lesson came as a rude though isolated shock to the child and, years later, Emily would think it had been richly deserved.

More recently, brother and sister had gotten along beautifully. Bryan lived in a small southern city. Several times a year Emily flew down to visit and suddenly swept into his modest home, which was as modest as a divorced college instructor with three children in tow could afford. She would radiate success at these times and was so full

9

of excitement and energy, like a big-city Auntie Mame with happy, optimistic talk for her struggling brother. "You always bring a real breath of fresh air," he would say in appreciation. Emily liked that. Emily also brought precisely picked presents for each child and, more important, a chunk of special time to be spent together. At some point during every visit, Emily and each child snuck off to a room or a park, just the two of them together for a few hours, talking, laughing, telling stories, and invisibly weaving that full sense of personal loyalty and extended family that Emily tried to spin wherever she went. Later, whenever Emily took one of her many glamorous trips abroad alone to Central America or Italy, a chatty card or two arrived for each child with a variety of foreign stamps, if the child collected them. A day or two before the youngster's birthday, a present would arrive in the mail. Invariably, it was just what the child wanted. How had Auntie Emily known?

One day a long letter arrived for Bryan. It was from Emily, who told her diary she was writing her brother this time instead of telephoning because she feared his rejection too much. Emily knew her brother well. She was asking him for a large loan or for him to cosign the mortgage on this house she wanted to buy with this fellow she'd just met. Bryan had always thought of his sister as living somewhere a few feet the other side of wild, so this proposal didn't come as a shock. He knew exactly what he would reply. So did she. In a few days Emily received her brother's refusal in the mail.

As usual, Emily took this rejection hard. It was very difficult for her ever to understand how anyone could not see things her way. She had been so clear and up-front, and it made such sense to her. What might strike some as brazen struck Emily's close friends as, well, Emily. She could be so determined about something that all else, including a friend's feelings, mattered little, so hard was Emily focusing on the issue at hand. Those without their own share of determination might feel stomped on by this woman with the beautiful eyes that could look so fierce.

Like the time Amy Hanson wanted those small Oriental rugs. Amy, the sister of a college friend of Emily's, was so excited when she phoned Emily about the auction the next day. She had seen Emily as such a caring friend ever since Emily had helped her through her mother's long dying days from cancer. Emily, who had her own developing fondness for these floor coverings that Americans prefer to hang on walls, seemed equally enthused about the auction. The next day Amy showed Emily the rugs just before the bidding began. Amy had calculated how much from her small savings account she could bid and she shared her financial strategy with Emily. The women sat together in the throng. As the bidding went on, there was only one other bidder, a good sign, Amy thought. Then she turned her head and realized something: The other bidder was a smiling Emily.

Amy's bright enthusiasm died instantly in an atmosphere of quiet betrayal. Without a further word she dropped from the bidding and developed a headache that required a return home immediately. Emily said okay, she had to pick up her new rugs and she'd phone Amy in a few days. But when she phoned, there was a coolness to Amy's voice. She said she couldn't make it to Emily's upcoming birthday party after all, which seemed strange to Emily. Was something wrong?

Most everyone was struck by Emily's determination, though some would call her pushy. Only a few, those who became good friends, pushed her back. That was all right with Emily. She understood. Like the times she asked to use Barbara Nelson's apartment. Barbara was traveling a lot, and Emily often had a number of out-of-town friends visiting. Could they save hotel costs and stay in Barbara's vacant apartment? That was okay for a while, Barbara thought. After she'd come home from a tiring trip and confront the dirty sheets and towels left by guests she'd never seen, Barbara soured on the arrangement. She hemmed and hawed guiltily with a silent Emily about why she didn't like the idea. Then, when Emily said she still didn't see why her friends—they weren't thieves, you know—couldn't stay in an unused apartment, Barbara finally blurted out, "Because I don't want them to!"

"Well," said an understanding Emily, "why didn't you just say so?" No more friends bothered Barbara's apartment.

That was one good thing about Bob. He didn't exactly push Emily back, but whenever she drew up and announced a Saturday schedule including her plans for him to go somewhere, he might say calmly, well, no, he couldn't do that today because he had his own plans. He

was going to be working in the garden all day and that was that. When
Emily said she had figured out the couple's finances and assigned Bob
to earn at least $17,000 a year, he listened and nodded politely.

Emily finally arranged financing on their first, and last, home. Only
those who didn't know Emily well figured she wouldn't. She convinced a bank that with her two paychecks she could handle the $230-
a-month mortgage payment. Her name alone was on all the papers.
The agreement with Bob, who didn't have any savings to put down,
was that his share of any future equity came through the investment
of his sweat. He was going to fix the place up over time, and he did.
Oh, how he did. Those six hillside acres with scores of surrounding
hard old oaks and soft old firs were a physical reminder of another
simpler time free of adult responsibilities, when the future was this
afternoon, when the summer days were long, and when he and his
two best playmates gathered in the woods for another meeting of
their secret club, where the dues went for shared milkshakes.

Bob never had liked rigid schedules. He got through liberal arts
college nonetheless, thanks to his extracurricular work in the school
theater. Not acting out in front of the crowd, but organizing the presentation, arranging the lights, constructing the sets, building a sense
of drama, and, most important, reveling in that warm sense of belonging that accompanies such temporary troupes. The shared drudgery
of preparation, the shared anxiety and anticipation before a perform-
ance, and the shared exhilaration of applause and satisfaction. The
shared belonging. It was like a large informal family full of people
who cared about each other and their work and created artistically
special moments that were so fragile, they were here and then gone,
like a cherry blossom. Bob sought out these groups after graduation,
for work and personal satisfaction. It was as if he were trying to revisit
the friendly country commune-type living of his childhood in eastern
Pennsylvania. There his immediate family included his mother and
father and two sisters, both more than ten years his senior and both of
whom doted on their "baby brother." There were also uncles and
aunts and, through the trees, many neighbors who were more than
just neighbors. So when Bob's mother fell ill with heart problems,
there were swarms of people, especially women, to help the household. As his mother's health problems continued for many years, Bob

saw his father doting on his mother. The sense of duty was indelibly etched in the boy's memory. During spells of weakness, when his mother had to rest for weeks at a time, Bob cared for her, too. It was the duty of every family member. Even when he wasn't carrying the weakening lady up to bed or down to dinner or fetching something for her, Bob knew he had to tiptoe about—Mom was resting. For years, "shhh" was the key word.

As the years passed, Bob realized that in reality the community was not as friendly, the family not as harmonious, and the encircling woods and streams neither as idyllic nor as large as they were in the little boy's mind. There were fights and alcoholics about. The tiptoeing was sometimes done less to disturb his mother's rest than it was to avoid stirring up his father's dark moods, which cast clouds over the household for days at a time, and for a long time after his wife died at fifty-one. These moods returned when Bob, the aging father's only son, announced that he didn't want to take over the family's dry-cleaning business. He wanted to earn a living in the theater, which actually meant earning a living in many odd jobs while working in the theater. Bob was a truck driver, a carpenter, and an electrician, and it was these skills that he employed to fulfill his end of the country-house bargain with Emily. It was working with trees and in the garden that gave him the most satisfaction, cleaning out old, dead under-growth, cutting back the suffocating vines and overgrowth, letting the bright sun fall in, and planting new things in the moist soil while a big dog or two ran around chasing faint rabbit scents.

Bob spent most of his time living at the country house when he wasn't working elsewhere. First thing, he bought a shiny new mailbox and had a private little ceremony out by the road, nailing it on the post, checking the level and the little red flag, painting his name on the side, and making it official; Bob Bauer had come home again. Then on Thursdays or Fridays he would take his van down the drive, pause to glance at the mailbox, and go to pick Emily up in the city for a few days together back in the country.

Less than a year after the closing on the house, they formalized their relationship in marriage. The ceremony took place in the house, in the bedroom actually, because it was the largest room in the place. Emily had decorated, or rather she had friends help her decorate the whole house with flowers, ribbons, ivy, and fir boughs from the property. Other friends did the cooking that weekend. Things generally went as smoothly and were as well orchestrated as Emily liked her frequent creative parties to be. Emily especially loved the crowd of happy family and friends orbiting around her that day.

Emily also planned a separate nonreligious ceremony. The couple had written and read aloud to the silent throng their own private promises to each other. Emily vowed "to be a loving and faithful wife, to be increasingly sensitive to your needs and always to act in ways that show my respect and regard for you, the most important person in my life." She promised, "For richer, for poorer, in sickness and in health to be loyal, including being patient and tolerant of your limitations and persevering with equanimity and gentleness during any times of difficulty we might encounter, to love and to cherish you and to be your wife in the sense of your female counterpart and partner, to do whatever will lead to a deepening of the bond between us as long as we live."

Then Emily and everybody turned to look up at Bob, who had always preferred backstage to onstage. But this scene was important to the director; he knew that. And, you know, somehow these created occasions of Emily's were becoming meaningful to him, too.

Bob cleared his throat, stroked his beard once or twice, and looked intensely down at the little scrap of paper in his hand. "We are all witness to the night sky," he said, "the dark shadows beyond the firelight." He spoke then of his deepening joy with Emily. He promised "to share, nurture, respect, and cherish you and to be available to receive long and loving kindnesses, to welcome and to treasure them, to recognize both our separatenesses and our oneness, to be willing to listen, to try and grow and be willing to laugh at myself in stupidity and both of us in foolishness. I promise to live our days together, plan our future, remember our past, and bite at our life with relish and greed, not nibbling like the riskless few." He paused to clear his throat again.

"Since I was a child," Bob said, "I have loved a few things and so I declare my love for you always. And with this I remember the depth of the traditional vows. I promise to love, honor, respect, keep, and cherish you till death do us part." Then he put away the piece of paper, never suspecting for a moment what living up to that traditional promise would fully mean.

The honeymoon was postponed for financial reasons. And the new Mr. and Mrs. Bauer resumed their new life, sometimes separate, sometimes together, always equal with a quiet love that ran deep like a river current. Now each segment of Emily's ordered life was fulfilling and exciting and under control, a husband who accepted—he had better—her need to aspire and achieve outside the confines of home, and a separate stimulating career with like-thinking female friends and several evenings a week to herself.

Those were exciting years, constructing a career, feeling herself something of a pioneer as a professional woman with students and patients eager and willing to pay for her thoughts and lessons. All of which let her go to the ballet, where Emily and Bob would hold hands and sometimes sneak a public kiss before the lights went up. Emily could buy nice things like the rugs or fine fabrics. On her earlier trips to Spain and Guatemala and the belated honeymoon to Italy, Emily bought many kinds of colorful fabrics—she loved their various feels and textures—and stashed them away in her apartment to be made into clothes for the children she knew she would have someday. Then when the youngsters had outgrown the garments, she planned to make a quilt with patches from all the different clothes and give that bed covering to the child when she or he left home. Well, maybe if Emily had a boy, he wouldn't be so interested in quilts. Good point. She'd have to teach him a variety of different values right from the start so he wouldn't be confined by old-fashioned thoughts that limited his appreciations. Then he'd like quilts. Emily would see to that. If she had a girl, of course, she'd grow up knowing she had to aspire to something great and that the sky was the limit.

Emily was constantly full of energy. She loved physical movement, especially bicycling and dancing and hard gardening. Growing up in southern California, where no one thinks of good weather or comfortable outdoor activities as limited to certain months, Emily relished being outside, even simply sunbathing. She wasn't just toasting herself; it was exhilarating, as if she could recharge herself through the sun. It was more natural to be outdoors, savoring the natural scents and sights, feeling free and fresh, doing things, even hiking, which

Bob loved, and then, afterward, feeling that pleasant sense of healthy sweat and gentle fatigue. Sometimes, when it was warm, the couple frolicked in their modest swimming pool, usually in the early-morning hours when the mist was still rising from the trees or late at night when the stars hung there in the dark like silent, celestial decorations so far above. Emily would savor these memories later in a different sort of silence during some long days and endless nights that had no romantic sheen.

For a while in the city Emily also studied dancing, but her amateur imperfections would ignite volatile frustrations. She wanted to be better than time permitted her to be, she said. After several months Emily changed to an exercise class. She needed a lot of time to taste all the things there were to taste.

Like art. Museum-going was a passion. Emily found writing professional papers so tedious that she procrastinated mightily, but the thought of ideas taking on a physical shape through an artist's eyes and hands was exciting. She dipped into various crafts. With some of the fabrics from abroad she made a large abstract montage to hang in her apartment. Emily was proud of it and said so. Everybody agreed that it was quite good. The montage seemed to depict a sunny sky with a brightly colored tree standing leafy, sturdy, and tall. But all the ground was gray and lifeless, and the gray seemed to be spreading up the tree trunk toward the limbs. Or at least that's what some people saw there.

■

December 6, 1979: I think I may be pregnant again. I'm not real good on intuition, so I'm not sure. I think of how much more complicated life would be with two, but I'd manage. Children are fabulous. I think Allison has helped me mature and another would even more. I'm still pretty self-absorbed. Sometimes I worry that all my happiness will be taken away from me now that I have grown accustomed to it.

■

Two or three days a week Emily taught in the city. And at other times when individual therapy patients arrived at her apartment, Emily would leave Allison with a kind lady in a neighboring apartment who needed the extra money. Alli would go there too when Emily had a dentist's appointment or was meeting one of the many women in her large circle of friends for lunch or a movie or a trip to a museum. In these caring conversations between pals, Emily could be a very good listener, which made the talker feel good and important. And Emily could silently learn things. Then when Emily spoke, her words carried more meaning and her friends, students, and patients, sometimes reluctantly, gained new insights into themselves and others, though rarely into Emily. She seemed an intelligent woman all right; not even her opponents on some faculty committees on educational reform could deny that. Emily was forthright, though some might have called it blunt. Sometimes she said things, even outrageous things, and let the verbal chips fall where they might, especially if she was angry or pouting.

Emily counted on the other person matching her forthrightness. Not everyone, however, had such strength or inclination, which was tough for them, right? She once invited Barbara to a New Year's party. Barbara said, oh, good, she'd stop by before midnight after this other party she had to attend. Emily said, no, never mind, if you can't be bothered coming for the whole evening, then don't bother coming at all. Some friend.

Barbara was stunned and called her back in a couple of days to apologize if she had hurt Emily's feelings. Emily said, no, fine, no problem, come by whenever you can. She was genuinely friendly.

That puzzled some. Then would come another one of Emily's personal touches. She frequently bought gifts for friends. But not just any gift. It had to be just the right gift, right color, right size, precisely what that person had said she or he wanted some months before, and Emily had remembered. Often the gift was even better because Emily had found a newer model with more attributes. Or maybe the friend hadn't realized how much she needed this item around her apartment, but Emily had. At just the right moment, she would breeze into the friend's place and present an exquisitely wrapped gift very simply, as if she'd just picked it up on the way over instead of having spent an entire afternoon taxiing from store to store just to find it.

Emily drew special strength and a strong sense of sisterhood from a small group of women therapists. They met monthly—networking, they called it—to talk and discuss cases and treatments and to share their excitements and disappointments. Emily wasn't quite so blunt then.

Often, two or three of the women would gather for lunch. They wouldn't just grab a bite anywhere. They would carefully select the place and the food—a delicate continental dish, perhaps, with a crisp salad and a wine or two and then a special coffee. They would savor the taste and texture of the meal as well as their affluence and urban independence. There were frictions, of course. One woman once confided to Emily that her husband wanted a baby immediately. The wife didn't, not till her work was further along. Emily said, no, the woman really ought to have the baby as her husband wanted. You could be truly creative with babies, Emily said. They were great. A woman at the next table leaned over then and said, "Excuse me, I overheard your conversation, and babies are no delight. They are a pain in the ass."

Emily's friend laughed out loud. But Emily didn't. In fact, she phoned her friend's husband and agreed with him—time for a baby now—which prompted some loud talk in that house during dinner that night and after dinner, too. Emily's friend didn't speak to her again for some time. But when the friend was briefly hospitalized, Emily promptly showed up—with a gift—and no more baby talk.

■

January 14, 1980: Sometimes I think what I would want to be remembered for. The first things that come to my mind are qualities I don't particularly have, like cleverness. I do have thoughtfulness; that is probably characteristic of me for a long time (and thoughtlessness). Perhaps my enthusiasm, loyalty, dedication. I would like to be remembered for who I am, but I think it'll be for what I do. Bob, in contrast, would be remembered for who he is.

■

Every day Emily allotted some time alone with herself—for some artwork or thinking or conscientiously adding to her diary. She blocked out some other time alone with Alli—for tickling or talking or simply observing. Sometimes Emily kept detailed, minute-by-minute notes on Alli's activities and the growth the proud mother saw. She addressed these notes to Alli:

"12:20—You are wiggling. I prop you up on a pillow and you stop crying.

"12:26—You are gently touching little plastic blocks. Never again will you have it so easy. You stretch out, arch your back, and cry.

"12:30—You make little sounds—'whoay.' I wonder why you respond to little sensations, like when I put a blanket on you, but nothing to a power drill next door."

On and on the notes—and the playing—went for hours, sometimes involving tape-recorded mother-daughter "conversations." There were times when Emily thought Bob could do somewhat more in the child care department. Some early mornings when Alli would start to cry too early by adult standards, Emily would stay in bed, pretending to sleep soundly, waiting Bob out. Soon, he would clamber out of bed and shuffle off to change and feed her. And Emily would feel good. But instead of going back to sleep, she would lie awake, ears alert, listening to the father-daughter encounters.

■

February 1, 1980: This is supposed to be the start of Alli's clingy stage. I'm interested to see how intense it is. I've noticed when she first sees Bob after not seeing him for a few days, she doesn't register much excitement. Her pleasure emerges only gradually over time. In contrast, she always gets very excited when she sees me, even if we have been separated only for a couple of hours. It's really very gratifying!!

February 10, 1980: I continue to feel very good, though I'm afraid the hemmorhoid thing will return. I'm famished three times a day, have only gained ten pounds so far. Not bad. Get nauseous sometimes. Already experience more difficulty climbing stairs. Not sure if it's just the weight. It just seems more of an effort. I get strange feelings sometimes, but then I'm doing more than last time.

■

Emily also liked organizing parties and then presiding over them at all times. Her annual Christmas affairs revolved around everyone making an original decoration for her tree. There were silly prizes for the best or most original, and she saved the decorations for the next year. Once, Emily reserved two large tables at a fancy hotel and invited two dozen friends to lunch and to help celebrate her baby and her fortieth birthday. She said everything had finally come together just right in her life. It was a fun time with lively conversation and good food. Everyone returned to Emily's apartment for a gourmet dessert and to play a personal trivia game that Emily had invented but some found a little forced and too revealing of private thoughts they would have preferred to keep private. Near the end of the afternoon at least one woman noticed that no men had been invited, and she thought back to the chattering birthday parties of her childhood when it was all girls or all boys. Are we grown up, she asked herself, or just bigger? And she smiled at her own answer.

Couples, however, were invited to another Emily family extravaganza, Alli's naming ceremony at the country house. There were too many guests for Emily's place settings, so she had friends bring some of their own, if they matched Emily's. Everybody chipped in with the food and cooking, too. Someone's son brought a guitar, so there was music, mostly folk songs from the sixties. Out in front of the house, with Alli blithely gurgling in a stroller and the many gathered friends watching, Emily and Bob planted a little star magnolia tree in the baby's name. Everyone had to throw a shovel of dirt into the hole. Then each guest was to read a passage from his or her favorite piece of children's literature, which made for quite a few bedtime stories for all the adults standing around in the sun on the front lawn. Emily loved it, and Bob seemed to, too.

At that fateful family weekend Barbara Nelson, Emily's best friend, met Bryan and learned for the first time that Emily had a brother. It was an encounter that sparked an immediate infatuation between the two.

Emily was busy preparing for the new baby. There were names to research the Biblical meaning of (Rebecca was out if it was a girl; she'd been too conniving). Emily had physical changes in her own body to monitor and wonder about. There were doctors to be told precisely how this baby would be born—natural childbirth this time, no matter what those men said.

■

February 27, 1980: Things seem to have settled down about the baby. I was mostly upset and worried over Bob's reaction and thought maybe I'd made a big mistake. I was worried that he'd resent me and the baby, that he'd stop wanting to have sex. But that doesn't seem the case. In fact, he's more concerned about me than the last time. I don't remember him asking how I felt before. The baby is so much fun to think about. And my minor tumble the other day doesn't seem to have done any lasting damage.

March 14, 1980: I sometimes wonder who I am writing this for. My aspirations to formal writing have rather diminished. For so long I thought of myself as someone with great potential, which would eventually be realized. But I am becoming increasingly ordinary. I want something to show for all my work. Why don't I feel more driven? Is it like they say about women, when they have children they put their energy in that rather than something more public? Maybe this is just a phase and later I will get drive. Right now, I just want a cozy, comfortable life. Very mundane.

Oh, another thing, I'd like some charisma or a gimmick, something to bring me recognition. I would like people to really love me and think I'm special.

April 3, 1980: I got angry at Alli. Last night, once again, she woke up at 4:30 and wanted a bottle and I thought this has been going on too long and has to stop. She can't just expect me to get what she wants when she's inconveniencing others. So I decided to let her cry it out. But she intensified her crying and I couldn't stand it. I gave her the bottle rather urgently. She cried even harder, wanting to be cuddled. I did it, of course, still feeling angry but also enjoying cuddling her. I wonder if I could line up a bunch of bottles and she could help herself.

April 16, 1980: I'm more concerned with how I look. In conjunction with my birthday and Barbara and Bryan's new love and courtship, I decided I really needed Bob to respond more vocally to me in this regard (many tears shed before reaching this stage). He has said two things. One, I seemed to look younger than ever, whereas he looked older, and second, that he liked a particular style dress I had on. For my birthday we went shopping and I got a new dress we both liked a lot and a new top (purple linen-like) to go with my slacks. I also had my hair streaked and I feel better. Though I still look at all thin women and hate them.

May 12, 1980: I am seven months pregnant and feeling very well except for tiredness and difficulty walking. It is a happy time in our lives.

∎

Because of Emily's concern with her age in this pregnancy, more tests were done throughout the nine months. As one result, the Bauers learned in advance that the baby was healthy—and a girl. After some heated discussions, they settled on Jene as her name. Barbara warned Emily that these "cute" spellings sentenced the kid to a life of spelling out her name for everyone. Emily thought the unusual arrangement of letters made a child special even before birth.

Emily told her friends many details about the pregnancy. And she asked many questions. Was their second more difficult than the first? Hers was. Had they had pinched nerves in the legs? She did. The leg didn't hurt so much as not do what it was told. And Emily, the child psychologist, got a doll made in time so Alli would have a "baby" too when her new sister came home.

■

June 11, 1980: What is this with me? Suddenly, I want to get everything in my life in order—my notes, patient summaries, my will, even my closet. I wondered if I was contemplating dying.

June 22, 1980: There is a part of me that resents that Bob and others can dip into Alli's life and then go off to do their own thing, whereas I'm always here and for that reason perhaps lose my specialness. If Alli didn't have me here, then she couldn't respond to the best in other people. I guess that's why motherhood is called selfless love. I guess I've never had that kind of relationship. I can see why I don't like the idea so well.

■

Jene's natural birth, meticulously recorded on color film, went uneventfully that summer, the doctor performing exactly as ordered. Every snapshot glowed with Emily's happiness. "Oh, Bob," she kept saying. "Our baby! Our baby!" For days she phoned all her friends, always opening with her trademark greeting, "Tis I, Emily." She was "on a baby high," as one friend remembers. Jene was so cute and healthy and responsive, and Emily had big plans for her and couldn't wait to see what she would become. You know, Emily said, you really should have a baby, too, or maybe another one. The friends would smile silently on the phone and say to themselves, "There goes Emily again."

It was true Emily could be a pain sometimes, and there was no small talk with her. But it was true, too, that she made up for it in so many ways. She was never judgmental about anyone. She was very tolerant of their quirks and so curious about life. She was an arranger, to be sure, but there she had a flair. Emily always seemed so interested in them and their experiences. Emily also knew or found out what was important to each individual. One older graduate student remembers Emily asking during her admissions interview what the student would do if she was not accepted. The woman said she'd go home and cry. When the university acceptance arrived in the mail, it carried a handwritten note from Emily: "Now you won't have to cry." So when Emily phoned about her new baby, everyone was delighted to hear from her, although when some of the women told their husbands about the call, they forgot to mention Emily's suggestion that they have another baby, too.

■

July 18, 1980: I realize I have the kind of personality that some people don't like. I don't want to be considered strident and intrusive. Yet I'm not sure I want to change the behavior that leads to that perception. I have been going through a lot of stuff about my pinched nerve and interacting with doctors. They all seem so defensive and have such little time to talk to me. I don't feel I can any longer simply turn myself and my body over to the authority of a physician, and yet at the same time it's very hard to make decisions without the required knowledge. I am probably overinvolved in this and it relates back to some unresolved stuff with my father.

■

Emily was also eager to get herself back in shape physically. She didn't like waddling.

Which is why Beverly Willett was taken aback when she and her husband Mike arrived six weeks later for one of Emily's gourmet meals—scallops and string beans. They found her limping still. Emily mentioned it only briefly. It seemed strange to her that a pregnancy problem continued after the pregnancy. It might even be a little worse. She had a doctor's appointment coming up. Would they like more beans? As Emily went to the kitchen, she was dragging her foot.

"Mike," said Bob, "what do you think this is with the foot?"

Michael Willett is a doctor. He doesn't like to talk about people's medical problems if they're not his patients. But, sure enough, at every party someone discovers he is a medical specialist and out comes a tale of their own medical problems—at least until they learn his medical specialty.

"What's an oncologist?" they ask.

"Cancer doctor," Mike says. And the subject quickly changes to the football season.

"Do you think Emily's foot is going to get better?" Bob continued.

The host was pouring some more wine at that moment so he didn't see Mike's face instantly pale. Beverly did. Worse, she heard her husband adopt that kind of level, noncommittal tone of voice that signaled danger to her.

"Don't know," replied Mike. "Depends on what it is. Emily, this is really delicious."

"Well, whatever it is," said Emily, "it can't be permanent. Handicapped is not my style." Emily, Beverly, and Bob laughed.

In the car on the way home, Beverly asked her husband what he had meant, he didn't know. He said he was worried because Emily's problem seemed to be progressive, but they were seeing good doctors. Lots of symptoms like that don't go any further. And they shouldn't interfere.

■

September 18, 1980: This has been an extremely difficult time. Have broken down in tears quite a bit and it's such an effort just to walk a few blocks. It is the first time I've been faced with dysfunction and I find the stress harder to handle than anything ever before. I am dependent on others' expertise and on a process over which I have no control. I am struggling for some degree of control. I know there's something to be gained from all this; maybe I'll get a new awareness of the feelings of people who have permanent handicaps. I wonder what it is like to be permanently crippled. Incomprehensible. But it is a challenge to operate within narrow limits. Probably eventually who knows when I'll be normal again.

September 20, 1980: I decided in the middle of the night that some-thing has to be done about my dependence on Bob. I resent it so much. He is so preoccupied with work that he has little left to give me personally. I wait so for him to come home and when he does, it's as if he's not here. I couldn't believe his conscientiousness last night in returning calls even to people he didn't want to talk to. I told him I'm the last one who gets something from him, which is true, except maybe he gives to himself last. And that is the basic problem. He apologized this morning so I know things ultimately will work out. Well, Jenie is crying. Must go.

An hour later. Jenie is sleeping on the bed. Alli managed to worm her way up and take Jenie's bottle, and I yelled at her, and both started crying. I'm not accomplishing a thing today. Bob and I really think alike. I try to be as concerned about him as I am about myself and feel modestly successful in this regard. Bob is my rock, my base. I love and respect him more than I ever dreamed possible. He's done his best. But sometimes it isn't right and I get upset. But I know it's not lack of concern.

Ultimately, I'm discovering one is alone in a fundamental sense.

October 8, 1980: More tears. Bob and Alli are out bicycle riding on a glorious fall day. Jenie sleeps peacefully on the bed. She is so ex-quisitely formed. I am feeling grateful for what I have. Larry called this morning to say Betty L. had died yesterday. I'm upset. Of course, I realized she was going to die. I had written her but not mailed the note. She is my age. I wonder if she gave up because she didn't have much to live for. There is a part of me that says I would fight and conquer and yet I know, too, there are some things that willpower cannot conquer.

■

Emily and Bob, who was spending more time in the city to help Emily, were seeing a series of doctors. Beverly expected that; Emily had consulted six or seven late in the pregnancy just to be sure it was safe to take a Valium now and then at night so she could get some sleep. She had become so uncomfortable lying down. So Beverly wasn't surprised when Emily said she'd been referred to yet another doctor about her foot. Beverly hung up the phone and rushed into the living room with the good news.

"They didn't find a tumor!" Beverly said.

"Oh," her husband said, sounding disappointed.

"Isn't that good news?"

"If it was a tumor," said Mike evenly, "maybe they could do something."

"What do you think is going on?"

"I'm not a neurologist," he said, and then looked down as if to read his newspaper.

The neurologist led Emily and Bob into an empty room he had found. No one was using it, at least for a few minutes.

■

October 13, 1980: I am afraid of falling. Maybe I need surgery. How invulnerable I have felt for so long.

■

The room was one of those small, green hospital offices with no diplomas on the wall, just a metal desk sitting there, lonely and adorned with no family photos, only coffee-cup rings. The drawers would be empty except for a few paper clips, crumbs from something unrecognizable, and a yellow plastic pen that no longer worked.

Dr. Berghoff motioned the couple to some hard chairs. He chose to stand against the front of the desk, closer to them. He leaned back, fiddling with the stethoscope in the pocket of his white jacket, then straightened up, folded his arms across his chest, and took a deep breath. This was all taking far too long for both Bob and Emily. For weeks now they had been shuffling from doctor to doctor, ending up with this nice, thirty-five-year-old specialist. He had put Emily in the hospital twice for tests, which seemed like a lot for a foot problem. They had done X-rays, blood and urine tests, and spinal taps. Her spinal fluid had a high protein content, which sent the suddenly hopeful doctor off in the wrong direction.

At first he had focused on the symptoms, not his suspicions. Maybe it was a pinched nerve. That hope died early. A tumor perhaps. But no again. Now he was getting that sad lump in his stomach once more, the one he could sense coming, the one that's not mentioned in the medical school textbooks, the one that feeds on hopelessness. It was harder being a modern doctor, he thought. The oldtimers knew all about what they couldn't do, namely just about everything. Now, the doctor thought, we can do so much to the human body with medicine and technology and machines. But when we come up against something we can't yet do, it's more frustrating. Infuriating. And frightening. It gets all tied up, too, in new legal and moral issues they didn't teach in school. It had been so very much easier when man wasn't making all the decisions.

Sensing his own personal alarm, Dr. Berghoff had moved into his cautious mode, trying to send signals of seriousness to the patient and her family with his tone of voice and comments. Early on he had wanted to ease the initial shock in case he finally did have to deliver even worse news. That's why he had said he hoped it was a tumor. That's why he had Emily back for a second set of tests. Bob thought the doctor sounded serious all right but so noncommittal, like Mike Willett a few weeks back. How can different doctors even talk alike?

Dr. Berghoff had looked and looked everywhere else. The second set of tests told him nothing new, and that told him something else. Still, one evening during Emily's hospital tests, he had started for home and then returned to Emily's room on a hunch, or a hope, hunting for an alternative diagnosis.

There she was with her husband and Barbara somebody, having a little wine-and-cheese picnic on the bed. The doctor had Emily do a few more muscle tests, pushing against his hands first with her good leg and then with her arms. Her arms seemed to have gotten a little weaker in the last couple of weeks. Only her movement was being affected, not her thinking. She was losing muscle tone, too. The doctor had said nothing about that. He hadn't laughed at any of the jokes that Bob starts telling when he gets worried. And the doctor had declined both the wine and the cheese.

Emily was anxious, naturally, but happy. How could she not be, right? With two nice kids, a career on the upswing, and a caring husband. They obviously had a very close relationship and good communications, which was why Dr. Berghoff could talk to them about this matter together, now.

Emily was quiet, sitting there. Bob started to tell a funny hospital story but stopped. He had an unfunny feeling in his stomach and a fear in his mind that his life was about to be changed forever. It couldn't be too bad, though; it wasn't cancer.

"Well," said the doctor, "you must really feel just about tested out, I imagine." He was uncomfortably aware that this psychologist before him was evaluating him, wondering if the doctor was hiding something. Those eyes of hers were powerful instruments of communication. How they could manipulate you. She was articulate, intelligent, incisive, and vulnerable. He figured she'd be skeptical for a long while.

He spoke very slowly and carefully. Patients get confused at times like this. If everything sounded too bad, even someone as intelligent as her could fall into denial, simply tune out the doctor and find another one with a more optimistic diagnosis. Or she could become an emotional hermit. Or maybe grow angry at those doing the most for her because that seemed safest. Emily was not Dr. Berghoff's first case of this disease. But she was to be the most intensely involving.

The doctor reviewed the tests and general findings. Then he paused.

"In my opinion," he said, "there is no escaping that you have motor-neuron disease." He waited. He usually used those words instead of the proper name. They seemed a little different, and he wanted to buy them some hope. But there was no reaction.

"What's Motor New Ron disease?" asked Bob.

"ALS," replied the doctor. "Amyotrophic lateral sclerosis."

Emily was silent. "What's that?"

"It's also called Lou Gehrig's disease."

Bob thought that couldn't be right—Gary Cooper died in that movie. And then it hit him. Oh, Jesus! Oh, shit! Not Emily, too. The doctor was answering Emily's questions, talking about the spinal cord and the nerves and how this disease cuts off the messages from the brain to the muscles. No one knows why. Or how to stop it. It often starts like this in a limb and spreads. Then, he was afraid, the muscles waste away. There might be some difficulty about breathing later, but they could talk about that another time.

Bob didn't want to hear this. He was trying to think of a funny joke, a very funny joke. But he wouldn't be laughing for a very long time.

"Am I going to die?" asked Emily.

The doctor paused a moment. This was like handing out a death sentence. Dammit to hell! This woman was just getting started in life. She was close to his age, with young children, and the doctor had come to see Emily as something of a colleague. Now she was asking about her death, as if it were up to him. Facing up to her death meant facing up to his own someday, too. It was always this way with these patients, if you cared. But for the ALS patients Dr. Berghoff had seen, and for their families who were just as stricken though less confined, death often became the least of their worries. It became less a feared end and more of a blessed way out of a life whose confines were overpowering its opportunities. Life for them gradually narrowed and narrowed until it was just an existence in a dark bed at the end of wires and tubes, maintained by machine and the will of white-coated strangers who could walk home at night to laugh during dinner and hug their children without the slightest thought. Secretly, the doctor also hoped that his brief silence would say yes to Emily without his words.

"We're all going to die," the doctor replied. "Some ALS patients live for ten, a few even twenty years. It can also be more like five, or three." He left out that awful word "terminal." He had taken the Hippocratic Oath to "do no harm." In his book, crushing all hope was harmful.

Bob and Emily didn't talk much on the drive home. They held hands at each stoplight.

■

October 18, 1980:

Dear Alli and Jenie,

Well, it is the end of the week when I found out that I have ALS, this disease which is at some presently unknown rate to destroy some or all the muscles in my body. You both are foremost in my thoughts, my joyous aspect of life in conjunction with my love for Bob, my best accomplishment. Thank God (and I have not yet come to know about such concepts—I have always done fine without thinking about them except in general ways, but I know in times of crisis people turn to religion, as it helps make sense of the otherwise non-sensical), I have you all. Somehow four seemed more a complete family than three. I wonder if at some level I knew. For, as I said to Bob this morning, the thought of another child now would probably be out of the question. And better Bob have two daughters instead of one because two spreads the parental concern and I don't want either of you to hang around to care for your dad.

Thank God (again I say that hesitantly), you have the father you do; the other best thing I ever did besides having you is marrying Bob. I told him this morning (as he was grieving, as he has been) that he alone would do just fine, although it's a big responsibility alone, and I had always thought he would die first and was very scared of the responsibility and aloneness. I said he knows who I am and he will just take in who I am and add it to who he is. This in addition to all the other loving people in your lives.

I am very saddened to think that I will not be here probably to see you go through all your stages (and maybe sometimes glad because at times you are and will be a huge pain in the neck); that is the hardest thing, because my work and my life are bringing things to fruition and I won't most likely be able to do as much as I expected. But then again, maybe one never does, who knows.

I try to think of what I am getting as well as losing from this illness and it is just beginning and I have much more to learn about all that.

31

October 27, 1980: Bryan has come for a visit. Bob has to work some-times, of course. So my brother and I went for the first of our second opinions today. These guys must have all gone to the same school. Before we left I had some time alone with Alli. She was all cuddly and wanted me to sing, but not the old songs, as if this is a new chapter or stage. I was a little distracted and forgot to say good-bye to her when Mrs. R. came to take them to her apartment. I could have handled it better, now that I'm more used to this (?!). I have Alli watch me get ready to go out (it's taking more time) and go down to the taxi with me. I want her to know what's happening, but I feel guilty. Not a good sign. She greets me "Mommy, Mommy," which is so nice. Maybe she understands this is a family crisis and is doing her part. Certainly better actions than when we brought Jenie home from the hospital. That was awful. It's so hard to figure out what is best to do for her, to separate out my needs for contact with them from their needs from me.

When we returned from the doctor's, Bryan said, "Let's do some-thing fun." And I wracked my brain and said, "Let's go for a walk." We all laughed. And I ended up crying.

November 1, 1980: Jenie, these days you are wearing all the clothes everyone has bought or prepared for you. Bob and I, and Alli, when we can get her cooperation, have drawn pastel colors on baby T-shirts for you. And Bob's sisters are making you things. As you might expect, they are always so tuned into things in so many ways. There is nothing more precious than giving of one's time—and hav-ing love and your health, of course. I had planned for us to do these shirts regularly. But, of course, I always plan more than I get done. Although I do get done a lot.

I plan to have things for you, like a dowry. I was thinking of the quilts, naturally, but it doesn't seem I'll have twenty years. Maybe I'll get a Christmas and birthday present for you for each year. But I don't know what your interests and tastes will be and you might not like my choice. But I'll do my best, and sometime later you might like it, so keep it anyway. I know that has happened to me. I hope so much you will love lovely things as a slice of beauty. If you don't like these gifts, then save them for your daughters or someone else in the family. But wait till you're forty. That is when you have a sense of what is and isn't important in life.

Jenie, you continue to have your fussy periods, which have no particular time or reason, and for some reason you always wake up in the middle of the night and it is getting harder for me to get around with you, even in the daylight. So Bob, of course, gets up with you. Usually if you are held, you stop crying. So you get held quite a bit. There is something so very satisfying in holding you.

Alli has taken to running from me when I'm trying to dress her. She, of course, knows I can't chase her. Dirty pool, I'd say.

■

That Thanksgiving weekend was a happy time in the Bauer household. Two dozen relatives and friends flocked to their country house, half of them sleeping over, on cots and beds and couches, and the smell of good foods and the sound of good times wafted through the old home, overpowering any sense of doom, for now. It was harder for Emily to move about; the house had numerous additions and each seemed to be on a slightly different level. The guests or Bob would often find Emily pausing at a stair or shuffling down the hall, leaning on the wall or her cane. Her arms would get tired from leaning so heavily on the cane. She wanted to be wherever the most noise and happiness were, and that moved from room to room. No one was accustomed yet to having a handicapped person around, so they'd all wander off to one room and a few minutes later Emily would be making her way in the doorway, sort of smiling. Someone would jump to get a chair, and they'd all be together again, singing and laughing and telling stories, eating and drinking with toasts to everyone and everything, including the cats. Emily sang very loudly; she knew all the words to the folk songs. One night she had too much wine and couldn't stop singing, and everyone tried to keep up with her. They couldn't but no one wanted to spoil her happiness. "Isn't this great?" Emily shouted. "I'm dying, but here we are having a wonderful time!"

There was a sense of adventure and determination to that weekend. Part of it was denial; few there had ever lived with a hopelessly ill close relative. She looked fine, except for the walking. They knew nothing could keep Emily down, not for long anyway. She had a special spirit. And hopelessness did not fit in. She made each of them vow to help her whip this disease. She couldn't do it without them, she said. They must all, every day, think of her walking normally again. She would do the same. Everyone promised they would. They'd all be in this together. Emily called it imaging, using the power of the mind to heal unhealable nerves and kill this bug or whatever an ALS was. Later, at home, the relatives and friends, especially the women, would privately try to picture Emily without that lifeless leg's awful limp, riding a bike, dancing, or jogging, something active like that. The picture came to some, fuzzy, but it was there. And Emily pictured them picturing her; it was good support like the cane, better actually, because thinking didn't tire her arms. Other friends had more difficulty with this process. They always got the image of a once-active Emily, a little smaller somehow, a cane in one hand and a half-smile on her face, leaning on the hall wall to rest a moment or asking someone to get her something. But the image didn't last long. It would evaporate in the demanding bustle of their ongoing, everyday, healthy lives—a phone ringing, a dinner cooking, a child crying, weeds growing, clothes washing. There were restaurants, movies, and ballets to go to, and country inns beckoning with bright lights and leaves. Sometimes the friends might seek a diversion to change the mental subject intentionally, turning on the radio a little too loud for a while or starting to read the newspaper only to realize a few minutes later that they hadn't retained a word. That might make everything all right until Emily phoned or until they were sitting in a highway restaurant on a weekend of antiquing when a family would come in, pushing a wheelchair with a member who had to be spoonfed, and whose soup ran down her chin anyway.

"Are you telling me," Beverly said to her husband out of the blue

34

the way spouses sometimes do, "that Emily is going to end up like that?" She was looking at that other table.

Dr. Michael Willett, who made the immediate, unspoken mental link, put down his silverware and glanced around, too, pretending to seek an arriving friend. "Yes," he said, casually turning back, "if she's lucky."

The Monday morning after Thanksgiving Bob noticed car tracks across part of the front lawn. When he followed them back toward the driveway, his heart sank. One of the city guests had wanted to protect his daughter's new shoes from the rural mud, so he'd driven closer to the door. In the dark he had also driven over the little star magnolia tree. Emily sobbed.

At night then, Bob took Emily up to bed in the room where they had been happily married. She noticed that he knew just how to carry her most comfortably. He would hold her there until sleep came.

■

December 4, 1980: Bob cries differently than I, breaking out with more force, like the other night at dinner. Alli took her napkin and dabbed his eyes, saying, "Don't cry, Daddy." Then she asked if Daddy wanted a Band-Aid. This Band-Aid business has become a big thing. She wants to wear one all the time. The other day she put two on my legs. Then when I was in the middle of the room, she took my cane away. I was really scared of falling. She said, "Walk." And I said, "Well, I'll try, Alli dear, but it's very hard for Mommy now." Later she gave it back. She said, "We get two canes." I said no, not even two canes would make Mommy's legs better. All she said was, "Sad."

■

By Christmas that year, the bright green leaves of summer hope had turned crisp and brown and fallen off the tall trees at the Bauers' country house. Even the evergreens seemed less green, more somber, as if they too were hunkering down for an unusually harsh time. It was a sparse holiday for the four Bauers that year. Although money was not a problem, spirit was. Santa Claus still came, of course. Emily still

had definite ideas on how the house and apartment should be decorated. The difference was that she couldn't do it herself. She had to
have someone else hang the boughs and mistletoe, the shiny balls on
the tree, and all the other symbols of tradition that were so important
to her. She asked Bob to do much of it, and he did. He was around
Emily more now, as she wanted. If Bob was busy somehow, Emily
asked the babysitter for help, or she called Barbara or some other
friend. Bryan, who seemed to find a lot of reasons to visit this north-
ern city now, was around at times, usually with Barbara. Everyone
was always available and more than willing to help any way they could,
they said. This made Emily feel very warm and very loved and very
powerful. Even her ex-husband made an appearance when word got
around about her illness. His business was going great; the money was
rolling in, apparently, because he gave Emily his company's taxi
charge account number. Whenever she had to go somewhere, she was
just to charge it. The least he could do. Emily thought that was a
lovely gesture. Sure, thought Bob, a lovely gesture that also happens
to be tax-deductible. But he didn't say anything to disagree. In fact,
he didn't say anything.

The four Bauers were spending more time together in the tiny city
apartment. It was a small one-bedroom place, still Emily's, judging by
the decorations. Bob asked if maybe it couldn't be made more his
apartment too, somehow, since he was there more now. Sometimes
he felt like he was just sleeping over in this woman's apartment. Emily
said fine, okay with her, although, practically, she saw little that could
be done. It already looked nice, colors matching and all. Maybe Bob
could bring in some of his books. Would he like that? Of course, Bob
would have to do all the changes. Not much got changed.

There wasn't much room for books either. The living room was
narrow, maybe fifteen feet wide without the shelves and twenty-five
feet long. Emily and Bob slept there in a large bed by the window.
The simple kitchen was at the other end, separated by more floor-to-
ceiling shelves. In between was a large wooden dining room table
with a deep, blond grain and a smooth feel that Emily loved. It was
round, which was important to Emily because it drew diners in, leaving no one out on a far end. Closer to the window was a low table and,
next to it, a big sofa—again, with a lush wood grain showing on the

end pieces—with oversized pillows that invited relaxation. This room would loom large in the lives of Emily and Bob Bauer in the coming months.

The girls slept in the small bedroom, with Gaucho, the all-American cat with an all-American heart condition. On the way to the bedroom on the right was a small bathroom, up half a step, which presented some difficulties for Emily. Because it now took her so long to maneuver herself anywhere, even on the same level, she had already had a couple of embarrassing problems; they would have been called "mistakes" if the dog had done them. Bear, as the dog was called, was Bob's pal, a very big pal, to be sure. So big, in fact, that some relatives wondered out loud why Bob would keep such a behemoth in such a cramped place under these trying circumstances. Bob never really responded except to say the dog was part of the family, too, and then he'd change the subject. But during their increasingly frequent late-night walks, Bear heard a lot more about Bob's feelings than any human.

■

January 14, 1981: I think of what I am losing and what I am gaining. I am losing the shape of my leg, which increasingly has no muscle and is flaccid. I am losing the ability to walk in the woods on a beautiful day, to be independent as I've been, to expand my life. I am gaining a sense of love I never dreamed people could feel toward me, a respite from everyday chores, and more time to spend with the girls. I still do the ironing—that's about all—and fold the clothes. I'm less tired than I can remember being for ages and seem to have more time for reflection.

■

There were not many things that Emily wanted to know about that she didn't eventually learn a lot about. One of them was ALS. Her brother had computer access to much research material, and she had him print out reams of reports on the disease. She got anatomy and neurology books from the library, or had someone stop by to get them for her. She bought and consumed books on healing, inspiring stories about cancer victims who beat the disease. She called the ALS Society, which sent a packet of material. She found that literature depressing because so much of it accepted the inevitable demise of the victim.

All the doctors—she had gone to several after Berghoff—talked that way, too. They all grew suspicious after spotting the muscle weakness and the faint twitching together. Not all twitching is ALS, one doctor told her, but all ALS has twitching. They warned her with stories about past patients who completely denied the existence of their disease for a while or forever; the horror had simply been too much for the mind to handle. The doctors said there were mental stages to diseases just as there were physical stages—denial, anger, acceptance, peacefulness, even fulfillment on a different level. Every case was different. The stages weren't always clear-cut; lots of times they overlapped. Some people moved back and forth between them, or stopped partway. That was understandable, given the pathological personality of ALS.

It is a particularly malevolent disease, a sort of slow polio that more often stalks males, usually older and usually dead within five years. Because humans don't need all their strength or mobility for everyday life, the disease is often far along before it is discovered. Relatively little research has been done on ALS because there have not yet been good questions to ask.

But ALS is in many ways the opposite of the better known Alzheimer's disease. With Alzheimer's, the patient might not know what day it is, but he could be out playing tennis. An ALS victim could be doing quantum equations in her head, but she couldn't scratch her own nose. The mind, untouched, is sentenced to sit there inside the once-active person and witness the slow decay of its vibrant bodily shell, finger by finger, joint by joint, muscle by muscle, function by function, as if millions of ants were slowly crawling up the body sucking its vitality from within. Walking. Writing. Moving. Standing. Waving. Chewing. Swallowing. Breathing. Talking—that was a big one, that wide wall of silence that grew and grew as an ALS victim could no longer seem to respond, and those around began seeing her as more helpless, like a baby; they can't talk either. Eventually, the books said, all normal muscular function goes except the bowels and the eyes. ALS patients are particularly vulnerable to pneumonia. But they can still blink. And shit. And smell and see and feel everything they could no longer eat and do. And because they can no longer move, they have plenty of time to think about all of this. And to drift down that long dark tunnel, catching ever-smaller glimpses of normal life as it passes by the lighted end, a life that once seemed to require their presence and participation but now goes on without them just fine, it seems.

Well, Emily knew all about denial. She was, after all, a psychologist and a teacher. She wasn't interested in denial. She was interested in determination. A couple of friends started to suggest that perhaps she was denying denial a bit too much. They were cut off, and sharply, by Emily's eyes as much as her words. Emily didn't need negative reactions, not at this point, not when her life hung in the balance, not when there was still a chance. She needed support from true friends. And hope.

Emily grew increasingly angry at the doctors, too. She said they were telling her, in effect, to go home quietly and wait to die. Which, no doubt, made it easier for them to cope with their own medical failure here. But Emily still had a lot of questions for the doctors: What about this treatment, or that one, or this experimental drug? And there was this report in the medical journal. What should they try now? The doctors told her, honestly, what they knew—it was all unproven—and that, sadly, much less was known than remained secret. But they didn't tell Emily what she wanted to hear most, that a determined patient had a chance. They didn't want to hear her either. And she found the so-called medical experts increasingly rushed in their conversations. Or they were unavailable by phone. Perhaps they were mentally dismissing her as another emotional, worried woman. This, or something, made Emily very angry.

The doctors suggested instead that a social worker come by to help with the adjustments and the physical and financial planning. How to reduce physical movement to conserve energy, for instance, or how to arrange a home to minimize barriers for the handicapped.

Or how to avoid making substantial family financial commitments now because some sizable demands were likely to come down the road. How was their insurance, by the way?

Emily didn't need that kind of negative thinking either. Not now anyway. Why give up already? The struggle had just begun. There must be other ways to heal, ways that don't require aging men with yellowing diplomas and condescending attitudes toward new women. Maybe Emily could do this herself. They said not to exercise, but if she was back in physical shape, back doing some exercises regularly, really pushing herself, you know, then she'd feel better, probably. And have more strength for fighting. Emily didn't need outside help arranging her personal life either; she had a large loving family more than willing to help with anything. Hadn't they toasted that with élan at Thanksgiving? Bob or somebody was always there to help, and Emily hadn't heard any complaints. They loved helping her; they loved her. Maybe this ALS disease would be the one that needed to adjust its thinking. Emily Bauer would become the first human being to whip it. The championship bout was about to start.

■

February 1, 1981: Occasionally when I write, my fingers don't work quite right and I make a letter too large. It is too subtle for someone else to notice. But it terrifies me. I want to stop this process from spreading to my arms. But I do not know how.

February 7, 1981: I want someone who can give me some idea of how I can be helped.

■

A friend once suggested to Emily that if she was so interested in—she didn't say desperate for—alternative cures, she had heard of a seer, a local woman who held séances. Maybe it was crazy. Maybe, the friend thought, hoping for some relief for Emily and herself, it might help. At least worth a try.

It was better than that, Emily said. An excellent idea. She asked Bob to set it up.

Bob had his doubts. He'd never been big on formal religion; a God of some kind, yes, probably, somewhere unknown and unknowable by humans. No one with any sensitivities could ever hike in the woods in the mountains the way Bob loved to do, but hadn't done recently, and witness the coordinated chorus of nature—the birds, the towering trees, the fragile flowers, the moss, and the little creatures so full of life who ran around on it. No one could ever watch this cycle of life and not believe in some higher power somewhere. Even before that awful afternoon in that grim hospital office, Bob could shed a tear, a joyous sigh, at the splendor from somewhere that existed in those woods. But churches with manicured lawns, organized by humans around rituals with set times and social hours, he wasn't so sure about. Bob could deal with fantasy and images on film, if necessary, but he preferred documentaries and hard facts in real life.

He had no illusions about a cure for Emily; hopes, maybe, but he knew the facts about ALS. He'd told Alli the truth at first: They didn't know what was wrong with Mommy. But he had let that stand for longer than he felt comfortable with, as the medical suspicions mounted. He remembered that not knowing exactly what afflicted his mother many years before had allowed his fertile childish imagination to spawn nightmares and daymares far worse than reality. He wasn't going to let that mistake be repeated.

He told Alli that Mommy had a disease that affected her muscles and the way she moved. That satisfied the girl for the moment. And it was the truth; it had to be. How could he raise two kids in his middle age—and he was going to have to do that now, or sometime, wasn't he?—and not deal honestly with them? Jenie was a different story. She was too young to understand, so Bob spent a little more time holding her and talking at her. That was fine with Emily. But she hadn't wanted to say anything special. They could see for themselves what was happening. And maybe, though Emily didn't say, they might drift away from her in fear. Emily, who was using two canes now, wanted loving people revolving around her. Even more than that, she wanted them not to stop revolving around her.

Initially, Bob didn't get in the way of seeing this seer, nor any of the healers, nor the therapists who would enter their lives at various times in the coming months. Not even the vitamin doctor. This was Emily's life, for now. It would be Emily's death. He was Emily's husband. Even when the neurologist took him aside and said that if the Bauers had all the money in the world, seeking a miracle anywhere might be okay. But since he didn't think they did, it might be wiser to hold on to the funds. There were going to be a lot of expenses.

Bob called him back and said how much he appreciated the doctor's concern. But he was going to have to support his wife all the way on this one. Who could put a price on his wife's peace of mind if she felt she was accomplishing something with a healer and was supported by those around her?

Bob was interested in the search process and in the sense of togetherness that grew from it, as long as one didn't expect to wake up one morning and find a crippled leg had healed overnight. Bob was really ready to believe when he and Emily walked into the seer's room alone together and the woman told them things about their daughters and their little personalities that were precisely accurate. Maybe, Bob thought, there are untapped levels of living, knowing, feeling, and healing within everyone.

■

February 14, 1981: I don't like this one bit. I haven't been dependent before and now I am.

February 27, 1981: We had a kind of wake for my old physical self. I have some faith that what I gain spiritually will equal or exceed what I lose physically. It is strange to know that whatever physical ability I have now is probably the most I'll have. Gone is the possibility of change and the frantic attempts at exercise in hopes of recovery. I sensed the futility of this but did not really want to face it. Going to the gym and "walking" up and down the hall for all that time— twenty blocks one day—was an act of hope, but on some other level, it was denial. To not walk, run, or dance again is hard. But now I say to myself I will continue to sit tall; I hope it will be possible.

March 28, 1981: I'm feeling really sorry for myself. I tried to talk to the doctor, and he pointed out there were some things worse than what I have. That's true. But somehow it doesn't take away the feeling of helplessness, depression, and why me? Much of the time I'm really strong and terrific and, I'm sure, glean a lot of admiration. But who does one talk with about how it feels to know you are dying? I expected to live into my seventies. Well, I'm learning things, but it's a hell of a price to pay.

I guess if I could go to the ALS clinic with a group at my same stage of disease and awareness, then I would. But my contact so far with social workers and even doctors has left me more depressed and frustrated, and I'm growing increasingly reluctant to take the energy and stir up the stuff it does. I would much rather focus on the healthy part of me than the sick; it is so foreign to think of myself as unhealthy. What did I do wrong? And I used to so blithely judge others who became sick!

March 29, 1981: Has it been only a year since that first foot problem? Faith and hope are supposed to prolong life. But right now I am lacking both. I will try more of this nutrition and meditation, but I don't have strong faith that will help. Sometimes I think I might by random luck be the one who beats ALS. But I also know the probabilities and interpret them that I am dying, and probably sooner rather than later. And I don't know if it would be better to die later rather than sooner.

Sometimes I try to concentrate on preventing whatever it is from spreading, but I can feel it already in all the crucial areas, other than swallowing, and I don't know if I have the inner strength to counteract that reality. Sometimes I think Bob will take a leadership role in this. When he comes up with concrete ideas on how we can fight this, like he did last week, then I feel more hopeful and less alone. But sometimes he just says, "I love you" (and I shouldn't say "just," as it means a lot and before this happened I never was as sure of his love as I am now). I think he feels as helpless as I do. He is tired and preoccupied about work. On one hand, I recognize the importance of his work and on the other, it seems outrageous for him to be giving the time and energy to that when I am dying.

But, of course, that is not quite the best of me saying that.

April 2, 1981: And I certainly don't think this is all for the best, although sometimes I try to think that way, e.g., this is a more dramatic death and perhaps people will miss me more—that is, if I die a dignified rather than a burdensome death. I've thought how the weaker I get, the less in control of my life I am, and I don't know exactly how I could kill myself once I've passed a certain point. I don't know if I should.

I was trying to think of what could keep my life meaningful. I think of withdrawing gradually from the world into my own thoughts. Then I think of Alli and Jenie and hearing about them rather than directly interacting with them. I don't know how I can take care of my present work, though I do have fewer patients, while being with children and friends and also preparing for an early death. I need two more days in the week. I think I'll record some stories for the children, as well as the scrapbooks. I should do the activities involving speech first. I'm terrified that will go soon. Yesterday, I realized I can't move my tongue side to side very quickly. How long was this going on and I didn't know? At least consciously.

I need someone who can deal with me and give me some hope on a consistent basis. But I'm also afraid to look for fear I won't find that person. Or maybe it's a fantasy. Each day I wonder who or what the next source of hope will be and then anticipate that will end as have the others. But maybe I should try. (It's funny how I assume this person will be a man, but when I think of who actually says, "Call me when you're feeling low," it's all been women—L., B., A., and mother's pretty good, too.) I was supposed to go out to the country tomorrow with Bob and yet I don't know. It's hard to get around there.

Mother is going home soon. She has faith and even if I don't, it's soothing around her. In contrast, most of the time Bob is as depressed as I am. I'd thought we'd go to flea markets, but that seems rather trivial. I'm very confused. I just don't know. I don't want to be real heavy, but that's the way I feel.

Mrs. D. called. She had nothing hopeful to say unless you can call it hopeful to say, "Let's hope you have five more years so you can raise your children." I think of how Alli has started turning to Bob, who spends much less time with her. I think of how I turn to Bob rather than my mother while she is here and doing much dirty work. It's all very confusing. When she leaves, I will miss her. I get irritated at her, too, for ridiculous things and feel ashamed. I treat her like a daughter treats a mother, as if she's there to serve me. She resents that, and I don't blame her. I resent it in Alli. And Mother has done it a lot longer.

■

Emily's mother came from California every few months. She found Emily friendly at first, warm and welcoming, and surprisingly eager after all these years to hear about her childhood. She wanted the old familiar stories as well as any fresh ones her mother could dredge up: About a kindergartner named Emily who would resist a teacher's help for hours while working on a puzzle—"I'll do it myself!" the child would demand. About Bessie Rodgers, Emily's favorite teacher of all time, the one who was so firm with her. And the memory about Emily's memory—her first, actually—of the Ferris wheel rides with her father. She had wanted to go again and again that day, whirling around so high and clinging to him. That was the day Emily's brother was born. Emily didn't remember that part.

These memories were the glue of the family; they could be recalled and recounted whenever some member wanted reassurance that, yes, we here are the same people as back then, despite everything. But like old glue, the memories were drying up and cracking. And they were getting harder to recall, as if the mother's memory, or something, was hardening around those once-colorful tales so full of life, leaving them preserve-dried and pale for some stranger to find someday, if he cared.

Emily's mother also found her daughter easy to anger now. Sometimes someone just walking into the room all bouncy and cheerful was enough to set her off. Of course, Emily had always been a headstrong girl and not a little defiant; her father liked that for some reason. But he was away and didn't have to live with it. His more recent memories, though, focused on the clash of wills between father and daughter, and on his relief when he could negotiate a compromise with Emily. Nowadays, Emily was just plain angry. That tone of voice! It brought back memories, sleepy but vivid ones, of all the times Emily would wake up after midnight and cry for the longest times. Even when the bleary-eyed mother fed her and sang in the rocker, the crying would go on, as if someone else was supposed to come, too.

Even then, the mother recalled, Emily had liked—no, craved— being the focus of attention. Remember the pout when she lost that school election? And her joy at being the emcee at the school plays with the microphone and everything? Here Emily was again, right in the middle of everyone's day and thoughts and activities, and smack in the middle of this very small apartment. With a huge dog. And who were these strange people—what did Emily call them, healers?— who kept coming in?

Emily's mother also noted, with a little parental satisfaction over the existence of some justice in life, that Emily's own daughter had taken to long midnight cries, too, or more like two A.M. cries. Everyone in that cramped space—and there always seemed to be someone sleeping over—could almost set their watch by the wails, if they could see as far as their wrist at that hour. Of course, increasingly it was not the former midnight wailer who would silently roll out of bed in the dark to prepare a bottle and quiet the complainer. It was Bob. Often Emily's mother could hear Emily giving Bob directions from the bed. She didn't always whisper. Bob would reply politely.

Bob was a saint, everyone agreed. A tired saint, quiet, long-suffering, caring. Everyone lavished praise on Bob, and that seemed to give him strength. At least they thought so. They could never be sure. Bob never complained. Sometimes they would try to draw him out, on the theory that pent-up emotions mean trouble. His sister might make a mildly disparaging comment about a current mood of Emily's and then pause for his reaction. He might nod, agree it was difficult sometimes, but then note how hard it is for the healthy to sense fully the frightening sense of isolation in the dying.

Emily's mother and their friends, even Barbara and Bob's sisters, could dip in and out of the ordeal unfolding in that apartment. Some friends visited Emily at the apartment two or three times a week because it was hard to go anywhere with Emily. Both of her legs were largely useless now, but she still resisted the wheelchair. When she did move about, she got tired very easily, leaning on the canes and swinging first one leg and then the other with her hip.

Bob was there in the apartment every day. They had given up living in the country house much. Bob would rise by six and get the children changed, clothed, and fed by seven, when he would have Emily's breakfast ready; Bob was big on bowls of fresh fruit, or maybe oatmeal, if it was cold outdoors. By eight, the girls were off down the hall to the sitter's, a wonderful Puerto Rican woman whose children were grown and whose apartment and flexible schedule were wonderfully convenient.

After Bob left for work, a struggling filmmaking partnership with two others, Emily would have the morning for her writing or reading and hour-long appointments with patients. Emily wasn't teaching at the university anymore—on sick leave, they called it, though she was coming to think she would not return in the foreseeable future. Beating ALS was taking more of her energy and time than she had planned. And she didn't like giving up such control, to anyone or thing.

Emily still felt satisfied with her therapy work with individual patients, though. The Bauers certainly needed the income, and she was going to be sitting here anyway. In a way, all this private time was nice. There were a couple of embarrassing moments over Emily's worsening physical clumsiness, like the time a patient arrived for her session and found Emily stuck in the bathroom and had to help the doctor pull up her pantyhose.

But most days Bob was around, just as she had requested. He felt guilty about not carrying his full share of work at the office, but the partners never complained or commented about it, not even when Bob volunteered to take a smaller share of their small earnings.

Bob would rather have been at work. But the fact was that he was feeling more guilty about not being home with Emily and the kids. So more often Bob worked around the apartment or did the grocery shopping, and there was always another appointment to get Emily to. He would carry her down to their old van and up to the doctor's office and down to the van and into the healer's apartment and back out to the van and up to their apartment and into the bathroom and out to the couch and over by the kitchen, where he would set up a chair so Emily could sit and talk while Bob prepared dinner. He liked to cook in a wok, although Emily often had her own suggestions about how things should be done.

Barbara stopped by at least one evening a week and made dinner, and one of Bob's sisters did the same. Besides the delicious chicken and pasta, Bob remembered each of those evenings as a happy oasis of laughter and stories and loving helpfulness.

■

April 7, 1981: I passed up reading the employment ads for the first time in many years. There will be no looking for new jobs. Partly a relief and partly a disappointment.

April 9, 1981: Where am I going to get my hope from? I wonder how much of my degeneration friends will be able to stand. I'd hate people to be relieved when I died. Sometimes I think I'd like to go out in a blaze of glory tomorrow or at least very soon when the image of me is a vital one. Amy said my daughters would have an image of me struggling against tremendous odds; Bob said he wasn't so sure. At the time I sort of hated him—it was like he was saying he wanted me to die. But another part of me thinks he is right. How did a nice girl like me get into a situation like this?

Mother says to note my blessings, which is true. Would I prefer to be killed in an auto accident? At least this way I can prepare. I wonder if I can will myself to die soon but remain vital. Seems like a contradiction. Seems like people who will themselves to die lose their spirit. I don't want to do that. I just want to be me. And I'm not quite sure at what point I will cease to be me. Maybe I'll know. Maybe I'll need help to die. But who can I trust? Who would I want to share that responsibility? It's a horrible one. How can one make that decision? Could I for someone else? I don't know anyone to ask to help me, someone that I wouldn't feel I was burdening too much.

What have I got, maybe a year?

■

Every evening ended pretty much the same. Bob would tuck the girls into bed in the other room. Emily would call in what clothes she wanted laid out for them for the morning. Bob would finish the dishes. Bob would carry Emily into the bathroom; she could stand by herself, once up, but was getting pretty shaky on the canes. Bob had gotten her an aluminum walker, which always seemed to be banging into something. Bob would help Emily undress and wash parts of her body. Then he would put her to bed. And hear her thoughts and desires on the coming day.

"Aren't you coming to bed now, too?" Emily might ask, a little coyly.

"No," Bob would say, beginning a burst of activity, "I have to walk the dog."

Bob and Bear would go out for a long while. "How long does it take for a dog to shit?" Emily would think, lying there in bed, alone. Then she would feel very fatigued. Instead of building strength, exercise seemed to tire her inordinately. Emily's eyes would grow heavy and she'd get that wonderful peaceful feeling she first knew on the beach as a child, that feeling so free of any care, when the warm waters took control and gently rocked the raft to and fro in uncertain soothing rhythms. And Emily would drift there, safe and asleep.

Until the cramps came. Powerful spasms, they would grip her motionless legs from inside and seem to twist the confused muscles into excruciating knots. The couple had been warned about these, but medical warnings somehow are never like the real thing. A grimacing Emily would groan and reach out for Bob before remembering that he was still walking the damned dog. But Bob was there. He'd be up instantly, his tall frame bending over her, quietly massaging her legs with those big hands and few words. After a few minutes, he would turn his wife over into a new position and arrange her legs as directed and remind her in the dark that he had rigged these ropes here from the ceiling so she could reach up and turn herself over anytime. Then Bob would return to their bed where he would seem to fall back asleep instantly. Until Jenie woke up at two for an hour or so, sometimes more. Then Bob was up with her, too.

■

May 15, 1981: I had a dream last night that I was making love with a very average-looking man with black-rimmed glasses. As we were getting dressed, he told me I had beautiful breasts and reached over and caressed them. I was very pleased and grateful. Associations: I had some sexual feelings for the first time in a while last night, but they remained unexpressed for a variety of reasons. I looked in the mirror while undressed this morning and thought at least some parts of my body, including my breasts, looked just fine.

That was the first dream where my legs were limited.

■

One day, out of the blue, Emily said she might try a wheelchair after all. Not, Emily quickly added, that she really needed it now or back when the doctors and nurses first suggested that vehicle for cripples. They said it would increase her mobility and daily endurance. Not, they cautioned, that she'd ever be stronger but that she could use her remaining strength more efficiently. At that time Emily's arms had still been strong enough to turn the chair's wheels herself. Now they seemed weaker to Emily. Anyway, she had plenty of friends and relatives who were willing to help.

■

June 10, 1981: Holly is in town for a visit and helped me get in touch with a lot of anger in me. She took me in the chair to the museum. I look at those people on the street who I know are far more mediocre than I, and they are walking around and I am not! Superiority, of course, has nothing to do with it. There is a part of me that thinks this is temporary and after I've paid my dues and learned, I will be able to walk. Holly knew just what I meant. But I hate many people's reactions, those who act like nothing is different, those who admire me for my strength and give no awareness of what I'm going through. Yesterday I told Bob I thought my legs were worse and all he said was, "Oh?"

June 25, 1981: I don't like going to the clinic. I see other people more disabled than I and I don't want to be there. I ran across, as I am collecting things for Alli's and Jenie's scrapbooks (that project progresses), an old report card of mine which spoke of how "Emily dislikes leaving an activity she is interested in" and how "Emily has a hard time letting others get their say in." I would say to some degree I've changed in the latter, although I do speak my own view and am very interested in my own ideas, but also learn from others.

How can I express my Self if I can't walk, can't talk, and can't use my hands? I'd probably find some way to communicate.

June 30, 1981: I guess I'll be forced to develop more humility. Sometimes, like now, I want to run out and learn everything else there is to know about ALS and find myself a cure. Then I think it would take a great deal of time and energy to gain such expertise and is that my task in life? Should I focus on saving myself or on leading my life and exercising the abilities I still have, and maybe discovering new ones? I both don't want to die and want to die while I'm still who I am.

July 7, 1981: A beautiful day! Bob brought me flowers today, as he does every week. I wonder sometimes if he would love me if we met now. He isn't crying so much about me, just as I'm not about myself. Yet I remember his grief and hope I never forget what it signifies.

July 9, 1981: I look at Alli and Jene and think they are so wonderful and so beautiful, and yet I see my salvation as getting more into myself and becoming more detached from them. A strange dilemma. In quiet times after I cry, like now, I lose my depression, actually feel quite content. In contrast, my time with them is very satisfying, but I am very conscious of my increasing limitations. And then I think of the future.

■

Bryan always came by on a Saturday, late morning usually, after he'd slept late from the ten-hour drive. This one Saturday Emily had a great idea. She wanted to go out in the wheelchair. Bryan could push. It was a lovely day. And it would be a kind of crippled coming-out party. They'd go around to all the neighborhood food and specialty and dress shops that Emily patronized and say hello, Emily was back in circulation in her new chair.

Emily was always trying to organize family outings of this sort to museums or arboretums or exhibits. Almost always Bob or the family would agree, although with the chair and the walker and the babies and the diapers and bottles, it became less of a relaxing outing and more of an exhausting expedition—for the wheelchair pusher anyway. Emily would sit there, bubbly again, organizing everyone. They were sometimes annoyed, silently. But they knew, or thought they knew, how confining it must be to sit in a wheelchair awaiting your doom soon. Emily was obviously gulping down these experiences like a thirsty traveler through time, grabbing them up as a squirrel does acorns and pine cones before the long winter and stashing them away safely for savoring later in a colder time. For the relatives the disease certainly was a primary concern, though not the only concern in their busy lives; they loved Emily for what she was and had done and because, but for the grace of God, they could be in her position. Emily was so appreciative and lavish with her praise when they did what she wanted. On the other hand, when they didn't . . .

The friends weren't trying to accumulate memories quickly. They could die, too, any day. The difference was that no one told them when. They wouldn't see it coming, wouldn't have time to count all the big and little things they would miss, like the ease of movement, the joy of hugging, the taste of turkey, the satisfaction of telling a joke, or laughing at one out loud. These outings with others gave Bob some company if he went along or some quiet time to himself if he didn't. He was looking quite tired.

So Bryan agreed to that outing with genuine enthusiasm. If the shopkeepers asked about her disease, Emily said, they would just tell them. She seemed pleased to have finally faced up to this creeping paralysis, at least as far as her legs were concerned. The family was pleased with this recognition. And no doubt her casual store friends would be, too.

So the brother and sister started out, almost ritualistically. Bryan quickly came to see barriers for the handicapped that he had never thought about before—tall curbs, potholes, narrow doors and aisles, and the silent stares of those in his peripheral vision.

"Well, hello, Mrs. Bauer," said the first storekeeper. "Long time, no see. What are you doing in a wheelchair?"

"I'm sick," Emily replied. "I can't walk."

"What's the matter?"

"I have ALS."

"Oh, I see. Well, when will you be out of the wheelchair?"

"Never."

The shopkeeper suddenly saw another customer who needed service immediately.

At store after store—the butcher's, the hairdresser's, the dress shop, the scene was the same: pleasure at seeing an old customer, concern at the wheelchair, ignorance about the disease, and, once they learned it was terminal, eagerness to change the subject. This woman seemed angry at them about something. The only thing that saved the afternoon was one woman, a clerk, who cried at the news.

That's the part Emily talked about when everyone gathered back at the apartment. They all agreed those others were callous or maybe too busy or too frightened of dying to show adequate concern. Animatedly, Emily talked with Barbara about her upcoming wedding to Bryan. That was when Bob suggested to Bryan the two men go for a walk.

■

August 29, 1981: At times I feel so full of good family vibes. At others I fantasize my not being here and people going on having a wonderful time and feel angry and resentful that I'm not there. And even darker are my thoughts that people aren't really doing anything tangible to make me better. And while I know I'm always on their mind, that doesn't seem enough. I want them to meditate with me. Or devise a ritual pageant for me. Or give money to the ALS society. I want people to sacrifice directly to help me and then I ask what makes me think they will or should do that. I don't express too much of these feelings, as they seem ungrateful and greedy. Yet I think something more must be done.

■

Bryan and Bob ended up in an ice cream parlor and ordered sundaes. Bob wanted to talk. He had to talk. For him, this was a flood of words. You don't know what it's like day and night, he said. There's always something, get this, do this. Bryan nodded. It sounded like an earlier Emily, only magnified.

Bob said at first he thought it was just him, you know, being too close to the patient and the situation and everything he and Emily had planned together for all those years ahead. But then, Bob said, he realized it wasn't just him. Some of their friends—just a few—but some had dropped out of touch. Emily's list of patients was smaller, too. Bob didn't know any of them well, but some just stopped coming or regularly skipped appointments, leaving Emily waiting, alone, in her wheelchair in the dark apartment. Those nights she aimed her anger at Bob, which he knew was misdirected, but that didn't mitigate the unpleasantness. At least two patients had confided that they wanted to stop coming but didn't know how to do it without hurting the doctor's feelings. Bob said he couldn't tell anymore who was the doctor and who was the patient.

It was starting to affect the kids, too, Bob said. The baby was still waking up wailing in the middle of every night. She obviously knew something was wrong, though Bob was doing the best he could, he thought. Alli had taken to misbehaving more. Sometimes she was downright obnoxious, which Bryan didn't need to be told. If her milk came in a blue mug, she wanted the green one. Whenever they went out, she wanted Daddy to carry her, just like he carried Mommy. Bryan knew the kid was crying out for more attention, but there wasn't enough time or attention to go around.

As Bob talked, Bryan's eyes looked past his brother-in-law's shoulder to a young woman hunched in a wheelchair by the front counter. She was trying to eat an ice cream cone while the bill was paid by her father or husband or brother—it was so hard to tell ages with the handicapped. But the woman in the wheelchair kept missing her mouth with the cone. A chill went down Bryan's spine—and not from his ice cream. He had just looked through a little window into the future.

When Bryan looked back to Bob, he was still talking. The ice cream was melting, but Bob was getting to the point. Can you imagine what it's like, he said, to carry someone all over and put them on a bedpan and then have to dump it? And then get into bed with that same person who can't move—he tried to crawl in quietly to avoid waking her—and be expected to make love to her? Now that her arms were getting weaker, it was like screwing a corpse.

Bryan didn't say anything, but he had already heard about the problem. Emily had confided to Barbara that her husband seemed to have trouble making love to her recently, and Emily said she needed his affection. Any woman, anyone, needs to be held and stroked and loved sometimes, especially at times like this. It's a necessity of life. Emily said she wished Bob would get some help.

55

Maybe he's tired, Barbara suggested. He was working very hard, up at all hours. Emily remained unconvinced.

Bryan told Bob that afternoon that he understood and had his full support, no matter what. Everybody knew how much Bob loved Emily and was doing for her. My God, no one could do more. Bryan said he'd do everything he could to help Bob. But Bryan didn't say anything about one of his other major concerns. Bob hadn't entered into this marriage bargain with any of these details in mind. He could just walk out the door one day, leaving the whole sad mess for someone else to handle, namely Bryan.

■

September 21, 1981: This is like experiencing one's old age prematurely. Bob tells me how much everyone loves me, and sometimes I feel it. But their lives can go on so well without me. He says I have to stay alive until the girls are adolescents, yet he doesn't mention our lives together. Well, I, too, think of them as reasons to live instead of Bob. Now I am thinking about things for myself, how I can improve the quality of my life, not how long it will be. But every different bodily feeling arouses such terror that I'm afraid I'm dying right now. I told a patient about all this, as my feelings now parallel hers, and she said some helpful things. The other day I was plotting my death with J. This week I want to fight like hell to be well. Yet the odds seem so against me. I guess I hate the thought of failure. I never would try anything where I thought I'd probably lose. But maybe now is the time to start doing things differently. Perhaps I don't want to be well, perhaps I want to be sick and special and see what that brings.

September 24, 1981: I gave J. my high-heeled shoes. But not all. I kept one pair in case.

September 29, 1981: Bob's friend R. told us about a healer who once cured a woman who had rheumatoid arthritis. When we met her, we both felt her tremendous energy and wanted to work with her. She told me a lot of things. She saw a mass in my pelvic area (where that Oriental healer saw an emerging cyst). She said I had serious misalignment and felt unworthy, despairing, and I'd have to choose life instead of dying. Then another of Bob's friends said he saw a lot of desperation in the way I live. I rose up and said I didn't agree, that I was very satisfied with the structure of my life since meeting Bob. I was surprised and pleased at myself because usually I am intimidated by people who I regard as more spiritually developed than I and feel vulnerable to their put-downs.

October 3, 1981: This second session with the new healer has turned me around. I felt like I was high on champagne. She gave me lots of encouragement and seemed extremely pleased with my ability and I was thrilled to be able to mobilize such energy and imagery because when I was working alone, nothing was happening and I was terrified that I didn't have the inner strength to beat this. But she said I do and she did a lot of healing on me through concentration, saying only, "Love is real."

Afterward she told me that what we were doing was God, that what I experienced was only one event along a continuum of that time tunnel that was endless and that actually things went much farther back, in fact, all the way to ancient Egypt. I had told her about a dream of being in another life, on the prairies and riding in a horse and buggy, and feeling myself falling off a cliff. She said it went back much farther and that in Egypt I was a woman possessing great wisdom. "You have wisdom," she said. And I said I was just beginning to sense that.

She said we would have to work real hard to reexperience all that and she thought I'd be cured in three to six months, that the disease certainly would not spread. We hugged, we were so excited, and she told me she loved me. She said I made her laugh, telling her what finks neurologists are and how I could hardly wait to walk into their offices and say, "Look at me!" I told Bob this, too, but he didn't say anything. I'm flying high now!

October 12, 1981: Tuesday I saw the healer again, and we got into a lot of heavy stuff (although in retrospect I wonder if what made it heavy was my expectation of what was supposed to happen). She said this was the first time I'd let a little light into the frozen parts of myself. Thinking about it today, I wonder how much of what I produced was to meet her expectations. Anyway, when she asked me to focus on my foot, one of the images I had was my foot flying with wings skimming atop the ocean with little waves to a shoreline, a barren one like the Maine coast. Then I had an image of a crocodile, which is cold and surviving and a sacred animal somewhere, I believe. Then an image of that coast and a lighthouse with a lavender beacon. She said lavender is a sacred color, and it's my favorite recently.

Then she asked me to go back to Egypt and see myself as an initiate into the mysteries inside the pyramid. This seemed a little strained to me, but I was game and said I went in and died. She said my disease was not part of myself but related to a past life, probably in Egypt, that I was a holy woman and doing quite well. I said I had been smothered and then I said, no, they hit me on the back of the neck, a quick merciful death. I said it happened because either I didn't have the inner strength or was in conflict with someone.

October 24, 1981: The healer and I have had a parting of the ways, since she is more interested in her imagery than mine and vice versa. She said my disease was due to a past life when I was a priest and was mean to people and hurt them.

That is my image of someone laying a guilt trip on me, and that is the last thing I need. Plus it is incredibly simplistic. She said that in times of transition foreign substances were spewed on earth and those who were weak got sick. But I couldn't come up with enough in my life to explain that. She is incredibly clever, as she said I would not believe her, which set me up in a no-win situation.

I do think the idea of reincarnation has merit.

■

For a welcome while, Emily drew sick-leave pay from the university, which was vital to the Bauers' financial survival with the mounting expenses for medical equipment and various treatments, two homes, the girls, and, of course, the healers, most of whom expected about fifty dollars an hour. But even when the university money ended, there was no talk of cutting back, not when it involved anything as important as Emily's life or salvation. There was some insurance money, though precious little, since Emily was not hospitalized. Bob's modest salary helped, and odd jobs, and some savings. They'd get by.

They did have to buy a medical bed for Emily, despite her abiding opposition. It was one of those motorized ones that tilts up and back. The girls were wary of the wheelchair; it seemed to swallow their mother every time Dad set her down in it. But they clambered up to ride on the bed that went up and down. Bob also rigged floor-to-ceiling doors in the living room to give Emily some privacy at one end, the end with the window. She would lie there for long periods, staring out the eyes of her window at the busy world passing by, unaware. Bob built those doors efficiently and quickly, hammering the nails in straight with frightening force. When Emily was resting, the doors were closed, which cut off all light from the outside, turning the home into a tomb.

Everyone had to tiptoe around. "Shhh" was the key word.

■

November 6, 1981: Another patient called to cancel today, so I spent the time imaging.

■

Money was also an argument Emily used against hiring outside help. Right at the beginning, the ALS people had said housekeeping help would become necessary as time passed and strengths waned; there would be enough strains on all members without worrying about toilets and laundry. Some ALS clinic workers had developed their own measures for the often unspoken stress of the disease's tyranny on a family. They watched the spouse's eyes for the telltale fatigue rings that spoke of long nights' work to catch up on chores and short nights' rests to catch up on sleep. The wrinkled wardrobe of victims' wives was an especially good indicator. How much the patient and the accompanying relative chatted while awaiting their regular appointment. Things were getting bad if the healthy member buried himself in an old magazine and left the victim sitting next to him, alone. If the husband simply dropped the wife off at the clinic, it might already be too late.

Emily went out to lunch with friends less, or they asked her to go less. They thought her increasing arm control problems might be embarrassing, when so much food would fall in her lap or on the floor and the waiters and other diners would look sideways and smile politely, saying that was okay, the cleanup was no problem. Bob still drove Emily to the clinic, and to the healers. He still waited at the clinic, but not at the healers'.

He did sit in on a few sessions of one larger therapy group, gathered around in a circle with their shoes off, the new members hesitant and smiling, the oldtimers joking among themselves. When they asked Bob about his feelings, he said he was feeling a little anger these days, but he really had nothing to say right then. The leader suggested Bob might reconsider later when he felt more comfortable. Bob nodded. Emily, however, did not hesitate. First of all, sitting in her wheelchair put her up higher than everyone else. And second, as a psychologist and patient she had been through these introductions before, the awkward initial time before people begin pouring out their guts to complete strangers because they are less likely to use it against them.

But the Bauers didn't stay with that group long at all. One of the women members remarked that she thought Emily was sitting on her

disease like a throne, its tragedy giving her added personal importance. Emily didn't say much the rest of that session. Neither did Bob;
it occurred to him that maybe he was, too. But an outraged Emily
repeated the story many times to others, who didn't seem to agree or
disagree with the other woman's observations. Perhaps they had an
experience with Emily like Barbara's, who had dropped in one time
and glanced at the Bauers' refrigerator. There, stuck on the door, was
a special curative diet from one of the healers. Only eight hundred
calories a day! This cure will kill Emily, Barbara thought. The healer
happened to be there then, and Barbara exploded.

"What the hell are you doing to her?" she said. "Emily can't walk
anymore. She's having trouble writing. Eating foods and sipping some
wine are some of the few pleasures she's got left!"

The woman left in a hurry. "Maybe you've gone a little too far into
this healer business," Barbara said to Emily. But then Emily exploded. Barbara had no right to come in here and treat her friends
that way. The woman was only trying to help. She'd helped many
others. What Emily needed most from her real friends now was not
criticism but love and support and, most of all, hope. She didn't want
to hear negative things, not in her house.

Barbara wasn't around much anymore, but she was in close touch.
She and Bryan had gotten married after a passionate courtship that
often seemed to annoy Emily. But Emily made it down south for the
wedding. Not all the family snapshots of that joyous affair included
Emily. Those that did showed her, in her wheelchair, on the side of
the groups offering toasts in the sunny garden or peering between two
people looking at the camera. No longer in the middle of each scene,
she was seated in a flowered dress amid all that standing happiness,
about three feet below the conversations. No one planned it that way.
Bob held her champagne glass between sips, though he talked more
to others.

When Barbara had described the diet incident to Bob, he
shrugged. He thought these healers were 90 percent charlatans and
10 percent worthwhile. The trouble, he said, came in sorting out
which was which. Maybe, he suggested again, there are other levels of
being than what he and Barbara understood. One person's nonsense

was another's salvation. "How do we know what it's like to be shrink-ing away?" he said. "If she feels better, then this healing business works."

One day, however, Bob did a little of his own healer-sorting. He arrived home to find a new healer meeting with Emily. Bob was walk-ing across the room to Emily when this healer looked at the two little girls, pointed at an uncomprehending Jenie, and sternly announced, "She is the root of this disease!"

In three quick strides Bob was by the man's side. He grabbed the fellow's coat and escorted him out the door, saying they wouldn't be needing his services anymore. It was then that the man asked for his fee.

"I'll give you something to heal on yourself if you don't get the hell out of here," said Bob, and slammed the door.

Emily did not argue.

■

November 14, 1981: Sometimes I think I'm using this illness to put me back in an adolescent stage of marginal involvement with the world. Also, there is a part of me that doesn't want to be defined as sick as if that subtracts from my power. When I get through all this, I'm going to be that much more of a person. This ALS label has brought a lot of attention to me and solidified my feelings of self-worth. But it is no time to be ruled by inferior motives like prolonged adolescence.

■

Healers from outside the family were all right. But not helpers from outside. Hired hands didn't care as much, Emily said. Half of them didn't speak English. They were unreliable, sometimes not showing up just because there was a sickness in their family or something. They might not even call, and Emily would sit there with her list of chores and no one to give it to. And when they did come, they often had their own priorities or routines. If they came to help Emily, she thought they ought to do some housework, too. If they came for housework, Emily needed another pillow or help to the bathroom or a massage for a leg cramp.

It seemed that none of them could do much of anything right. Emily was full of criticism before and after they left, with the servant sometimes closing the door a little too firmly for someone of her station. Sometimes Emily sent them home early. If they couldn't get anything right, what was the point in staying? Emily would detail her displeasure to Bob that night and have him do the unfinished chores. Around mid-evening Bob often excused himself from the apartment—had it grown smaller in recent days or was that just his imagination? Maybe Bob would take the garbage to the chute. He would stop by the pay phone in the hall. "I don't know how long I can stand it," passersby could hear him say. "It's 'do this, do that, get this, get that, go here, go there, do it now.'" That passerby may have thought the man was complaining about his boss.

The ALS social workers had seen all this before in all the many forms that each unique case presents. For a patient to accept outside help required accepting the need for help, which meant accepting the continued progress of the disease. Hired helpers, who knew all the tricks, were less susceptible to the guilt that terminal and long-term diseases spawn among healthy family members and friends. "Terminal guilt" the social workers call it with a knowing smile during their coffee breaks. That gives an ALS patient immense powers over the family. They can't quit and go home; they are at home. The realistic family, watching the daily wasting process, begins to feel the narrowing confines of hopelessness and the leadening burden of forced cheerfulness. The focus of life turns to death and degeneration. And although modern medicines and machines can offer no cure, they can prolong the process.

A patient might resist and resist and resist every inexorable step of the disease. Then the losses accumulate, day-to-day concerns become paramount, and the denial becomes a dam under mounting pressure from reality. Finally, a patient accepts the loss of yet another movement, only to discover that the disease hasn't waited. It has moved on to other muscles. Despair seeps in. And anger.

There was plenty of family to help keep the Bauer household operating. If Emily needed anything and Bob was gone, she just phoned a friend or other relative and asked them over. Sometimes the friend said she was busy with classes or patients or a doctor's appointment. If Emily told her how badly she wanted to have lunch with her, she usually came around. She would skip the class or change the doctor's appointment at the last minute and bring in some of Emily's favorite tacos or sushi. Some of them remember those times as among the happiest ever, so appreciative and intense was Emily.

Emily tried to keep a regular routine of these visits. There always seemed to be a special project for them, too. Her fingers and arms weren't operating as well as they used to, and she seemed a little short of breath at odd times, too, but maybe that was just her imagination. As a result, Emily had fallen behind her schedule on all the projects she was planning to leave behind, in case she didn't beat ALS. There were the quilts, which a whole quilting group took on. There were long hours spent with her diary; her fingers were missing the right typewriter keys more often, but she felt better having expressed herself to herself. There were the scrapbooks for each girl and the family. Bob got slightly annoyed whenever he looked at them. Emily had the habit of cutting out the silhouette of every person in a snapshot and rearranging the pieces on the scrapbook page to represent a new reality. Bob preferred natural scenes, though his short, sharp remarks to Emily recently dealt with other things. In the world according to Emily's scrapbook, there was little room for empty woods or mountains or even a wheelchair, just crowds of smiling friends and her children, arrayed around her and glued into place, so they couldn't drift off.

■

November 19, 1981: The healer says Jenie is from another dimension, to which Bob says, "Bullshit!" But then he tells me that when he was feeding her at one A.M. the other night, she stared at him for twenty minutes without blinking or diverting her attention; he timed it. When I'm alone with Alli sometimes she will move the phone out of my reach, with a gleeful look. It is like she is possessed by the devil, or enjoying torturing me. She can make me so aware of my limitations that I would like to take out all my anger on her and hurt her back. On occasion she has hit the baby. I wonder if she is retaliating or simply senses her advantage and exercises the power she has. At other times she is very sociable, feeding Jenie and bringing me things. I know I was mean to my brother, not to be mean, but to get my way.

November 26, 1981: Sometimes I feel like a scared little girl and all I want is a mommy to put her arms around me and tell me everything will be all right, somehow.

I called Dr. Berghoff today and was encouraged by his interest in me. I started to tell him about an ALS symposium I went to and all the alternative forms of therapy I've learned about, but he cut the conversation short. Putting myself in his place, I guess I wouldn't want to hear a patient start telling me about new treatments I should read up on. But perhaps I'd listen more. I put myself in the role of the professionals I'm dealing with and they, like I, hadn't and haven't any idea how it really feels to be in a position like mine. It's new for our society. I'm getting a lot more compassion and humility, but it seems an unfair way to have to learn it. But probably I wouldn't have otherwise.

December 4, 1981: called E. to come do some light housework. Funny, a while ago I was delighted to have someone else do the chores. Now, I'd like nothing better than to be able to do some. But I get so tired. I do so little now and I see it as an avoidance because all things are so difficult.

I know I called E. in just because I feel such despair. Like when I called the healer and she came in and held me for an hour and I paid her $50. It seems crazy, yet basically it was just what I needed. But who can hold all people going through such things? Professionals? Mate? Therapists? All of whom have enough else to deal with. (I think of that one therapist who, when she heard Bob mention he did

65

all the cooking, said with a ring of obvious disapproval, "How come?")

I think of what Bob is going through; today, simultaneously I told him to go to work and to go pick up Alli at nursery school. I guess it's just I'm so needy and distressed by all this.

December 10, 1981: I hate doctors. I hate when they ask how much life insurance I have. I hate when they say they're just being realistic. I hate Berghoff saying I probably won't get better. And I hate that psychologist who enjoys helping me adapt to my illness. They, of course, are right in a reality sense, but I hate that in their quest for reality, they give me no hope. Let me be the doubter and reality-oriented and let them be the healers. I hate my mother referring to the day I won't be able to move and adding, "But that's a long time from now."

AND I HATE HAVING THIS DISEASE. There is nothing to do but struggle. I won't give up hope that things can be different. I don't know if I would want to live without any hope. Deep inside I will never give up hope.

I think of the smugness of others, that one woman (an occupational therapist?) who said to me with a ring of criticism, "Why don't you do the cooking?" How the hell does she know what it's like to maneuver in a tiny kitchen and apartment? Let her try it for a while before she's so quick to judge. Oh, and I can see the part in me that is like her, that is so certain about everything. Boy, am I learning a lot.

And thank God for Bob. I would give my life for him, as I feel he gives to me on that level. In my bad times I wonder what I give to him. I just realized I don't know what it is about me that is important to Bob. I try to feel we're both getting something from this. I'm lucky to have him. He understands.

■

Emily felt short of breath more often. She thought it was like drowning and it terrified her. She might wake up at night—well, she always woke up at night and called or nudged Bob to turn her over—but breathing now sometimes felt like sucking in air through a straw. It would come, but not enough soon enough. Such work for something that had so long been taken for granted! It reminded Emily of what she imagined drowning to be like—sinking, frightened, gasping, coughing, dreaming, sleeping. But not peaceful. Emily, in mental flight, would waken Bob to be with her. Sometimes he would hold her in the dark, and that was soothing, though Emily noticed that her husband no longer kissed her full on the mouth. He'd give Emily a little peck on the forehead as if she were a little girl. And maybe a pat, while he asked about her day as he went about the chores. Those days of passion were gone, too, she figured, at least for now. Bob was big on hand-holding and cuddling sometimes. Thank God.

The Bauers got a respirator, a portable model that Bob could hook on to the wheelchair. Not that Emily had to have it, of course. It had been like the wheelchair, not really necessary, she would say, just more convenient. Easier for everyone, Emily said. She was still resisting the idea of a motorized wheelchair, which made no sense, since there was always someone available to push the chair. You had to recharge it and everything. But the respirator made sense now.

The respirator had a long, clear plastic hose the diameter of a fifty-cent piece. With her stronger left arm Emily lifted the mouthpiece to her face and inhaled a few breaths whenever she wanted. That got more oxygen into her system and eased the strain on lungs and heart.

For Emily, like many of those with breathing problems, the option quickly became a necessity. She wanted that equipment right next to her every single minute. The sight of a reclining Emily pausing in a conversation, lifting her left hand to her mouth, keeping the elbow tight against her thinner body, became very familiar to those around her. The equipment's gentle hissing sound would become familiar, too, in a sinister way like a snake, a constant aural reminder of reality.

■

ANDREW H. MALCOLM

December 18, 1981: The severe stress with Bob continues and is as much a source of distress as the disease. It seems an inevitable consequence. I think my physical condition and its endless frustrations have stirred all our vulnerabilities. Bob oozes silent rage. I always look forward greatly to when he comes home and love being with him, but we don't really have that much to talk about. I try to express what I'm going through, and I wonder if it is all very boring. I'm somewhat interested in his work but mostly just to know what makes him happy or unhappy.

December 20, 1981: I wish I had a consuming passion to organize my life. I look back on the beginning of all this when I had so many action-oriented plans and ambitions. People ask me about writing a book, and I say I don't know what the point would be. An outcry? A demonstration of valor? Maybe something on the impact on the family. But that is so complex it makes me tired.

■

Emily was looking forward to Christmas that year. They were going south to Bryan's for the holidays, driving to save money. Thank goodness for the van; it had room for the chair and oxygen, and the four Bauers, too. Bryan and Barbara had just moved into a gracious old brick-and-stone manse with a fireplace, frolicking squirrels, and far too many wet leaves to rake. It was just right for the newlyweds and Bryan's three fast-maturing children from a previous marriage.

But five plus four equals nine, plus one respirator and one wheelchair and one large dog with four legs, and things in that house were suddenly a little tight for the holidays, especially since Emily had to be in a ground-floor room. They set her up in a den bed with a light and books, a radio and TV, and a view out into the tall, old trees. They also put an old cowbell on the bedside table, just in case Emily needed help.

Emily needed a lot of help. The bell rang quite a bit, especially if Bob, Bryan, and Barbara were in the kitchen making a meal and chatting together. Emily also had numerous suggestions for putting up or moving Barbara's holiday decorations. This annoyed Barbara a great deal; Bryan could tell by the pauses in her replies. This house was Barbara's nest now, not Emily's. But Barbara said nothing. She would move the wreath over a little, as Emily suggested. After all, this well might be Emily's last Christmas. Humor her. They were going to have a good time whether they liked it or not.

They did, however, develop several unspoken strategies for dealing with reality that week. They took turns answering the bell by day and night. And, of course, the bell would awaken at least one baby. Each adult discovered urgent errands outside the house. Even after returning from the store, they'd remember a forgotten item—paper diapers or some other necessity. How stupid of them! And back out they'd go for a while, Bryan or Bob or Barbara. They might smile at each other after leaving the house, feeling so clever and relieved and guilty about both. They'd open the car window and take a deep breath of that fresh cool air and think of that respirator back inside, its wheezes seeping through every room in the house like a malevolent cloud. Then they would change the channel and drive away from it all for a while.

Emily couldn't understand why her brother's household was so disorganized, all these errands that seemed so necessary. Sometimes Emily suggested an outing, to the zoo or somewhere that was fun and open enough for two baby strollers with two fussing babies and a wheelchair with a portable respirator and a happy woman attached, all being pushed by three adults who told their presiding tour guide in the wheelchair what a good time they were having.

It took much longer than planned to get to the zoo. Back at the house, the two families, minus Bryan's teens, who had their own plans, all piled into the Bauers' rusting old van ready to go, and just as Bob put it in gear, Emily's voice came from the back: "I don't want Alli to wear that color dress today." There was a pause that seemed very long, while the eyeballs of the three adults turned toward the vehicle's ceiling. Then Barbara, who had fed, bathed, and dressed both toddlers, stepped deliberately from the van and went inside with Alli to change the child's clothes. No problem.

A few days after Christmas, Bryan and Barbara were standing in their back door, waving and smiling broadly as the Bauers drove away.

The newlyweds didn't see the Bauers every two weeks or so anymore, so they had noticed some changes. Emily was definitely weaker. She could talk okay, sipping on the oxygen now and then. But the right arm was useless and thinner. She looked gaunt, and her appetite was smaller. Bob looked pretty well though tired, and he did seem to drink more this time.

And there was a palpable tension between Emily and Bob. It flared up now and then, when Bob admonished Alli for not eating all the beans Aunt Barbara had made and Emily interjected that the child didn't have to. The disagreement was a mild one, but it didn't end there. There was more verbal shoving, which the other adults pretended not to hear and the child watched intently. Bob didn't choose to spend any more time with Emily than necessary. He was kissing only her forehead, they noted. And then one evening after Bob had bathed Emily and they were all sitting together sipping wine, Emily launched into a long talk about how wonderful her ex-husband was, how he must still like her, don't you think, and all the things he was doing for her—the taxi charge account and sending a secretary over once to type some things. Emily thought that was so thoughtful. And Bryan thought Emily was being so Emily.

Bob was silent that day, but back in New York when a couple of women friends were over one Sunday and Emily was choreographing their afternoon in the apartment sorting photos and memorabilia, she wanted Bob to rearrange a shelf stacked with shoeboxes full of fabric scraps. He did so, but intentionally or not, the boxes did not end up as Emily had envisioned. She told him to move them.

"I'll move them all right," he said, and flung some across the room toward her, before stomping out for a while. Emily said she was shocked. She told her friends it must be all the stress of her disease. Yes, the stress, they said, nodding.

Soon after, Emily suggested the family go away for a midwinter holiday. Puerto Rico, maybe. Who knows when the next opportunity might come? They could take along the attendant they hired most days to help Emily. She made this suggestion knowing full well how much Bob disliked lazy beach vacations. On a previous trip to the Caribbean he had vowed he would never go again. Boring! And right now he was feeling that he could not take a breath without Emily telling him to do something. So it wasn't surprising when he rejected Emily's idea, although he did come up with the money for Emily, the children, and the attendant to go and to stay for several weeks. The sun would be good for her. And it might be good, after all, for Emily and Bob to spend a little time apart, he said.

Emily told some friends that it was a great idea. She was becoming increasingly concerned that both girls now were turning first to Bob for help. This trip would give her a chance to be alone with them as a mother, well, sort of alone because besides the attendant, Emily wanted a woman friend to go along, too. She asked several friends, one by one, if they wanted to come—good times, lay around in the sun, warm waters. They said it was tempting, but they couldn't afford it or didn't have any time off coming. Then, Emily called several relatives, who were awfully sorry, but they couldn't make it, either. Emily really wanted a trip companion, someone who cared about her and not just because of a salary. Good female company and help, too, of course, sometimes. So Emily looked farther afield, and one night telephoned an old college friend in the Midwest. That woman was flattered, but she didn't know if she could. She had her own children and a working husband, but it had been, what, six months since she'd seen Emily and Lord knows when, or if, a next chance would come, given the seriousness of ALS. So maybe she could work something out after all. For a week or so anyway.

She did. Emily was very excited. Something fun to look forward to and, who knows, perhaps this new vitamin therapy would take hold, maybe. There must be fifty bottles of pills they had ordered from Mexico somewhere. If you had all the money in the world, Dr. Berghoff had said, these kinds of searches for longshot cures might be worthwhile, but—

Bob interrupted him politely, again.

Emily and Bob were sitting at the kitchen table the night before the Puerto Rico trip. Emily wanted each day's doses of different-colored pills and capsules arranged in individual plastic bags. Make everything easier down there.

She grew quiet a minute. "Look," she said in sudden despair, "at what we are reduced to doing—sorting quack pills." Bob looked up and handed his sobbing wife a tissue. He hadn't felt much for Emily in nearly a year—other than anger, of course—not since the reluctant fading of his initial enthusiasm for combat with a terminal illness. But he had to be realistic. He looked at this woman across the table, the confident woman who had approached the less confident man that day in the bicycle registration line. "Do you ride here a lot?" she had asked, all perky and curious. All she could talk about now was this damned disease. And she was crying over some phony vitamins.

"It'll be all right," he said. "You'll have a good time with Janice."

Janice's incoming flight from the Midwest was a little late, storms or something, so she had to hurry over to meet Emily at the airport gate for the Puerto Rico flight. She saw the wheelchair from a distance. But who was the black woman in the white nurse's outfit? And the babies? Were they going on vacation, too? And a typewriter? And what were all these boxes and bags of vitamins?

They began boarding then. "Children and those needing a little extra time first." Just before he left, Bob told Janice what to do in case Emily had trouble breathing. Trouble breathing? *Trouble breathing?* What was he talking about?

Due to bad weather, the plane, fully loaded, sat on the ground for two hours. By then, the trip toys and puzzles for both Alli and Jenie had grown very old. And so had Janice.

Bob found himself feeling relieved when he saw the wheelchair disappear down that airport ramp. So many days to himself. He hadn't figured out what to do with himself during that time, except work. It had been so long since he had such free time to spend, he had forgotten how.

He was a very angry man, and there were many things to be angry about. First came fate. Just how the hell had he been steered into this unbearable situation? Life didn't seem to move along in a line anymore; it was a huge, cube-shaped mass of pain with no beginning and no end and, like the ocean Emily and Janice were soaring over, it went on and on and on without a shore or visible progress. How long had Emily been sick now? One and a half years, nearly two from that first stumble. What's that in minutes, do you suppose? Bob's life had become one long series of minutes—no chunks of untimed delight when the hours flew by—just an endless series of minutes, one after another, and each moving as slowly as time does when the clock is closely watched.

Bob loved his little girls. In fact, in many ways he was living more for them now than anyone else, including himself. When he met Emily at the age of forty, he was not looking to be a daddy again, or even to marry again, probably. Helplessly watching his new wife slowly decay and, no doubt, die was not part of the bargain when he and Emily signed on together and exchanged those earnest vows. No, sir. Nor was taking this kind of abuse.

Sure, she was scared. Sure, she knew she was dying—she had to—though they never discussed it. A couple of these half-baked healers seemed to have some human insights and provide some comfort for Emily, more than Bob could, obviously. Emily saw them as all part of her extended family, the support group. But Bob knew they weren't going to stop the unstoppable. He had to be realistic and protect himself and the girls. If Emily hoped too much for a miracle and lost, she'd be dead and safe. If Bob and the kids did and she lost, they'd be shattered for years, three more victims smothered by the same disease.

Bob was angry at himself for putting up with Emily's treatment of him. He hadn't when they first met; that's probably why they got along so well then. But she had changed somehow as soon as the sentence was pronounced, become simultaneously more demanding and more vulnerable. Any more talking tough to her seemed inappropriate. He wasn't even sure if he cared enough now to spend that energy.

He couldn't even talk with Emily about work. Besides, that was depressing. Emily had enough troubles on her mind already. She didn't really seem to care much, and he didn't really want to think any more than necessary about all the years of labor and partnership going down the financial tubes. He couldn't talk with her at all about finances—how could he say that this much money was too much to spend on her life-and-death battle? How could he begin to make plans for the future, a future without Emily, when she was right here, alive and verbally kicking, and looking to him for hope and care? With Emily now it was easier to stick with the pro-forma talk. And safer.

More disturbing to Bob was the fact that he liked all the good words and encouragement he received from friends and family for being such a dutiful husband. It made him feel good. He felt badly about that, too, as if he enjoyed having a dying wife because it made him extra special somehow. Like that kid in the third grade who'd been such a schoolyard celebrity for a few days, loving every minute of it, because his father had been killed in a car crash.

Bob knew that he didn't deserve all that praise. If they knew how angry he was at her for getting sick. If they knew how important she had been to him. If they knew how important his love was to her. If they knew how he had withheld that affection to get even; she had tried to tell that to some of their friends, to show how Bob was being precisely perfect on superficial things so he wouldn't have to relate on a deeper level. But they had dismissed that, condescendingly, as hollow, the way people often do when a handicapped person makes a point. If they knew how much Bob wanted some affection and understanding himself. If they knew.

All good things must come to an end, Bob's parents would say at the end of his boyhood birthday parties. But what about the bad things, don't they ever have an end, too? Bob had found himself wondering sometimes when Emily would die. A horrible thought, or wish. He knew it was bad. He was afraid she could go on for years. He was afraid she wouldn't. He was afraid of thinking either one. He was afraid of living with her, so alone together. And he was afraid of his anger and of being all alone in the world without her and with two desperate little girls.

Why did he feel so lonely amid so many people?

A few days after Emily left, Bob was at the airport again. He wasn't looking for anyone other than his son, not consciously anyway. The kid—well, he was in his twenties now, not much of a kid anymore— had worked and saved and spent several weeks wandering through the Orient. Bob was there that afternoon to pick him up. So was Marjory, the kid's mother. Bob's ex-wife.

Bob hadn't seen her in years. She was aging well, neat, sort of attractive still, immersed in her career now. Unmarried again. Still. To her, Bob looked, well, like Bob, a little scruffy, still tall and strong, with that sexy deep voice. That was Bob behind that beard, wasn't it?

That was new, since the divorce anyway. Part of the new me, Bob said. So what have you been up to?

Marjory knew about the marriage to the younger woman, but not much about Emily's illness. Oh, no, a shame, it really was. Her father had died not long before. He had ALS, too. No, it was Alzheimer's, another one of those diseases that locks everyone up for a long while and sucks the stamina from the living as well as the dying. She was still trying to forget it. He had lingered long thanks to all the machines and specialists. Every time he'd get pneumonia, they'd pump in the antibiotics and bring him back. Amazing what they can do nowadays. That was the hardest part, knowing the ending three chapters before the end. But enough about sadness already. What's new with you?

They talked for a long time, waiting for their son, and then, later, over a quiet dinner. Just for old time's sake. They were comfortable together, the bitter edges of their relationship having been dulled by time and other experiences. Marjory thought Bob was "safe"—he was married—not like some of those guys out for a one-night quickie. Even after more than a decade apart, they found they still had much in common: the son, some friends, the continuing careers, though Bob's finances were as shaky as ever.

Marjory had buried herself in her work for the security, and so she wouldn't have time for anything else. The few times she did try the middle-aged singles scene, she was appalled. It was so forced and superficial. Everyone seemed so desperate and lonely. No, there wasn't anyone special in her life at the moment. After work, she would just go home and eat and go to bed. Cooking wasn't all that much fun anyway, but cooking for one was really the pits. By the way, where was Emily? Oh? And the children? For how long? Well, Bob would have to come over for dinner sometime. Just for old time's sake.

That's the way it began.

Emily loved Puerto Rico, still. She had chosen—just for old time's sake—the same isolated old hotel with its open bungalows where she and Bob had stayed so very long ago.

It was so sunny and warm there, like the Hawaii of her childhood when the minister's daughter would wiggle her toes into the beach and feel the warm sand enfold them. Except now, of course, she couldn't wiggle her feet. Or her legs. Or one arm. The other hand was feeling a little funny sometimes. During the day Emily lay there in the heat, soaking up the sun thirstily. She and Janice talked; what a help she was with the children, dressing them and feeding them. Now Emily had the time to talk with them more, to teach them motherly things like matching skirts and blouses. No, Alli, she'd say, we don't wear plaids and stripes together.

One time Emily asked her daughter if she remembered her mother ever walking. Alli said no. Emily sat silently for a long while. Then she remembered it was time for more vitamins.

In the afternoons after a nap—Janice needed one, too—Emily wanted to go down to the water. Neither Janice nor the aide could push the wheelchair through the thick sand. Usually there was a nice man to be found who would lift Emily into the warm saltwater and, with Janice or the aide or perhaps both, would help her float there, holding her head up, while she drifted and dreamed for some moments, her eyes closed. It was good to be carried and strange to feel her limbs moving again, drifting with the rhythmic currents. Soothing, too. Her legs felt so light. Emily never wanted to come out of the water—just like the little girl in Hawaii.

Late afternoons were spent cleaning up, or being cleaned up, and dressing, or being dressed, for a ritual cocktail hour. Janice and Emily sat on the porch together and chatted about silly things and, once, suicide. Janice had had cancer and she knew how dooming such thoughts could be, and how liberating just the thought of freeing herself was at moments, even if it was through self-destruction. The two women watched the sunset together. The days ended so abruptly there. And the nights seemed so long. When the sun went down, the two women fell silent for a few minutes, one more day gone. One time Janice heard Emily muttering to someone far away—"Please," she said, "this far and no more."

At the end of that week Janice felt bad about leaving Emily alone with the children and the attendant, who would have preferred to be elsewhere. But Janice's life had to go on; she had to get back to her own family, no matter the love she felt for Emily. She telephoned Emily's brother from her home. If you want some quality time with your sister, Janice said, you should join her in Puerto Rico for a few days. She's lonely. She can still talk. You'd drop everything if it was her funeral, Janice said. Well, skip the funeral and be with her when it counts.

Bryan said he'd like to, he really would, but he had classes almost every day that week and faculty committee meetings and a conference coming up. Barbara was busy, too, but they were glad Janice's trip went so well and that Emily got this trip in. Good for her.

Emily couldn't use the typewriter anymore, one more thing gone, her one reliable outlet. It meant she couldn't do her diary alone. She'd have to dictate it into a tape recorder, more work for a friend transcribing. But those thoughts and observations had to come out somehow. Meanwhile, she mailed tape recordings back to Bob, dictated by candlelight, as the power failed frequently. They were full of earnest wandering thoughts on their lives and dreams and Emily's fears.

Often, these thoughts kept Emily awake—maybe that was why she felt so tired most of the time. "I sit here," she said, "and I plan our future and all this stuff and I get myself so worked up, I can't sleep. It seems so stupid. I wish I could stop. I get sick of all my thinking." On the phone Bob said he was, too—sick of always having to think, that is. Wouldn't it be nice just to float through life a while and not have an assigned port every day.

Emily thought they ought to simplify things, but she didn't know if that was possible given two children and her physical condition. Compared with the idyllic life of rural Puerto Rico, she found the thought of city life and its pace back home increasingly distasteful and stressful with everyone running around professing such concern for issues and others when all they really cared about was themselves. "How can we live so isolated amid so many people?" she asked.

In Puerto Rico, Emily said, she could stare at a flower and draw it for three hours and feel she had accomplished something; if she'd done that at home, with all its strictly structured schedules, it would seem like a waste of time. Even their country house seemed confining now, Emily said, its various floor levels, gravel driveway, rough grass, and thick woods confronting her with her narrowing limitations at every turn. "It's always, 'I can't. I can't. I can't.' I'm getting to really dislike moving." She couldn't even chase the big mosquito in her room at that moment, Emily said.

"It ain't easy for someone like myself," she said, "who's always loved so much variety." And she'd had some dreams involving her disability. In one, she came out of a movie and couldn't find her parked car, the one she'd saved for and bought as a teenager, and Bob had to drive her on a long detour to find it. Or she was riding in a car, a convertible, with Janice. Several times the car veered across the center line. Several times Emily turned the wheel back. Then it shot up an embankment and began to turn over. And she awoke. "There were two me's in that car," Emily observed. "One who goes along with others. And one who takes the wheel and takes charge. And when it ended, I didn't know if I was going to survive or not. I just wonder what that's telling me." Oh, and she was concerned with inklings she sensed in friends' letters that perhaps the Bauers were imposing on them, asking for all kinds of help. But maybe she was reading too much into them.

"And I keep thinking of how you must feel," Emily told her husband, "because you don't even have the time to nourish yourself. I would like to be able to give to you at least some of what you've given me. But how? It's a real dilemma. And I'm worried that when I come back, my survival will be precarious in some sense I don't understand."

When Emily and the children returned home, Bob seemed more relaxed, and more attentive, at least for a while. He said her tan was beautiful. Everybody did.

■

March 22, 1982: It has been a long time since I have written. It feels like a holocaust. I must be entering a new phase, because all my attempts at understanding and explanation seem feeble in the face of my growing anger and frustration. As I told Bob today, "I am tired of this script and want to change it." But as he replied, "There's not much I can do about it."

I spend most of my time lying in bed or going to appointments related to my condition. My arms are now largely useless, although I can still caress the children when they're lying with me. I've started having dreams again. They are pleasant and ordinary, and my mobility is not an issue in them. Roland, one of the healers, says that when a disability doesn't permeate the dream life, then it is affecting only the more surface layers of the self. And I had a strong sense that no matter what happened, everything would be all right.

March 26, 1982: I don't care what the healer says about the disease being confined to my spinal cord, there's something going on there. I can feel twitches in my neck and head. If I can't be whole or complete, I don't know if I want to continue to be. It's not the being dead that frightens me; it's the dying.

April 6, 1982: Things go on normally. I wake in the middle of the night crying because my hands are going now and it's harder to lift the respirator hose to my mouth. Even my reading is difficult because of turning the pages. I can only do small paperbacks now. Big books and newspapers and magazines are gone for me. The attendants are changing more often, which means they don't like who they're staying with. The healer said I must pray and love God. I know I'll come around, but not without a fight. Not for me that syrupy position: "Isn't it wonderful to be sick to be brought closer to God?" I still maintain a huge mistake was made and that all this was meant for someone else, although I wouldn't wish this on anybody.

I wonder what, if anything, I will be left with.

■

One day, abruptly, Bob decided to sell their old house in the country. It didn't cost much to keep it, but Emily didn't like being there anymore. And Bob didn't like Emily not liking being there, with the trees and the garden, the grass and the pool, none of which Emily could use anymore except to look at and watch others enjoy. Selling the house would leave one less thing to think about, though Bob did all the time anyway, the late-night swims and the embraces under the stars. God-dammit! The way things were going with these healers, the Bauers were going to have some financial wounds to start healing pretty soon. Emily did not oppose selling their dream house. That made Bob even angrier.

The moving out went smoothly, though Bob was silent throughout. He left the mailbox behind. Emily had some friends over. She supervised their help, wrapping and packing. They all pitched in and had a very social time, but later that evening, back home describing the day to her husband, one of the friends realized that she had spent the afternoon folding and boxing fabric scraps and tissue paper—*tissue paper!*—that Emily was determinedly saving for a future that would not come. After that, when Emily phoned for help, the friend was often unable to come over.

∎

April 20, 1982: I was just telling R., who's typing this, that my shiatsu teacher gave me the following prescription: 1) Don't use my respirator so much. 2) Read a story to my children. 3) Have my friends bring in comic books and read them to make me laugh. And watch funny things on TV, no news. 4) Move all the plants away from the window so I can take a sunbath daily. Can you imagine an American doctor prescribing these? Fresh as a spring breeze these ideas hit me. As I was thinking this, I longed to be really silly, like ten-year-old girls are silly. I've always wanted to enjoy comic books. Maybe now I can allow myself that. I still take myself far too seriously. You'd think I'd take a hint from the way my body behaves, basically like a ragdoll.

May 5, 1982: Today I saw an old friend I haven't talked with since my wedding. She heard I was sick. I was very cautious about our meeting; people are so well intentioned but it's become so tiring to respond to them cheerfully, and truthfully. But our meeting was warm and delightful. She is going to come on weekend afternoons. It will be a big help to ease the pain of Bob being out with the children, which, of course, I want to be, too. She will help with the scrapbooks or whatever.

May 20, 1982: A lot of my life I've felt different. As a mother I was beginning to feel not different. And that was good. Now I'm different again. Only more so. It's funny how now that I'm sick, few people view my observations the same as before, as if I'm no longer a trained child psychologist. Yesterday I noted when Matt and Suzanne were here, Bob addressed a question about Alli's behavior to Matt and then to Suzanne with the implication she was the child expert. And no one asked me anything.

June 22, 1982: A few nights ago I dreamt that I was a bird and I was flying over farm countryside with green fields by the sea. I was quite large and had powerful wings, and the sense in the dream was one of joy of moving my powerful wings up and down, which enabled me to fly so high and see the sights.

■

The gasping began in the late morning on that July Saturday. Long desperate pulls for air that strained Emily's body, the top half anyway. From her hips on down was limp. Emily had been in her reclining wheelchair; they had returned the motorized one since Emily couldn't control it anymore. Emily said she was tired, and Bob lifted her onto the bed for a rest.

Bob's cousin Fred was visiting, and the men were talking animatedly in the kitchen when Bob noticed Alli standing in the living room, looking toward the window kind of funny. He followed her gaze and there on the bed was Emily, her mother, his wife, silently struggling, her back bowed the wrong way with each frantic gulp. Her arms flopped uselessly.

Oh, Jesus, Bob thought, this is It. Emily's eyes were rolling up.

Fred grabbed the girls and took them to the playground. Oh, God, thought Bob, oh, God. He was worried, very worried, and a little hopeful, too, if he had been honest with himself, which he wasn't until later. Bob grabbed the oxygen mask and strapped it over Emily's nose and mouth. He talked to her. And held her hand. She always liked that. It was awful watching her gasp for life, like a flopping fish out of water, her eyes wide and wild. He rubbed her head with a cool cloth and did some quick thinking and regretting.

They had talked with various doctors about this day, but always in generalities, never specifics. The doctors had gotten the impression that Emily, like most patients in America, didn't want to talk about death, and that Bob realized what a crucial decision time that un-scheduled day of breathing difficulty would be: Should the Bauers let life pass at home, quietly, the way it used to when doctors made house calls and the elderly and ill died upstairs in the bed where they had likely been conceived and born? Or should they seek help from the people and the machines of these vast medical institutions whose regimen of treatments for a variety of logical reasons took on a life of its own with a force and momentum that patients and families often found forbidding and difficult or impossible to control?

One way, it would all be over, the disabilities, the suffering, the anguish and anger, the fighting, the mourning and sense of impending doom, the love, the potential, the life. The other way, it might still be over. Or it might go on, the life, the potential, the love, the sense of mourning and impending doom, the fighting, the anguish and anger, the disabilities, the suffering.

The husband and wife had never decided which it would be. They couldn't face the decision back then, not when there still seemed hope, not when such talk would have admitted defeat. To bring it up later seemed to seek it, to foreclose the hope that Emily leaned on more than any cane or walker. And now, here it was, time, The Time. But Emily was unconscious. And Bob was numb.

He began yelling to her. "Emily!" he said urgently. "Emily! Emily! Wake up! Emily! It's me, Bob! Wake up!"

Her breathing eased a little. The oxygen was working. Her eyes were closed. Her hands cold. He rubbed them. He pulled the blanket up. He talked to her. He had to get through. He knew what he wanted, but he had to know what she wanted.

For brief moments she wakened and looked around lazily, her eyes unfocused and wandering. Bob talked to her, but she didn't hear in there. Or couldn't hear. Or heard but couldn't answer.

Bob's breathing was slowing, too. What am I doing here? he thought as the long minutes turned into an hour, two hours. I could just let her go, sit here with her and help her struggle for the last time, frightened and frantic. "Since I was a child," he had said, "I have loved a few things and so I declare my love for you always. I promise to love, honor, respect, keep, and cherish you till death do us part."

Or he could help her drift away, take off the mask and sit with her through the last gasps. Who would know?

He would.

"I promise to live our days together, plan our future, remember our past, and bite at our life with relish and greed, not nibbling like the riskless few." This could not be his decision. He couldn't kill her. He had loved her. He still did.

"Emily! Emily!" he said, slapping her face gently. "Wake up!" Her eyes opened very wide. She looked up at him, terrified.

"It's okay," he said, "I'm here. Emily, this is It. This is what the doctor told us about. It's gotten to your lungs. What do you want to do? Do you want to go to the hospital?"

She paused a moment. Then nodded.

"You want to go to the hospital?"

She nodded.

In a flash, Bob scooped her up off the bed. He set her in the wheelchair. He flicked on that respirator. From her back he held the mask to the face of his limp wife as he raced down the hall to the elevator and out the lobby and down the street to the emergency room, the longest six blocks he had ever seen. And when the crew of strangers in white coats whisked her away, Bob stood there, alone and gasping, and wondering what had he just done.

Two doctors, a man and a woman, worked on Emily all afternoon. They knew just what to do. They were devoted to saving this patient, which is what Emily had become. A case. They were so efficient and thorough and they had all the latest equipment to help.

They checked and adjusted her blood gases, got nutrition dripping into that frail body and plenty of oxygen flowing into those weakened lungs. Her color started coming back. They checked Emily's pulse, of course, and her chest, making sure she was not filling up with fluids. They stuck tubes down her nose and mouth. They wired her to a monitoring machine that sent constant readings of her heartbeat and blood pressure to a green bedside screen and another one at the intensive-care nurse's desk. They adjusted the machine precisely; if Emily's rates strayed outside the settings, the alarms would sound.

Later, they would also cut open a large hole in Emily's throat to ease her breathing. They sucked out a fair bit of mucus there, too. The doctors stayed around through their breaks and meals. It was marvelous medical work, just like they had been taught to do. Textbook. They had saved her. Pulled her back from the brink. Very satisfying. Reward enough, before they went on to the next case, for the long hours of concentration on a Saturday. There would come another Saturday when no medical team would have the chance to work on a slipping Emily. And that would not happen by chance.

The medical duo didn't know much about this woman. They knew she was down and out when they got her. A little young for ALS. They hadn't concerned themselves with her future; there wouldn't be one at all if they'd stopped to chat with that tall bearded fellow who brought her in. The guy sitting in the corner, maybe muttering. The husband, right? We'll give him the good news in a minute. No time for idle talk in a busy emergency room this size, just enough time usually to deal with the immediate, STAT. If Mr. or Mrs. Bauer had not wanted maximum help, why had they come to the hospital? No time to think about that now. Not their job.

Eventually the tracheotomy had to be done. A neat pink hole in the front of her throat. Emily's weakening lungs could no longer provide adequate air. The tube was inserted. The full-time respirator took over her breathing, according to its dials and alarms. They could set it to make every other breath, leaving Emily's lungs to work part-time. They could set it to monitor her own breaths and if they weren't deep enough, the machine would add the extra kick. Or they could set it to wait and breathe only when she didn't. Every few minutes the machine would even insert an extra-long breath, a mechanical sigh. With all the tubes, Emily couldn't talk now; she never would again.

■

August 10, 1982: I've now been in the hospital a month. Some friends read my lips and write this down. I've just found out my stomach is not digesting properly, and the days go by and I'm here and my family is there and it gets harder. The thought of not seeing my children at home and holding them is unbearable.

If I was at home, I could not do much, but at least I'd have the pleasure of seeing everyone in their daily activities. Right now, I can't see how I'd have that in a hospital visit. At the same time I worry about the effect if I was at home, and the children would see me and my nurse and my machine. Sometimes I cough and choke and that might frighten them, too. I don't know how they would feel about bringing their friends home and seeing their mother so different than other mothers.

August 12, 1982:
Dear Allie and Jenie,

I lie in my hospital bed and I think of all the plans I had to do things with you. When you went to the beach, I wanted to be with you, to go in the water, to build a sand castle, and to put on your suntan lotion and dry your hair. The main reason your father and I got married was so we could have children. I looked forward to the future.

I know Bob is doing a wonderful job to give you a good home life, and you have many other people who love you and help bring fun into your lives. I have strong respect for you two as people. I do not worry that you will be less because of me. My pain is in not being with you—the fun and the fights. It's hard to believe, to accept, that this is the way things are and will be. It all seems like a nightmare that I will wake up from. I looked forward so much to being a mother. I can't believe I won't have this chance.

August 14, 1982: I think of you, Alli, going to nursery school. I wanted to take you and pick you up and talk to you about what you did. I lie here thinking about both of you all the time. When people come to visit, I ask them about you. And I can never get enough. I'm very sad.

■

Steadily, the word spread through the wide network of family and friends that the expected hospitalization had finally come and Emily was out of that tiny apartment and no one knew how long it would last. It couldn't be long though; she'd been sick for well over two years.

There was always someone coming to see Emily. And she cherished that. They would bring a little something as a gift—flowers, or perfume, and always cards to add to the standing array on the mobile bedside table, where the humorous rhymes fell flat whenever the table was moved. Knowing how much Emily liked to read, one visitor who hadn't seen her in some months brought a new book. After seeing her incapacitated, he didn't leave the book, pretending instead that he was reading it himself.

The visitors came down the hall tentatively, checking room numbers, seeming to tiptoe as if they feared offending one of the high priests of this temple of technology; different rules applied here, different from the other world, the world of the living, outside. The visitors could tell this from the wandering wings of the institution, each numbered. Is this a hospital or the Pentagon? one husband whispered just before his wife's eyes scolded him. They could tell it from the strange language that seeped from the ceiling's public address system. They could tell it from the strange equipment in the halls being wheeled officiously by, its myriad arms and dials speaking of and to other complex worlds somewhere. They could tell it from the indecipherable name tags on everyone's chest and from the temple workers' special uniforms, colored according to their rank. If they're supposed to be so sanitary, why were they wearing that garb out in the halls? But the visitors didn't dare ask.

The visitors could tell it, too, from the people and the shells of people they glimpsed within the identical chambers as they moved slowly by the rooms, hopefully toward the helpless Emily's hopeless room. Sometimes the people they saw were just lying there at the ends of all those wires and tubes, seemingly asleep. Some, drawn and pale, sat by the windows staring from hollow eyes out at the unseeing city. Once in a while, an electronic alarm sounded by one bed and a small mob of medical saviors quickly appeared from nowhere, jamming into that room and squeezing some worried-looking visitors out into the hall. The door would be closed then for some kind of ritual within.

■

August 18, 1982: I wish I was there to celebrate with you how terrific each one of you is every day. I try to send you love by imagining putting my arms around you. And I wonder if you sense this.

August 21, 1982: I would like to be with you when you girls need me. It's hard for you and for me to have this. But I want you to go to other people when you need to, when you're hurting or need to talk. Don't feel it's only your mother you can go to. I hope you will always feel loved and be able to return love. That's what I found out the most about being in the hospital: how precious love is. I wish I could express love in more ways. But I do feel it deeply. I hope you can understand and love, too. I hope we can find some ways to communicate. I hope in some ways I can be a mother to you.

September 2, 1982: I got Bryan and Barbara's flowers, and they were purple and beautiful. Nothing warms my heart more than flowers. I have to be careful; sometimes I have a roommate with asthma. I miss people coming over at all hours and making dinner and talking. Of course, I'm not home either.

I'm trying to think of some way this whole thing has some value for all of us.

■

Emily's visitors, pretending not to see, moved on in their search for someone, something familiar and friendly in this mysterious world where people eat alone together at the same time and incredibly jolly TV hosts are continuously sincere in full color to excited contestants high up on the hospital room wall and to silently staring patients below in bed. "Here's the answer for you folks at home," the happy man would say. But his viewers here were not at home, or maybe they were but didn't know it.

Eventually, the visitors found Emily's door, way down at the end, checked the name and number, and peered around the corner to see if they were disturbing a priestess or Emily or that person in the other bed.

When Emily saw them, the room filled with the light of her smile. The smile would move the tubes. For now.

■

September 6, 1982: I got a letter from Mother and a poem. I want to hear whatever she wants to tell me about, especially her religious experiences. I found a Catholic priest here who's been coming to see me, and he's quite helpful. And a lot of friends are coming all the time.

I feel better each day, though sometimes slip back. I don't know if I'll ever really accept my situation, but I'm doing the best I can. The time goes by fairly rapidly. I probably watch more TV than I should, although I try to be selective. I was watching the afternoon soap operas, but I stopped. I don't read very much. I like when people read me the Psalms. I spend time each day praying and meditating.

It was so wonderful, Aunt Ethel's and Uncle Richard's visit, their coming all that way to see me. I know it was hard for them with my not being able to talk. But they were very patient and did not get upset when I got upset. I think of them every time I put on that Chanel body lotion. Maybe I'm getting some inner peace.

September 9, 1982: Alli came to visit twice, and that was both wonderful and painful. She was very sweet and loving. She crawled up on the bed and wanted me to put my arm around her. It made me feel very good. After she left, Bob said she got very difficult, so it must have been a strain. She asked Bob if I was going to die and if I would say good-bye. I was very proud that she can ask these questions, although it makes me sad. She also asked why I couldn't come home and if she would become an angel after she died—she said she didn't want to. Really a wonderful girl.

Jenie visited once and was very charming but kept her distance. That, of course, brought me pain very much. But it's understandable.

■

The care that Emily and the other patients received was very professional and thorough and often caring, as caring as possible when the caregivers changed every eight hours and could go home to care for their own families. They checked on Emily regularly and asked how she felt, and Emily nodded or shook her head, and the woman, while busying herself with bedside maintenance chores, started idly guessing out loud what the problem was. You have a headache? You want a drink? You have to pee?

Emily took her medicines at the right times or, rather, they gave them to her at the right times prescribed at the nursing station by illegible directions in a large three-ringed notebook that the family was not allowed to see. The name card on the blue binder said BAUER. The card slid into a metal holder on the spine, for easier replacement when the patient left, as they always do somehow. The medicine came through a needle or in her food down the tube or in a disposable plastic bag and hose that hung overhead for a while. Emily was turned over frequently to help prevent bedsores and pneumonia, which kills quicker than ALS. But pneumonia has a cure and so, naturally, it must be fought vigorously by those who control the weapons.

Emily ate regularly and well or, rather, she was fed regularly and well, eventually liquid through a tube up her nose and down her throat straight to the stomach. This saved her having to chew food. Emily couldn't always swallow anymore, so the artificial feeding saved her from having to swallow and maybe choke. Sometimes, if she forced a burp, Emily could get a faint taste of food on her tongue. And chemicals.

■

September 16, 1982: My stomach's gone bad. Sick all week. Some of my faith is shaken, but I'm trying hard. I won't let it get me down. Maybe I have to accept that this is going to happen with my stomach and there's not much they can do. Something else to go through. I worry about losing weight. Maybe I have to accept being thin. All these changes. I feel grateful when I feel good.

September 24, 1982: Last Sunday I was telling Bob how positively I'm beginning to feel inside me. There's great joy at seeing Alli and all the amazing things that she comes out with. Although I don't see Jenie, she is remarkable, too. I feel very blessed by this. Also I feel closer to Bob than ever before. And I feel we are together as a team, though physically apart. Sometimes I feel very happy, which surprises me. I didn't think I could be happy under these circumstances. I am coming to believe in a personal God, along with a God within me.

■

The three Bauers who were not hospitalized quickly fell into a new routine that quickly came to seem normal. Bob was up by six; he was awake by four, but he didn't get up until six. He made breakfast for the girls at seven. Soon after, he delivered Jenie to the same family babysitter down the hall and took Alli to nursery school. Then he visited Emily and maybe got some grocery shopping in or ran an errand or two or three for Emily. Then he went to work. Then he came home and collected Jenie and Alli at the sitter's and made dinner and got them to bed. He asked some friend or sitter over nearly every evening so he could run down to the hospital for another visit. There, he delivered a bouquet of daisies and daffodils, her favorites, and fed his wife with memories of the day.

Bob found he needed these visits. He knew he should visit and he wanted to. He loved Emily; he always had and always would. He wanted the visits to build new bonds on a new level. Theirs had been a passionate relationship at the beginning and it had been maturing into a deeper one until that day in the doctor's office, the day that pruned hope. Not right away but soon after, emotionally their love started to slide down that slippery slope of fear where it is every man for himself, and women and children, too.

Bob found his anger waning somewhat as the months passed with Emily in the hospital. He still couldn't understand why this had happened to them, or how they would get out of it, spiritually and financially. Now that she was in a hospital, the insurance picked up much of the cost. But there was a time limit of some kind on coverage, though he did not want to look it up. The $22,000 from the house sale would go only so far, especially since he had hired private nurses to be with Emily much of the time in the hospital. With these others caring for Emily full-time now, Bob had more space, literally and figuratively. So did the children. The family. The friends. Even the dog no longer acted so high-strung.

There were many lives, healthy lives, to be led. So much to do and see, and it included caring for and being with a physically declining Emily. But Bob was coming to feel that he did not want the lives, the hopes, the living, to be dominated by the frightened, the worried, the dying. For sure, one of the four Bauers was very sick. But three of them were not. The three would do and care and love the one, but no matter how lonely the end seemed to Emily, they couldn't die, too, just to be with her.

Bob always pictured it like a family journey down a long, unfamiliar road, the four of them briskly pacing along under cloudy skies. Now one of the four was going slower and probably would stop for a rest soon, forever. Looking back, the others, especially the older one with the beard, would feel a powerful sadness, but they would go on; they had to. They had so far to go, especially the younger ones. "Is Mommy going to die?" the child had asked her father, taking his hand and sending him back a long ways. "Alli," he had said, remembering how much he had wanted to hear an answer, any answer, years before, "I think so, yes. But I don't know when."

■

October 7, 1982: I thought I would talk about my life in the hospital. I wake up around seven and try to meditate. Usually a woman from one of my healing groups comes at eight to meditate and rub oil on my body. Then I watch TV and eat, if I'm eating. Then Lucy gives me a bath and changes the bedding. That takes an hour. Friday is my busiest day, when E. and A. visit in the morning. Otherwise, I listen to music.

Between twelve-thirty and one, I turn on the TV and watch soap operas until four, unless I have visitors. I have them two or three times a week in the afternoons. And I don't mind missing the soap operas at all.

From four to six, I like to read, if Lucy is in a good mood. She turns the pages for me. What goes on between Lucy and me during the day affects my well-being. Most of the time she makes me feel like I'm a big problem. But at the same time she takes good care of me, that's true.

At six, I watch the news and get fed. If Bob comes to visit between six-thirty and seven-thirty, that is the best time of the day, because he can understand me so well.

My night nurse Eleanor comes in at eight, and we work on photo albums and scrapbooks and watch TV until it's time to go to sleep around midnight. And there are some visits during the day from physical and occupational therapists.

On weekends I do not have my regular nurses. If the new person doesn't lip-read, I must spend much time explaining. I'm always nervous about having a new person, although most are quite nice. So I don't get bored. There's lots to do.

October 19, 1982: I've been having a lot of dreams. They all have the theme of moving from place to place. The moving refers to my journey. I don't know where this is all going, but I have fine things to take with me. I think so much about my family, but they are not in these dreams because I'm going through this transition in life alone.

For the past two weeks I've been having trouble with my stomach. It blows up with gas, and I get very sick to my stomach. I cannot eat solid food. I must struggle to avoid being depressed and upset. Here, I can barely manage not being able to move and scratch the slightest itch and now I have to deal with this on top of it. It is really too much. I have moments wondering if the struggle is worth it.

Then, of course, when I wake up, as I did this morning, feeling better, I feel so grateful just not to feel sick.

October 26, 1982: My stomach problem is still bad. Anytime I'm fed, I never know if my stomach is going to blow up. I am very weak. I hate to be so totally concerned about myself physically that nothing else seems important. And then different nurses come, and I must deal with them not understanding. I try to communicate, but it's usually so hard. With Bob, I can, but everyone else is difficult. I get a lot of hot flashes. And I'm very tired. I long for peace and rest. And I've begun to think again about dying, more positively. I am afraid of pain and don't want any more suffering.

This makes me very sad.

■

Much of the time on those weekend days that the healthy know as so leisurely and the bedbound know as so endless, Emily would have to entertain herself. She would watch TV if football wasn't on. Or she might watch her heartbeat on the electronic monitor and try to make the digital readout go up or down just by willing it. That was the limit of her exercise. Once or twice, Emily got the nurse to move her bed and wired body over by the window so she could watch for her family. She watched for a very long time. Then Emily spotted their familiar coats and walks even from so many floors up. When Bob and Alli walked in her door, Emily had already warmed the room with her smile.

Those regular visits by Bob and Alli—Jenie being deemed a little too young yet—were the highlights of Emily's week that fall and forever. Alli usually brought some schoolwork, most often crude crayon drawings, which Emily wanted posted right by the bed where she could see them constantly.

Alli would also climb on the bed to cuddle with her mother. Bob would wrap Emily's limp arm around the child. Alli would lean close to her mother's mouth, trying to decipher the silent lip movements amid the slow, rhythmic whooshing of that nearby machine. Bob would lean down, too, and repeat Emily's words out loud so that she could correct them with a shake of her head and so Alli would learn how to play this game. "What . . . happy . . . no . . . happen . . . a . . . no . . . school . . . at school. At school? Right? What happened at school?" Alli couldn't think of anything of great significance, just the ordinary stuff, which is boring to talk about but exactly what Emily wanted to hear. Bob might prompt his daughter about some incident involving her friend Jason or the teacher. And Alli then gave a brief edited version.

But it was hard and not very interesting for very long for the child, and Emily could take only a certain amount of this before the head-shakes became angry with frustration. Bob would stand up and turn away then as if to straighten his back and take a break. Whether Emily still had something to say or not, there was then no interpreter to see her speak. Alli would scoot off the bed then to explore somewhere, play with the TV channel changer, or chat with Emily's roommate, who could talk. And whether Emily was ready to end this dialogue game or not, she was left alone on her bed, limp but thinking.

Nurses came and went at various times. Or Emily nodded toward the bedpan and Bob would slide it under her under the sheet and then remove it a few minutes later and clean her. But when it came time every few hours around the clock for the nurse to suction the hole in the front of Emily's throat, Bob would rather have been somewhere else. Emily, like other patients with tracheotomies, could no longer cough, so to avoid infection and keep the incapacitated from choking to death on their own body fluids, the hospital's maintenance manual for patients like Emily dictated regular cleaning of the hole.

There is some debate, at least among those who have never had it done to them, about whether it is painful to have one's throat vacuumed through a hole. The nurse would talk gently to Emily while concentrating on the hole, but Emily would wince. And Bob, who had been present for both babies' births and the breathing troubles, would excuse himself for a few minutes and take Alli away from that rasping, mucus-sucking sound.

■

November 5, 1982: I have something I want to do. I was thinking of what I could do for Bob. I would like to give him something, because he gives me so much. There aren't that many things I can give him. But I can give him time—by his not having to visit every day, sometimes twice. I will miss him a lot. But he seemed relieved.

November 12, 1982: I cannot remember the details; last Saturday night I began to have more difficulty breathing. After a lot of commotion it turned out I had a small pneumonia. I had several days of being very tired. The last few days I've felt better, both emotionally and physically.

■

Emily's pneumonia was, of course, fought aggressively with all the medical means available to every shift. The pneumonia was beaten, decisively, so that her weakened lungs could be inflated and deflated properly by the breathing machine. And the hospital people could feel good and satisfied about all that on the way home at night or dawn. Although, of course, nothing could be done about the underlying disease, which was too bad but didn't seem to need so much thinking about.

All that medical effort, so Emily, the jogger, the bike rider, and the active working mom, could lie there, seeming to float on the rhythmic suck-and-whoosh of the respirator. Unable to scratch herself, and acutely aware of it and of everything else going on in her sixth-floor rectangular world that had but one way out.

■

Thanksgiving 1982: I don't know why this happened to me. But I do believe that the future will have beauty in it and I will understand why. I do know that I influence other people and there is some purpose to that. I still feel sad, but I don't feel so upset, though I am wondering about death. I'd rather be whole and be with my husband and children. I am more afraid of pain than dying. What happens after you die sounds more interesting than the way I have to live now.

■

Knowing of her friend's passion for fabrics and colors, Janice bought several pieces of different material and some stuffing and sewed little pillows from them. There were satin and cotton and corduroy, among others. Visiting friends put these pillows, one after the other, on Emily's stomach and lay Emily's hands there. And for long hours the woman, motionless everywhere else, caressed the pillows with her long bony fingers. Each sensuous pillow, each touch, felt good and unleashed a flood of memories within Emily—her first slip, her prom dress, Alli's play pants. Looking up at that familiar pale-green ceiling, Emily smiled that warm, family-famous smile of hers. The visitors looked at her and smiled, too, and noticed, without notice, that it was only a half-smile now. One side of Emily's mouth didn't move up when told.

■

December 2, 1982: I've been very upset because I haven't been sleeping. My night nurse gets mad at me. I wish I was a better patient. I don't know what to do. Sometimes I think I cannot go on because it's so hard. I feel like this when I cannot sleep and when the nurse gets mad at me.

December 8, 1982: My stomach's been better. I wish there were more ways I could be better.

December 12, 1982: Both Alli and Jenie came to visit me twice. The first time a friend of mine was here—a therapist—who's very sensitive. Both children loved her and drew pictures with her. She helped both get on the bed. Both were very affectionate with me. Both children were amazing in what they said. One of the things Alli said was the sun has the power to make scribbles go away (i.e., fade them). Jenie was concerned about showing her anger and needs some help. She's always nice.

It was a visit that left me feeling that both children are doing very well, and they were wonderful to me. Having my friend here made a big difference; they needed a woman. The next time Bob brought them the children wanted to call someone on the telephone to come here. Finally, they sat down and drew pictures. It was so much fun to watch them work away. Alli's picture was very beautiful: Jenie's has a lot of anger. She talked and drew about the house where Bob and Alli live. I was not in that one—and she showed her anger about that. I felt very sad.

The visit was a good one, although different from the other one.

December 15, 1982: I have been feeling very down. I do not know why I am living. When I thought the whole family would go through things together, I felt better. If I am helping people in my family, I feel better. The only thing I can do to help them is pray. That's what I decided to do, so I feel better.

Then I thought some more. I do not have to be here to pray. I could be on the other side, praying. So that means all I really have to do is prepare for my own death. That's where I am now. I feel very sad, but also I feel peaceful. I think a lot about the children and how much I miss them. I have to say good-bye, and that is very hard.

December 17, 1982: I've been thinking about my funeral. I want the priest who visited me in the hospital to conduct my funeral. I want all the people in my address book to come. I want there to be good food to eat. I want there to be flowers. I want people to say what they want during the service. I want my body to go to the ALS Foundation for research. I want to have a casket because I think it's very tangible. I can't believe I'm saying all this. I worry a lot about pain. I don't want to have any pain.

December 19, 1982: The healer I am working with promised that when the time comes, I will just go. But first she said I have to prepare. That's what I'm working on now. My dreams are of going on trips. Once I went to a public building in Morocco. In another trip I could not find where I wanted to go. At the last minute I finally remembered where it was. I was going to a shop where the clothes were colorful, simple, youthful, and fun. I think that's how my soul has to be—but I'm not there yet.

December 21, 1982: Christmas is coming, and I asked Bob to make a party, which he did. Alli picked out the tablecloth and the napkins. Jenie did not pay attention to me. She got very angry at Bob and pulled his hair, hard. Alli offered me food and she sat on my lap and made a scrapbook of pictures for me. Bob was very upset about Jenie.

I feel very bad; I want to help her so. I asked Bob to bring them when my friend, Anne, the therapist, was here. But he took them to his sister's for the weekend. Anne and I had a good time anyway. She makes me feel really creative, and we did a lot of work with imagery.

■

Bob was having trouble, with himself, with work, with the children. Everything had to be done; there was no time for fun, not even walking in his woods, which they had sold. He felt very lonely and isolated, even with all the people around. He was seeing Marjory some weekends, when others took the children for a day, and he got over to her place on the rare evening, which could be relaxing. But it was not going as smoothly as he would like. There were lingering resentments and hurts from their marriage. He was so desperate for friendly female company, and felt guilty for that. With Marjory, it seemed that the pressures within him were so strong that all he did was talk about things he couldn't talk about with anyone else. His emotional need left little time or energy to give Marjory anything. She had her own loneliness to live with in that city and she resented this greed in Bob. Their arguments would be patched up artificially, without the tenderness that promotes healing.

Marjory felt sorry for Bob, and for herself. He was, after all, the father of her child. They did have some good times, in between the fights. It was very good to lie there together at times, like old times, and to hold the large man, and to be held by him. Bob couldn't talk about this with Emily.

He couldn't talk with Emily about work either. You can't saunter into a hospital room where a woman is lying motionless, dying, unable to even shit by herself, and complain about a balky camera. "What a day I had!" he could have said to the woman who would give anything to have just one such bad day outside the hospital, or to hear about it in detail. "First the cat threw up during the night. Then the van wouldn't start. Then there was all the traffic. And I got a call from that computer company canceling their order. But here I am, safe and sound. I rode over on my bike. How was your day?"

On the mammoth scale of life and death that Bob had come to face daily in the living and dying of his wife and family, such everyday concerns came to seem pretty petty and mean, like worrying over the death of a bird in a nuclear war. "How? Who? How . . . was . . . your . . . die? No, day," Bob would say, reading Emily. "How was my day? Oh, fine, not much happening really. The girls are fine. I was at work, and Richard sent his best. Yes, he's a nice man. That's about all, really. Oh, I see you got some new cards. Let's see, who are these from?" No, Bob couldn't talk with Emily about work.

He couldn't talk with Emily too much about the children. If he told her how often they were bad, fighting him and each other, it would greatly distress her. She'd start issuing Emily Edicts on what he should do with them, yet more things for him to do and arrange. She did that anyway. If he told Emily too much about the trio's happy times, she'd get to wondering just how much they really did miss her. "Seems like you're getting along just fine without me." So, things couldn't seem too swell on the outside. No, he couldn't talk with Emily much about the children.

He couldn't talk with Emily about Marjory, either. At one point that autumn, Emily had suggested Bob ought to find a female friend, someone to have right now and maybe develop a new relationship with for the future. Bob couldn't watch her eyes when she said that; he was too busy reading her lips, and guarding his own expression. There was no longer a tone of voice to help read Emily, but Bob's instincts told him to be very careful on this one. He figured Emily was saying this to get him to say something back. She was good at that. So he said what she wanted to hear, that he loved her and that maybe someday he would come to love someone else, though never the same, which was all true. But right now, he said, it was the two of them, together, fighting this disease and raising the children, and sharing life, which was not true. He could share her dying in that bed, but she couldn't share the living in his world beyond these walls. It wasn't the life they expected, or wanted, he said, which was true. But it was a life, which was true maybe. No, Bob couldn't talk about his need to be held, too. So he didn't.

Emily cried then, which she seemed to do more now. They were silent sobs. Silently, too, Bob wondered, then and later, whether his words had made her happy or sad. She was right here, close by and so far away. It was becoming harder to communicate anything across this growing gap. He had to be so careful about what he said and how he looked; Emily was watching him like a hungry hawk. Emotions that he had once taken for granted as natural had now become so tricky and dangerous, a different kind of terminal disease. To Bob, happiness and sadness had come to seem the same, both painful. There was no relief from either. Would he feel happy when Emily died? Or sad? Or both? And which was which? So Bob wondered what Emily thought that autumn day. But he would never know.

■

December 28, 1982: Last night I had a nurse who was a nightmare. She would not try to read my lips. She totally ignored me. I could not communicate. She would not move me. When I asked for a bedpan, she told me to wet the bed. How can I ever deal with this? I feel so furious and so helpless. And also very anxious.

I cannot seem to smile, even though my nurse asks me to. I've been very anxious and I don't know why. Last time it happened it was because of a talk with my night nurse, Eleanor, who can read me. We were "talking" about preparing to die. She was matter-of-fact about it. She told me to be grateful for what I have. What do I have? I feel just horrible. I feel so down about everything. I really like Eleanor, so it's hard to be mad at her.

I don't feel like I have anything to look forward to. My nurses may stop working with me. The husband of Lucy, my day nurse, is sick. And the other one got married. Bob is going away at the end of the month to Morocco. I feel I'll be without the people I need the most.

Even Jenie. She was angry at me and didn't want to come visit. Alli has been sick and she did not come to visit. A lot of people come from one of my old healing groups and massage me. They are wonderful and I don't know what I'd do without them. But I feel I'm not making the progress spiritually that I should be. My husband Bob says I should not think that way. He says not to judge myself that way.

My friend Vicky tells me that every time I don't get sleep (like last night) I'm very depressed the next day (like today) and that this has been true throughout the illness.

I don't remember.

December 30, 1982: I have been excited and looking forward to talking on the electric larynx. The speech therapist has been coming to help. I don't know why they didn't think of this before. I am very thankful. I hope the children will be able to understand. My friend Sara suggested I start with nursery rhymes and the alphabet.

The other thing that makes me feel good is that Janice brought me some nice new nightgowns. Also I have been working on the scrapbook and I have all the old pictures my father gave me put into the scrapbook. Now I'm working on photos of me in the 1960s.

I worry about what I'll do when I finish the scrapbooks (I do them with the night nurse).

■

Emily had gone through a platoon of private practical nurses during her lengthening illness, both regulars and weekend fill-ins, at home and in the hospital. They came from the agency for a few weeks of more or less regular duty, and then there was always something that pulled them away, much as they liked working for Emily, they said. The patient would get depressed for a few days. Then Emily would have to go through the frustrating routine of teaching the new nurse her required routine, without speaking. Emily liked to bathe in the morning, for example. There were reading times and thinking times and times for listening to music and times for watching TV and lots of talking times. That had become much harder, since for Emily to say anything, the nurse had to stop all activities and stare at her lips. Sometimes, if she was really tired, or perhaps fed up, a nurse wouldn't seem to understand Emily's orders, even when the patient's lips repeated them. And the nurse, whose training did not include lip-reading or psychology, would straighten up and say, "Well, I'm sorry, but I just don't get what you want, dear." Then she'd go on about her business as Emily silently mouthed the orders again and again, while no one watched.

When Emily was nervous, she could push her temperature up, even without moving. At those times she would want the pillows puffed up more frequently. Often they were puffed up wrong. Or she'd want frequent sips of water, in the days when she could do that. Anytime the nurses dozed off or were the least distracted, perhaps chatting with a hospital nurse at the door, was when Emily would develop an urgent need of some kind.

Emily was the easiest to care for in the late morning, when her stomach was working, and the nurse would put a little set of headphones on Emily's ears and turn on a cassette tape of classical music. Amazing what some violins can do. Emily would lie peacefully for an hour or two, listening, floating somewhere. Sometimes the nurse wouldn't hear the little click when the tape ended. She'd continue to read or nap. Then after a while, the nurse would catch a little movement of Emily's mouth and realize the tape had ended some time before. She'd flip the tape then and play the other side.

Unlike many of their other patients, Emily didn't just watch television; she watched certain shows that were on television, which meant the nurses had to pay attention to the time and channel. How could she stand newshour after newshour? Why pay attention to all that outside stuff from within this self-contained institutional world that had its own news, its own births and deaths, successes and failures, its own social structure and social values, its own language and smell, its own fears and secrets, gossip and protocol, even its own TV channel? Whole careers can be spent in one of these medical mammoths, striving, achieving, winning and losing medical and bureaucratic struggles, without having any inkling of what's going on across the street. Or at least not acknowledge it. No time, you see.

Lucy and Eleanor were different, though, more patient, for one thing. They came from outside that specific hospital's specific fraternity. They went with their patients from hospital to hospital, from home to home. They had stuck with Emily for many months and would be there for as long as Emily's journey took.

They had their tiffs with Emily, Lucy especially during Emily's days back in the apartment. Sometimes Emily would get into one of her more demanding moods and Lucy, a little older than the patient, would be accommodating and maybe do a household chore or two, just to be helpful. Then Emily would come up with other things to do and better ways to do them. It seemed that Lucy, a black who ran her own household just fine as the single parent of two youngsters, could do nothing right on those days. And Emily would suggest she just go on home. Okay, said Lucy, and she'd leave. In the morning she'd be back, cheerful and smiling again. Emily, the psychologist who hadn't read the booklets on care for the ALS patient, would greet Lucy with an open arm.

Eleanor had come on the scene later. A widow who was confronting her mortality in an impending heart operation, she had experienced her own losses in life and would prove a subtle but significant influence on her patient's life—and death. When Eleanor was hired, she followed in the white-shoed footsteps of numerous other nurses, night and day shift, who figured patients should be sleeping at night, not still trying to fill scrapbooks, photographic and mental. And certainly not seeking to organize their treatment or making some hopeless attempt to fight the quicksand of a terminal disease like ALS. Just accept it with dignity.

Eleanor had seen patients like Emily before. Clinically demanding, she called them. They choose to go on the respirator without realizing what that means; how they lose control then, how that decision forever involves teams of specialists and institutions with their own ambitions and fears and rules that do not always concern the patient's family.

Eleanor had seen these patients filled with anxiety that spilled out in predictable if trying ways. They couldn't pace the room or wring their hands; they had no control over their bodies anymore. So they sought control of the world around them, the arrangement and movement of people and things, debating things that didn't need debating, reorganizing things that didn't need reorganizing. If they couldn't dominate themselves, by God, they were going to dominate something, or someone. The handiest, safest subject around was the hired hand. Eleanor figured that some means of control might calm Emily some. So she brought in a little battery buzzer gadget she had used before and put it on Emily's hand. All Emily had to do was touch her forefinger to her thumb—she could still do that usually—and a little bell would ring. Not as loud as a cowbell perhaps, but it was enough to give Emily a sense of control.

The two women would sit there together, Emily reading her daily newspaper and Eleanor her latest paperback novel. When Emily finished one side, she'd touch her thumb, the bell would tinkle and Eleanor would turn the page and resume her own reading. Other nurses didn't like that idea, or it seemed that way, because they routinely forgot to replace the worn-out batteries. Then Emily would lie there, motionless, touching her forefinger to her thumb with no one hearing.

Of course, there were times when even a patient Eleanor had to get away from her patient for a while. Then Eleanor would arrange for a hospital floor nurse to come to the door of Emily's room. "Eleanor," the nurse would say, "could we see you out here for a few minutes, please?"

"Sure," Eleanor would reply. "Excuse me, Emily. Be right back." And she'd follow the other woman out the door, sigh, and softly say, "Thanks." She'd go sit for a blessed few minutes by herself in the coffee room while the hospital nurses peeked in on Emily occasionally. Then Eleanor could purposefully stride back into Emily's room. "Well, now, how are we doing here, eh?"

Emily liked Eleanor a lot. She was always full of ideas and accepting. The nurse would arrive a few minutes before eight P.M. and an Emily who appeared to be fading at the day's end would seem to perk up immediately. Her eyes grew brighter somehow. That is what everyone remembers about Emily after everything else went, her hungry eyes, how they could hug you, and stab you. Eleanor spent long, closely directed hours helping Emily cut up photographs on the bed and assembling a pile of family scrapbooks to show two little girls someday, when they weren't so little anymore, what their healthy mommy looked like a long time ago. There was one photo of a smiling Emily in a skimpy swimsuit. "Not bad," she told Eleanor with a crooked smile.

There were warm times passed with friends, especially with Vicky Francen, who was to spend many long hours of her life fighting Emily's death. She came to the hospital religiously at least once a week to read Emily's lips into a tape recorder for transcribing into her diary later. And sometimes Emily "talked" with Eleanor about what they would do together when Emily went home. "Home?" said Eleanor. "Is that what you said, home?" Emily nodded. Surely, all this treatment couldn't last forever. Just the other day the hospital person said that this institution was for acute-care patients, not long-term chronic patients, so the hospital had something in mind. Emily's stomach was improving. With a respirator handling the breathing, what's the difference between a hospital room and Emily's apartment? Eleanor could come there. More comfortable. And Emily could again watch her children going about their daily routine of growing up without even knowing it. Emily said she wanted to die at home, when the time came. Not in one of these impersonal institutions full of strange people, strange equipment, and talk-show babble where happy families and classical music were foreign.

Meanwhile, though, Emily would be talking okay with this electronic larynx, after some practice, of course. Eleanor or Lucy or a therapist would hold the little box up against Emily's throat and the mother of two children who had just learned to speak, would try to learn how to speak all over again. The sounds were slurred; maybe they had waited too long, overanticipating Emily's resistance to this therapy, too.

Emily sounded like a monotone computer speaking Russian. She grew frustrated. Everyone was encouraging and told her to keep trying, knowing how important the effort can be in physical therapy, regardless of the practical results. So hour after hour Emily practiced making sounds, all different sounds, and then hours of practice assembling them into words and sentences. Everyone said she was doing well. One way or another Emily was determined to escape from within herself. Imagine being able to talk again!

She knew what she was going to do to surprise her girls. She'd have Eleanor hold the box up by her throat and when Alli and Jenie came in next time, their mommy would say, "Hello, Alli. Hello, Jenie."

■

January 4, 1983: I was hoping Alli would be interested in talking to me with my new machine. But when she came in, she was very afraid of it. She put her hands over her ears and shook her head. Please, God, is there some way to help them not be so frightened of it, of me?

January 6, 1983: I am feeling fed up and angry. I've had to deal with a lot of relief nurses. There is nothing I can do about anything. I'm so used to being able to do something to make everything better. I hate it so much. I am not accepting my situation at all, which somehow I was supposed to do, from a spiritual point of view. I think I want to scream. I cannot even do that. Bob has gone to Morocco and I cannot go anywhere. I just lie in this goddamn bed. I cannot go anywhere. I hate it. I want to be able to go somewhere and do something. I don't want to blame Bob for what's happening to me. I don't think it has to do with him. I think it has to do with the nurses; they are here all the time.

January 7, 1983: I have a therapist friend who comes to help me with this. Vicky says I must turn to myself now. I feel sad about what I'm missing in the world. My cousin Diane was just here. I am so sad I cannot go to her wedding. It seems so unfair to have to miss it. I would love to be there so much. I could help her plan it. I want her to take lots of pictures to show me. She said I have had many wonderful celebrations. It's wonderful to hear her tell me what a good time she had.

January 9, 1983: I forgot to write about Christmas. It was fairly okay. I had some presents here for Alli and Jenie to open. They were very involved with the dolls I got for them, feeding and changing them. Jenie feeds herself now. Alli brought a picture of a house. I don't really interact with the children. There is nothing I can do with them.

I watch them carefully. My friend Sally was here—she hadn't come in a long time—and she acted as a substitute for me. Bob was here, too. I miss the visits where the children make more of a fuss over me, although it cannot happen every week. They do not say much to me. They do look at me a lot.

■

When the plane's nose tilted up Bob began to relax. He had driven the girls to stay with his cousin and his wife, who were childless and had only an inkling of what they had gotten into with the Bauer brood; after fourteen days, they would return to childlessness, and thankfully.

Bob knew very well what he was getting away from—everything. Except Marjory, who sat next to him, their long legs stretched out together beneath the seat in front. It seemed to Marjory's friends that she was going out and going away more during the last ten months. She was dressing a little more smartly, too; was she coloring her brown hair a little to subdue the gray? Her circle of friends wondered if there was a new man in her life; they knew it wasn't one of them. Soon after takeoff, Bob's head nodded over onto Marjory's shoulder. That felt good to her.

For Emily, Bob's two-week African trip was mainly business, though no doubt he would get in some mountain hiking. For Bob's relatives, who suspected and approved but said nothing, the trip would be a well-deserved relief. They had seen some changes in Bob starting after the hospitalization, as if he had been freed to make a decision of some kind. He was more assertive. On his hospital visits, which came three times a week now, Emily produced a list of errands or research for him to do. Bob said okay, he would try, but he had a couple of business appointments and he had promised the girls a trip to the beach. When Emily silently insisted with her lips and her eyes that all these things were essential, Bob said, "No, I'm sorry, Emily. I can't do everything for everybody. I will try to do what I can." And Emily did not like that.

Emily also did not like Bob's response to her casual remark about going home, and soon. "Absolutely not!" he said. He was unusually adamant for Bob. She would need round-the-clock care, he said. He couldn't give it. In that tiny apartment under those circumstances there would be no room for anyone else to live—five people and the machines. He was having trouble just with the kids and himself, Alli having become a very demanding little girl. Bob said he'd bring the kids by the hospital lots of times. Besides, the insurance wouldn't pay—hospital care, yes; home care, no. The institutional incentive was clear. Emily said there were only twenty-two more months left on the policy's coverage. Bob had paused. He said he had enough things to worry about this month, let alone twenty-two months down the road. Emily stared at Bob a very long time during that visit. But he was unmoved.

■

January 12, 1983: Every day is as depressing as the last one. I'm watching more TV. I feel so uncomfortable all the time, like that ache when you want to turn over in bed. But I can't until someone thinks of it. A friend said I have the best and the worst. The best are the friends who come visit me. I am very lucky. And they are very lovely. Some massage me; it feels so good to be touched.

I pray every day now. I talk with God. I ask him why this is happening to me, and for strength to deal with it. I thank him for all the good things, like visitors. I feel like I'm living in hell. I am afraid of suffocating on the respirator.

Today another healer came to see if he can help me get better physically. The idea of getting better is so wonderful: To be with my children, to be off this respirator, to be able to talk, maybe walk. He says this will happen. But I am afraid to get too hopeful or excited. I cannot understand how God can let me be like this. Most of the time now I feel as if I can't go on. I've tried to think of how to die. I'm afraid I will live on like this for quite a while.

I wonder how Bob is doing.

■

Bob was busy the whole time, as he liked to be when relaxing. Too much free time lying around leaves too much time to think—about the withering woman back in a United States bed, about what he was doing in this bed in Morocco, about how he felt about himself— which was not good. So Bob did his brief bit of work, then he plunged into an almost furious round of leisure activities. He and Marjory walked through the bazaar and a long series of shops. Bob bought Emily a few pieces of fabric, but he took a pass on the Oriental rugs. She didn't need jewelry anymore; the only thing she wore, besides her wedding ring, was the amulet a cousin had made from small pieces of silver donated by family members as healing tokens. Emily loved the idea and insisted on wearing the necklace every day, even though it hung near the breathing hole in her throat.

■

January 13, 1983: The art therapist came to work with me. I used the Magic Marker in my mouth. I've done several drawings that I liked. I can't do it for long, as my neck tires easily now. The therapist is very helpful and encouraging.

■

Bob and Marjory took a bus into the sandy North African mountains for a couple of days and hiked around there with a group for hours. Bob was very talkative, remarking on almost everything he saw, which was almost as tiring for Marjory as the climbing and walking. They ate late, long, leisurely meals together in nearly empty, white-tiled res- taurants that did strange but delicious things to chicken and vegeta- bles. They had some minor arguments, of course; that was a habit with them. And they made love, often, with a desperate flavor, as if they knew time had run out but the buzzer hadn't sounded. That was getting to be a habit, too.

Emily was mildly shocked to see Bryan walk into her room. He hadn't visited in a long time, though he sent many messages through Bob.

They must talk often. Where's Barbara? What a pleasant surprise! Or was it, judging by the look on her brother's face?

"Hello, Emily," he said. "How are you?" He went to kiss her—but where, with all these tubes and wires? He ended up pecking her on the forehead, and patting her arm. God, she'd gotten small! Bryan could remember when he'd thought Emily was the third largest person in the world, after Dad and Mom. Now she was this helpless, uh, hopeless thing who couldn't reply to any questions without that nice nurse to interpret. At least there weren't any of those fruitcake healers about. Bryan wasn't sure he could restrain himself after he heard from Bob about the one blaming Jenie for Emily's sickness. God in heaven, what were these people thinking when they said such things?

Bryan was sympathizing strongly with Bob these days and weeks. The men did talk frequently by phone; it saved Bryan the long drive and all the long thoughts about life and death, Emily's and his own. For a while Bryan and Barbara had visited once or twice a month, regularly passing on news of their visits to Emily's distant father; Emily had asked him not to visit. On one trip Bryan made Emily a kind of alphabet eye chart where she could point with her eyes in the direction of certain letters and visitors would move their finger along the rows until Emily blinked. Spelling out words that way took a very long time, though it did speed up as the months wore on. To cut down on the boredom, regular visitors soon learned to confine their questions to ones requiring yes or no answers. It made for one-dimensional conversations. But it was so much easier.

For their visits, Bryan and Barbara left home Friday after work and spent most of that night driving, got some late-morning sleep, and saw Emily right after lunch. The first thing Emily asked, in those days when she could still talk, was, "How long can you stay?" And Bryan would reply, "We have to leave in the morning." Emily, who would have loved to spend all those hours driving across the countryside, looked disappointed. "What's the point in coming then?" she said. And Bryan got to thinking, especially after the tracheotomy, when visitors spent all their time talking at Emily, you know, what was the point? So he and Barbara cut their visits back to once a month, and then every other month or two. Emily didn't say anything, except she got in her little dig. "Hello, stranger," she would say. But Bryan would ignore it.

Bryan felt he shared a common experience with Bob: the tyranny of a demanding Emily, though he wasn't sure how well Bob would take such a comment. So he never uttered it. Now in Bob's understandable absence, Bryan was about to support him against his own sister, to crush the fondest flickering hope of the dying member to protect the hopes of the living members to go on. Once, it had been their dream that Emily would come home; now it was their nightmare. One day, both would come true.

"Emily," Bryan said, "the hospital says we've got to move you. . . . What did she say? . . . Own? Home? Oh, home. No, Emily, not home. That wouldn't work. It wouldn't be good for the children, or Bob, or you either. We've all discussed this. I agree with Bob. It's the best thing if you go to a special place that can care for you properly. They have the equipment and the people. You can have the same private nurses. And it's close by, so Bob and the girls can visit regularly. And maybe you can visit home sometimes, who knows? But you can't turn that little apartment into a hospital room where four people live. How could the girls have a friend over to play? They have a life to lead. It'll be best this way. Really. It'll all work out."

Judging by Emily's eyes, which is all her friends and relatives could do by then, Emily was not convinced. In fact, she was downright furious. She didn't scream. She didn't say anything. She cried. Then she stared at Bryan, hotly without blinking, with narrow eyes as her brother paced about the room talking about everything he could think of except the move. He glanced at her as he paced and talked, and she was still staring at him, her eyes following his every move. In the heat of her gaze Bryan's inner guilt was consuming him. He told Emily then that he had to go. He told his wife then that he didn't see any point in visiting much anymore. The Auntie Mame he wanted to remember wasn't really there.

The move to the chronic-care facility came within forty-eight hours. A bed had suddenly become vacant, as they do now and then in those places where the subject of going home doesn't even come up.

■

January 18, 1983: The move was very hard. It was very disorganized. And my head kept flopping around. I asked them to put me on a stretcher, but no one saw me.

Bob's sister and two other friends helped. I cannot get over my good friends. Vicky comes all that way. Lots of times I've been in a bad mood and not very good company. I'm used to reciprocating with my friends. I don't think I am now.

I was accustomed to my hospital room. I miss that routine and their familiar faces. I feel very tired. I miss my hospital room. I can't eat very well. And I realize I can't look at the patients here. I don't like the way they look. I think they are ugly. They look bent, and their eyes go off in strange directions. Now I'm afraid that I'll start looking like them. I wonder what Allie and Jenie will think of me. I know Bob has mixed feelings, too.

January 19, 1983: Lots of people came by today to say what they were going to do for me. One possibility is to lower the air in the trach and learn how to speak that way, somehow. Other possibilities are to use a portable respirator, so I can get around, and a printing machine. It is hard for me to do all of them.

January 20, 1983: All this adjustment has been very hard for me. I do not feel very well. I do not have any advantages. All my life I had advantages. That's because I was very smart. Now that doesn't help. I'm smart. But I can't even breathe on my own.

January 23, 1983: Both my nurses have been talking to me about my attitude. What they say is to accept my situation. I try to adjust. But I know that I really don't want to adjust at all. I look around me and this is how I have to live. I don't want to live like this.

There are children near me who do not seem upset. I look at the others and want to know how they adjust. Also how they go to the bathroom when they sit in the wheelchair all day. They just sit there with nothing to do. I don't want to be like them. I have no choice. I would prefer to die.

January 24, 1983: I woke up this morning thinking how I would try very hard to adjust. I said to myself: I'm going to have a goal—I'm going to my cousin's wedding in July and Bob's nephew's wedding in October. That's what I'll do. I'll just decide and then I can do it.

Then I sat in the wheelchair for four hours and I got very sore. And very tired. And I wet myself. Why must everything be so hard? I have not accepted. It's like that play I saw when I was pregnant, *Whose Life Is It Anyway?* I feel like that man. I have no more choices. No one asks me if I want to do this, to live like this. Professional people assume that I want to live. Their jobs depend on it. I think I should have a choice.

It's funny, though. My breathing tube came off over the weekend, and I called for help. I waited for a little while and I thought, "Can I go through with it?" But then I got very scared and called for help, even though I was disappointed in myself. I could not be quiet with the bell on my fingers. I had a chance to die, but the will to live is still strong.

It's very hard to let go.

January 26, 1983: Alli asked to come see me! She was waking up crying in the morning. Bob says she told him she misses me. I had been very worried that she did not miss me. So I was very happy to hear that. The visit was okay. She spent some time with me. She would not talk with me directly. When I asked her questions through Bob, she asked me if she had her boots on the right foot. When I said, "Yes," she didn't understand. I felt terrible. I must have faith that she got something just from seeing me. Jenie played around and looked at me some. I don't know how she felt. She was very far away.

It would be wonderful just to talk with someone.

■

It was a large place. It still is. Always full of many people. Only some of them, the ones in white clothes, leave each day. The others, the pale ones in faded green smocks that tie twice in the back, are home already.

Made of bricks and stone a long time ago, the building stands strong, several stories tall, its large windows staring out blankly like the eyes behind them. The hall walls have two colors—a dark green swath running the length of the corridor about as high as a head in a wheelchair. Even the old radiators that creak and groan when the unseen steam seeps through them are covered with the same colored swath, many layers of it. The other color is a lighter, wider band of green covering the rest of the walls and running as far as the eye can see, way down to the end of this world where the people in white appear so small, running back and forth. The color scheme was designed, several administrators ago, to make an otherwise impersonal hall seem brighter and cheery. Some paint is always flaking.

The wards are large rooms running off the hall. Each ward has a dozen beds. Each bed has a patient. Each patient is still, though some make motions at times and talk about themselves to visitors who have not yet arrived. Each stall—patients stalled there between life and something else, waiting, always waiting—is enclosed by thin drapes hung from a ceiling track. That is for privacy, so that the folks in white can whip the green curtain around and enclose each little world for a moment, or the moment.

But the flimsy curtains cannot contain the sounds of pain and fears and conversations and dreams. They cannot contain the sounds of machines that keep them all going. There are machines that go beep. There are machines that buzz. Machines that flush. Machines that whirl. Machines that suck. And there are lots of digital readouts and clear plastic bags to collect the various fluids that emerge.

There are also emergency machines on wheels that are rolled up to the bedside of a very still patient whose smock has been torn off. A man in white pounds down on the bare chest. A woman in white sticks a needle in the body. A second man in white places two cups on the very still chest. He calls, "Clear!" as everyone steps back. And with a muffled thunk the body jumps from the foreign current.

If nothing happens, they do it over again. And again. And again. With an admirable dedication to someone else's life. Until after a long while someone will say, "Enough," and the crowd quietly melts away.

But if everything works out well for the well-trained people in white, after one or two thunks the digital readout moves again. The line on the screen is no longer straight. And everyone smiles, everyone but the patient. Yet another victory. If only he could celebrate, too. If only he knew.

Of course, there are the respirators, the breathing machines that keep everything going, pumping pure air in and foul breath out. To some, the building itself seems to breathe in and out with the rhythmic wheeze-and-whoosh of the machines, so pervasive are the sounds of life-giving, death-denying air being forced into the sick.

■

February 6, 1983: A lot of things have happened. The doctor did a test and found I have a hole in my throat. So they put another tube in. On Friday, they tried another test, but it was too full of mucus (and very painful). It has been rescheduled for this Friday, and I am frightened. I'm tired of all this.

February 8, 1983: They say they are going to put an alarm on my respirator. I said I didn't want that. My nurse told me they will anyway. She said I could ask them not to revive me after the alarm goes off. But I have to make it legal. Bob is talking with the administrator.

February 9, 1983: I had a dream: I was leaving home. My mother and Alli were there. They were very upset. I felt pulled toward them, but I left anyway.

■

Once, Americans didn't need a special place to be allowed to die, and legal papers to approve it—in case the living left behind got to arguing in a court. Once, death came where it came when it came, once. No heart restarts. No machine-inflated lungs. Until 1950, about the time Emily's hospital was reaching middle age, a majority of Americans died at home, likely lying in the same bed in the same upstairs bedroom where they had first breathed and, later, moaned through the flu. Perhaps, too, it was there that they had conceived the children now gathered somberly around the bed with the friendly family doctor who delivered them all, and tended their cuts and bruises, and broken legs and mumps and ruled out polio one thankful day. Now with his little black bag on the bed table with his stethoscope, wooden tongue depressors, and that miniature flashlight for the ears, the doctor was painfully aware of everything he could not do. So was the family, whose simple hope was to make the passing as comfortable and peaceful as possible. "The old man's friend" was what they called pneumonia then because it brought the sleep that led to the fog of forever before the pain from other ailments could set in too badly.

Then along came iron lungs and powerful new drugs and more machines with a diagnostic and curative sophistication undreamed of by the old doc upstairs who had always thought, mistakenly, that there were powers beyond him making the decisions.

These were expensive and sensitive machines being invented and reinvented. They required cadres of technicians to man them, tend them, aim them, and train those who would destroy sick cells by radiation or dissolve kidney stones by sound waves, or peer into a malignant cell, or rearrange genes. The machines wouldn't work in the patient's home. Machines need much more room than humans, stronger floors, more electrical power, and more protection for bystanders from the unseen rays that can see and the magnetic forces that erase the memories of passing digital watches and cause metal pens to fly across the room.

What individual doctor could afford the gear to perform such miracles? How could anyone seriously expect this apparatus to make house calls? Or the busy medical doctor anymore, for that matter? The ones who, faced with this avalanche of new knowledge, data, and techniques, could no longer know all there was to know about the body's

117

operations. They had to specialize in just parts of the human body—kidneys, livers, eyes, even hearts that needed replacing.

So the patients began being drawn to the institutions, like pens to that magnet. The specialists treated them, one after another, and felt good, and made good money. Some patients recovered and thanked God and, of course, Dr. What's-his-name, who had spent several minutes with them several times and then wrote a formal letter reporting back to the family doctor, who filed it in case there was a lawsuit later. Some patients died bitter or happy or unaware of anything, which may have been just as well. Others recovered but wished they hadn't, having been saved so they could fall victim to something else, something perhaps more painful, for which there was no machine or cure yet.

It sometimes seemed to the oldtime doctors, who were passing away themselves as the years flowed by, that their young replacements, the specialists, often displayed more interest in the special diseased organ than in the special life of the diseased. This bothered some, but what could anyone do? People were living longer. That's what progress was all about, a few extra months or years, another football season to watch, another anniversary to celebrate, another grandchild's face to see and kiss.

There were others who thought a few more months like that was a man-made living hell, or would be. So they signed advance medical instructions, "living wills." Bob did, too, stating he wanted no extraordinary measures if serious illness ever struck and there seemed little chance for significant recovery. Above all, no respirator—that's where it all begins.

Some doctors chose to pay attention to such documents. Others chose to pay more attention to the rising number of malpractice suits filed by or on the behalf of patients dissatisfied with imperfect treatment or imperfect results, though the doctor, unlike the manufacturer of medical machines, offered no warranty. The doctors saw the rising amount of damages awarded and the rising insurance premiums they had to pay and pass on to their patients, the living ones. So when the time came for important decisions and, as usual in medicine, the outlook was uncertain, maybe the doctor would make the safest recommendation: Do everything. Or nearly everything. Or something;

there was always something new to try. Few of the worried families, including the Bauers, were prepared at those times to say, "No, wait." So as the country moved through the last fifteen years of the twentieth century, 80 percent of the 5,507 Americans who died on an average day did so in a hospital, or those special institutions where they went after the hospital to wait.

The administrator of Emily's institution was friendly and understanding with Bob. The request for a "Do Not Resuscitate" order was not unprecedented, although the hospital didn't feature it in the brochures the way it did, say, the solarium or the physical therapy sessions. Did Bob know exactly what this meant? How important a decision it was? It meant that if the patient's heart stops, it would not be restarted—let nature take its course sooner rather than later. Quietly. Unofficially, it was perfectly appropriate in some hopeless cases. Now, if Bob would just sign these sheets here—they were for his protection, too—then those meaningful three letters, DNR, would be written on page one of Emily's file at the nursing station. Mrs. Bauer would have to be consulted, of course.

■

February 13, 1983:
To all those concerned with my welfare,
from Emily Bauer:

I have decided that I wish each one of you could experience endlessly what it is like not to be able to move, to use one's arms or hands, to breathe, or most important, to talk. The degree of discomfort, deprivation, and frustration makes the quality of life unacceptable to me.

I had such a rich and active life before and I cannot accept or adjust to this. I look around and see how others spend their days and I do not want that. I am being challenged to define for myself what is essential for living. I know I have more to learn about this. Animals do not talk. They sleep a lot and never think about the quality of life. My intelligence may be a disadvantage.

I worry a lot about the muscles of my tongue and lips. They are working less well and this could progress to where I lose the ability to have my lips read. The pain I now feel from not being understood by most people most of the time is so great. I do not want anymore. The degree of frustration I feel cannot be described.

February 14, 1983: People who visit say I look better. I'm not sure I feel better. Things look very grim. I had my tube taken out yesterday to prepare for a test today, the painful one looking at my throat. The doctor did not come. I did not have the test. They replaced the tube.

February 15, 1983: I saw my reflection today: nasal tube, trach tube, hair unstylishly pulled back. My eyes are bagged and drooping because I have not been sleeping due to ill-fitting trach tube. But I still look okay. My friends are right: the essence of me is still here.

I got a letter from a student. She said all the things she had learned from me. I was "a very good teacher" and gave a lot to students and children. Now I do nothing except this writing.

I still operate under the assumption that life is about developing one's abilities. I was never exposed to dealing with insurmountable limitations. The American way, the Western way, is to overcome limits. I watch a lot of news on TV, and their stories of disabled people always show them coping and surmounting difficulty because we all need to believe it is possible. Why not a story on me and the ways I do NOT cope? Like when I cry from the pain of sitting without being able to move. Or the times when I am not understood and the helplessness and frustration I feel.

How could I have been better prepared? Should we educate to deal with the insurmountable? Central to at least middle-class youth is a belief in limitless opportunity, while longer aging today and illnesses involve narrowing of possibilities. I guess I will never be a philosopher, as the rebel scientist always seeks the exceptions.

February 16, 1983: This morning I woke up after a good night's sleep—sleeping is one of the few sensual pleasures I have left—and looked at the hyacinths from friends and the burgundy and white orchids in a lovely Japanese-style vase Bob gave me for Valentine's Day. And I felt happy.

I love to look at flowers. I think it would be worse not to be able to see—worse than not being able to talk. Imagine not being able to see Alli and Jenie! They visited this week! I get such pleasure from watching them move, play, and interact. Alli is so lithe and airy and prickly, while Jenie is solid, earth-grounded, and amiable. They are so full of energy and spirit I am glad God and I brought them forth.

I could have been like the two men in cubicles near me. Ed, who can talk, and Charles, who can't. Both paralyzed from the neck down. Both twenty. What if I had been twenty instead of in my forties and never had the friendships and loves, Ph.D. and work, travel and skiing, swimming and biking, and, most important, Bob, Alli, and Jenie? What do these men have to draw upon for self-comfort? At least I can tell myself I've had a rich life. Yet maybe having a rich past is a hindrance in that one expects more. Ed's reaction to having nothing to do ever, not even to watching TV while in intensive care, was far more accepting than mine would have been. When I asked the nurse to ask him what he did all day, he simply said that he stared at the wall. I would have been crying from the frustration.

February 19, 1983: The day begins with my six o'clock feeding through my nose. I have deep yearnings for some of the delicious food I see people eating so casually on TV. I think often of the taste of Chinese food and good hamburgers. Then I am given a sponge bath and have the chance to see my thin body with atrophied arms and legs, and I recall how they used to look. It is very hard to accept this body that neither looks nor acts right.

■

The number of Emily's visitors had fallen off at the new hospital. For one thing, it was somewhat harder to reach. Perhaps unconsciously, the planners had placed the chronic-care hospital a little more out of sight of the healthy—fresher air, they said. The "novelty" or "freshness" of Emily's illness had worn off. It was clear that Emily's disease was not going away. Every visitor to the bedside world of Emily Bauer had to confront the specter of creeping death, hers and, someday, theirs. Please, God, make it quick, they would say on the way home.

They had to confront, too, a once-vibrant Emily who was shrinking before their eyes, week after week, as if that wheezing respirator thing was sucking her life out instead of blowing it in. This was the same energetic woman who, always being a little late, would run up the stairs and bounce into the room, and everyone would turn to look at her entrance with all its bright colors and strong movement. Emily always liked being the center of attention, ever since her infant days. Someone always came to her in those days. But now they came less often—you know how it is with kids in school or a husband on the road or trying to work and run a household at the same time.

When visitors did come, they stayed for shorter periods. There was only so much they could say at a person. These adults wouldn't ever expect a response from a baby, except maybe to quiet down or smile or burp. But it was very disconcerting for many visitors to waltz into Emily's cubicle with a cheery "Hello." There she was. The body resembled Emily, but it didn't talk like Emily. It didn't suggest playing a game of some kind or singing a folk song from the '60s or ask after their welfare. It just lay there. It didn't even move like Emily. The only things that moved in that bed now were Emily's two eyes. If she was awake, they turned to greet visitors and follow them everywhere, like the eyes of a painting on the wall of a haunted house.

They could be warm eyes or happy eyes, angry eyes or sad eyes. Some thought they saw inquiring eyes or suspicious eyes. All saw crying eyes. Of course, they could only guess why the tears were flowing. Was it something they said? Had they forgotten something? Did she hurt somewhere? Did she need help of some kind? When they checked the sheet of instructions by the bed, they saw that one blink meant yes and two blinks meant no. There were so many teary blinks. Was that five blinks? What did five blinks mean? Do they mean yes,

yes, yes, yes, yes? Or no, no, yes? Or yes, yes, yes, no? So, many visitors just gave up and sat by the bed, holding their friend's cold hand, until they noticed how late it was getting and remembered all they had to do at home before dinner.

There were fewer healers calling on her, too. This hospital frowned on them, made them feel uncomfortable, as if they were somehow suspicious, just because their methods weren't taught in accredited medical schools. Emily's physical condition had deteriorated rapidly since the move, so no one, not even the healers with the medical school degrees, could claim their treatment was working.

One man did continue to visit, however. His name was Mikhail. He believed not so much in mending the temporal body as in tending the soul within by massage and meditation, which were not designed to cure terminal diseases, unless you considered tension and stress to be terminal diseases. All of which suited Emily fine; she was realizing she couldn't do much about her body.

Emily had some nice bright nightgowns, the ones Janice had bought, sewed up the front, and slit down the back for her. Emily's eyes looked excited when Janice, who had wrapped them as a gift, opened them in front of Emily. The eyes said thank you. It took two people, Janice and the nurse, to try them on Emily—one to hold the body sitting up, the other to pull the bed clothing up the arms and over the shoulders and tuck her back into the bed without pulling out one of the many tubes or wires. That was the big project for Janice's visit that day, and the big excitement, too, judging from the immediate need for the bedpan. They put on the nightgowns and Janice recalled where they came from and when she got them and what the choices were and why she picked these colors and how she got them with her sister, who was sorry she couldn't come too today. Sometimes it seemed as if Emily's healthy visitors were really visiting Emily's healthy nurse, so intense were their conversations and so interested were their responses, creating conversations for the benefit of a silent someone's ears. They were desperate to find anything to talk about. There was something about the door to Emily's cubicle that made many people sigh on their way out.

Not everyone saw the bright nightgowns, because Emily had taken to wanting the sheet pulled up to her neck, the woman who liked revealing sweaters now preferring to be fully covered. But she very much liked the idea of wearing a bright color and of a man with strong hands calling on her, caring for her, about her. How could anything about Mikhail's attentiveness be wrong when she couldn't do anything to respond? Except maybe seem to moan sometimes. Bob obviously thought less of her as a woman, a wife, and more of her as a burden. At least he hardly ever touched her. Well, he did touch her—they held hands like they used to at the ballet—but it wasn't like before. Emily wondered why.

Mikhail heard of Emily from a fellow student several months before. He just showed up at the first hospital one day and asked Emily if he might visit once a week for a couple of hours. Emily blinked once, very quickly. Now the chronic-care hospital informed him of its hours and rules—no drugs, foods, or medicines to be given. Mikhail arrived when no one else was visiting, usually on a Saturday. He checked in at the nursing station and greeted the private day nurse, who waited outside, somewhat suspiciously at first.

Mikhail felt nervous before these visits; Emily was his first regular exposure to a terminal case. Emily was always so alert and so welcoming with a smile and then, later, just those eyes. The visits over the coming many months almost always turned out to be good conversations, at least that's the way he remembered them. For a few minutes he chatted about the events of his week, his girlfriend, and asked after Emily. Then he asked her to think of a part of her body, perhaps a shoulder or leg. Sometimes he spoke to her softly; sometimes, there was silence. But every time he slid his strong hands beneath her bony body and massaged her back, wherever he sensed tightness, trying to break the monotonous rhythm of the respirator. Or he might work on the shoulders or neck. It felt very good. He thought this woman developed an awful lot of tension just lying there.

It all made Emily feel special again. It pissed Bob right off. Of course, he said nothing. The two men had met awkwardly one Saturday when their hospital visits overlapped, briefly. Mikhail thought Bob was like a big bear; he obviously loved Emily very much, though he clearly thought less of the visitor. Bob figured if this guy, who never knew Emily, could give her the physical touching she wanted and craved, the one thing Bob could no longer bring himself to do lovingly, then Bob told himself that was fine with him. The nurses noticed that whatever Mikhail did, Emily was calmer for hours after his visits. The nurses also noticed that Emily's husband no longer came to visit on Saturday.

■

February 24, 1983: This morning a bouquet of springy flowers arrived, and I have enjoyed looking at every petal of each flower. They were sent by Bob. I especially appreciate the thought because in the last few days I have shed a lot of tears about us, and they still keep coming, suggesting I've tapped into their pool of deep grief.

I have thought about his struggles, raising the children largely alone. We discuss Alli and Jenie often, but he deals with them. I have seen tiredness in his eyes and cried that I was not there to help him, knowing how much children need a mother. And as I say this, I add, or is it they need more than one parental person? How will Alli fare in femininity? She has many others to go to. She does not miss Mother, me.

February 26, 1983: I have noticed how my professional status as a psychologist exists only to the degree others choose to give it to me. My doctors are illustrative. One said, in my presence, "This is an intelligent woman." The other called me Dr. Bauer. Most call me Mrs. Bauer or Emily, which I prefer. But I note that some who call me by my first name introduce themselves by their last name. Another reminder of the status of being a patient.

■

On Wednesdays Emily had another regular visitor right after lunch. His first name was Stephen. He was the psychiatric social worker assigned to Emily's ward. He was a sensitive single man with an appreciation for the individual as well as the massive medical bureaucracy that he had chosen to work in, with its political currents, ethical shoals, and moral reefs and the vast unfathomable depths beyond. Steve was troubled by some of the cases he saw—like the man who visited his wife every day for three years though she was in an ALS coma right to the end, as they all damned well knew she would be right from the start. He was troubled, too, by the families who wrote off their patient from day one in the chronic-care hospital. They rarely visited, rarely even seemed to think of the patient, filing the shell of a person away in some sanitary hospital to die, officially, among strangers in white coats and digital readouts in green lights sometime sooner or later, preferably sooner—was it illegal to just kind of unplug him? That way they could get on with the business of forgetting and living, because the business of living with death was a whole lot easier than living with dying. Until it was their turn to be filed among the strangers and readouts.

Steve, like the physical therapist, the occupational therapist, the nurses, and Emily's doctors, made it a point to step into Emily's world the first day after her arrival. They each had conversations with Emily, though these were not easy given the difficulty of communicating. These hospital staffers met in an old conference room down the hall at a shiny, worn table made of wood.

They reviewed their new patient's records, including the psychiatrist's report from the first hospital, and gave their own evaluations. They seemed agreed on two points: Emily could be a very demanding, uh, person. Thank God for the private nurses. They'd seen that before lots of times, patients who can't control their fate trying to control everything else. They agreed that Emily knew what ALS was and that she knew she had it; some patients came in there unable to move, still claiming they had a minor nerve problem that would heal itself any day now, if only the patient could find a decent doctor.

Bauer, Emily R., clearly was not accepting reality. She still thought family members could have, ought to have, the same relationship they had with her before the hospitalization, as if the disease wasn't invisibly killing parts of others, too. It looked like the stages of her disease had moved along too quickly for Mr. and Mrs. Bauer to work out new accommodations at each level of disability. She still clung to false hopes in all sorts of miracle cures; had everyone seen some of those characters who had come by to see her? One—was it Michael some-thing?—seemed okay. A gentle sort.

First, Steve thought they ought to cut back on some of these fel-lows. And gals, excuse me. Not Mikhail maybe, as long as he went by their rules—had they been explained?—but the others, especially that vitamin guru. Tell them that visitors were being restricted pretty much to immediate family due to Emily's condition. Second, there seemed a lot pent up inside Emily. She was brimming over with rage or something. Did everyone pick up on that? Okay. Well, this woman is very intelligent, as you know. She was a child psychologist, before. What if we moved some of the children in around her? Maybe Nicole and Lewis? Give Emily something to watch and think about instead of those two paraplegic men, and herself. Stephanie, can you see to that, please?

Now, third, is there any way we can tap into her need to communi-cate? She seems very frustrated when you misread her lips or she can't make herself clear. I share that frustration around here some-times—and I can speak.

The artificial larynx is out, I think, don't you? Too late for that now. What about the printer? Put the switch under her head. She can still wiggle her head some, can't she? Why don't we try that and see how it goes. How does the family seem? They had brought up DNR already? That one kid seems to have very little to do with Emily. The other one sometimes, but she's starting to withdraw already. The husband, too, I think, though he seems very dedicated. She's one of those who just lives for these visits, doesn't she? I hear about them a lot. You too? That husband is a dutiful man. Did we warn him and the friends about keeping anybody with a cold away from the patient? Maybe put up a sign. Bauer wants to see me next week.

■

February 28, 1983: My area has two children in it now. They are both of good spirit and undemanding. It is interesting to watch them. They have many visitors, people from the hospital and outside. Even so, much of their time is spent sleeping or watching TV. They don't com-plain or seem depressed. Just now the boy, Lewis, who is twelve, sat in his wheelchair one hour doing nothing, not fidgeting, not eliciting attention, seemingly content. Later, he got an earache and began whimpering.

March 1, 1983: I am getting better with this printing machine. There is a board with letters on it and a cursor that moves along under the letters. When it reaches the letter I want, I nudge a switch under my head and it stops. I nudge again, and it prints out that letter on a tape next to my bed. I nudge again, and the cursor starts moving again. It can go slow or fast. I am still very slow and make many mistakes but I am getting faster. It is a laborious process.

Why didn't someone think of this before?

March 2, 1983: This morning Nicole, who is eight, had breathing problems, which is very frightening. She cried out loudly and clearly what she wanted—she wanted to feel better. Her behavior was more appropriate than Lewis's with an earache. Today Lewis showed anger when told he was being put to bed. All he did was drop his head and lower his eyes, again not direct or assertive. He had been over by Nicole, chattering happily. The nurse did not ask him what he wanted to do. Amidst her banter, she told him she was not to be given a hard time. He did not say anything.

March 5, 1983: The two children last night were calling people on an imaginary telephone. Nicole called her dead aunt. They had an animated exchange lasting about twenty minutes. Part of it was silly sounds. One child would imitate the other. They were very animated.

Earlier Lewis was waiting for his mother to visit. When he was being dressed in the morning, he said he was waiting. When he was being fed at lunch, he said he was waiting. At dinner, while the nurse was feeding him, she casually told him that his mother had called to say she was not coming. Lewis told the nurse she was a liar and he did not like her anymore. The nurse laughed and pretended to be insulted but continued to be warm and kind.

March 8, 1983: Nicole had bad dreams and began whimpering and crying. A nurse came, tried to comfort her, and then told her to stop, that she was a big girl. Then another nurse came and comforted her. A third nurse tried to find out what was bothering Nicole. Nicole asked her not to be left alone.

March 12, 1983: The sound of the breakfast cart interrupts the silence in this cubicle where I live now. It is fairly cheerful. I remember how offended I was when I first arrived, to think that I, with my sensibilities and taste, had to live in a place of no beauty. However, it is a kind place.

The two children who live by me—Nicole, who is eight, and Lewis, who is twelve—were talking. "Lewis," she said, "will you be my valentine?" And Lewis replied, "I love you." Nicole retorted, "That is not what I asked you."

It is getting near eight when my night nurse leaves. I was worried about communication, as she was a new nurse. With comparatively little difficulty, I communicated to the night nurse that I wanted to show the card used to spell words to the floor nurses, as my new nurse could then go to them for help, if they knew how it worked. (Dorothy, the spelling card is in the drawer. The print machine switch often needs to go under my head. It slips out a lot. I blink three times for this. Thanks for hanging in there with me today.)

I need my nurses so much. They give some comfort, companionship, and ability. I am the only one here with a nurse. Others must lie in the same position for hours with no one to talk to and not able to do anything. Some don't even watch TV.

March 15, 1983: I said to Bob again that I could see him in another relationship someday. I also thought of his own needs although not as much. But when I asked him this time, he told me of wanting a relationship and someone to make a home for him. I got very upset. I spent a day expressing my feelings and fighting for our relationship. He told me of feeling such despair that he thought of suicide. Along with everything else his business is on the edge of bankruptcy, and they lose money on projects he enjoys.

He said it was very hard to live reactively due to my illness, and he must get control and go on with his life and meet his needs. He told me how he didn't want things this way and was in a rage most of the time, and sometimes is very angry at me for being so sick. He said he had to be realistic and that I was looking at our relationship as if it was 1977, whereas it is 1983 and I live at the hospital and see him only a few hours each week.

■

A couple of months earlier, Bob returned from Morocco refreshed and resigned, and relieved, too, once he heard the hospital move had been made. The chronic-care hospital was a grim place, all those bodies arranged all around, waiting. Bob hadn't even known such places existed, before. He had no idea either, like a lot of people, what They could do in hospitals nowadays. He read the papers now and then, no TV, but he did read. Were all those machines and techniques invented secretly somewhere and then trucked in at night when no one was watching? Or had he not been paying attention for years when all this progress was accumulating? Who ordered all this medical technology? Who controlled it? Who said when to use it? Sure, they consulted with patients and families. But the way the doctors usually shaped their presentation in those little conference rooms, there seemed little else to do but go along with what the doctor ordered. When the same doctor or maybe a different one announced later that a new complication had come up in their loved one's treatment, something that was frightening enough even if they could have pronounced it, the relatives might wonder why this possibility hadn't been mentioned at the beginning. But, of course, the relatives would never openly question the doctor. Besides the stethoscope, he held a lot of power in those broad jacket pockets.

More importantly, who decided when *not* to use this technology? Who could say, "No more"? Every time a conversation drifted toward that dangerous area, eyes were lowered and feet shuffled. How come all a patient or relative had to do to get maximum treatment, the works, every machine, every kind of ray and electron analysis imaginable, was say to one doctor two magic little letters: O.K.?

But if someone wanted to do less, to say, "No, wait," that became a throat-clearing problem requiring further ethical explanations and meetings on morality and consultations with higher bureaucrats and patronizing suggestions for further consideration. Just let's see how things go in the next few hours or weeks or months—at $1,000 a day or more in some intensive care units, which is never discussed openly, at least by those who don't have to pay.

Bob wasn't paying anywhere near that much. The insurance company got the basic bills, and wrapped them into all their other costs and adjusted their premiums up accordingly. So Emily's expenses were only several hundred dollars a day, plus the nurses. He hadn't known about the problems of medical control until he became deeply involved. Afterward, when he could have warned others—watch out for the respirator decision, for instance—he didn't even want to think about it, let alone speak out. And he was alone. This technology certainly had a way of isolating patients, treating them alone as single individuals, usually naked—their clothes having been hung on hooks beyond their reach—and not as full-fledged members of a larger society united for self-protection. And it isolated the uncomprehending family, too.

When those thoughts crept into Bob's mind, he figured maybe Emily's case was somehow unique, that she was the only deathly-ill patient and he and the girls the only dying family to wander in saddened isolation and wonder if this impressive, admirable white-coated struggle to maintain life in a body that could no longer move or talk was perhaps merely prolonging the dying. Because They could prolong this life, of course, they would. Naturally, Bob said nothing of these ill-formed thoughts to anyone, except maybe Marjory. Who would care outside this one family, the business of being a medical patient seeming as lonely an affair as Bob could imagine? He knew these thoughts about death were heresy, seeming to challenge the old black-and-white ethics of life at all costs in an affluent age of grays, seeming to suggest something close to suicide, which is not illegal, or aiding suicide, which is. So he said nothing. He just felt guilty for having thought such terrible thoughts.

He was pleasantly surprised when Steve, the psychiatric social worker, turned out to be warm and receptive. Steve told Bob he didn't think Emily's desire for a DNR order would be any problem. They would acquiesce to nature stopping the heart. He offered to see Bob, too, anytime. He said he knew there were a lot of pressures on patients' families. He knew, too, but didn't say that he saw a distance developing between this husband and wife. It was a fundamental change in their relationship that Steve had seen separate others many times before. It couldn't be hurried. It shouldn't be hurried. It couldn't be stopped. They were withdrawing from each other. Bob had felt this for a long while. Emily was just starting to sense it, and it was becoming a great source of anxious preoccupation and depression for her. This usually led to a loss of self-esteem and self-worth. That had to come, Steve knew, if Emily were ever going to stop flailing at the fates and see herself honestly as sick and disabled.

The question—the fear—in Steve's mind was whether or not enough time remained for Emily to follow her own course of recognition. Steve had seen ALS patients slip into long comas right about now. He called them "gray nowheres."

This was all relatively new material for the professionals to handle. A generation or two ago, there wouldn't have been so much time for the happy, healthy memories of this family to go dry around the edges and grow moldy in the middle; in the old days, Emily would have been dead a year ago.

Emily's dreams, which Steve read in the diary pages she sent him, involved men all right, but not Bob. She also talked, or wrote, a lot about friends, those children near her, and her own children, but her expressed thoughts about Bob were becoming more scarce.

Which was not all that bad if it meant she was starting to let go.

Steve tried gently to validate those thoughts of Emily's that he deemed best for her mental condition, a gradual acceptance of the inevitable without a sudden determination of doom. Like a psychiatrist, Steve seized on the thoughts he wanted her to pursue and ignored the others, without seeming to discard them. There was no more talk from Emily, for instance, about going home, though Steve suggested that an occasional afternoon visit might be arranged.

Emily was much less interested in current affairs now beyond the world of her ward. There always seems to be a good deal in newspapers that doesn't concern its readers directly. Now there was nothing in them that did concern Emily and her shrinking world. Some days Emily's notes talked of nothing but dying; she couldn't wait; she wanted out. Other times she was excited about spring and the coming weekend's visits by the children; she wanted them here; she couldn't wait. Ambivalence, Steve told himself.

He sensed that something was cooking in that intelligent woman's head. She had inquired a bit too much about Charles. Both of the paraplegics had been moved down a few spaces to make room for the children to be near Emily. One afternoon Charles's breathing tube came loose, just slipped off, it seemed, and the alarm did not sound. Someone may have forgotten to throw the switch back on after suctioning his throat that morning.

Anyway, Charles lay there, silently suffocating, unable to move or signal, while the rest of the ward's world went on about its business just a few feet away. The respirator kept blowing the air down the tube and sucking it back out. None of it was getting to Charles's lungs. After a very few minutes, his eyes slowly closed, as if he was going to sleep.

A few minutes later the voices from the soap opera on Emily's TV were interrupted by a nurse's voice addressing Emily's wardmate. "Charles," said the nurse, "Charles, wake up. *Charles!*"

An alarm went off then. "Code Blue!" the loudspeaker said. "Code Blue!" But the large crowd that responded wore white. They came running down the hall, or at least that's where Emily assumed they came from. She could turn her head only slightly now, and the curtain was half-closed. She could see the bustling personnel rushing by just beyond the foot of her bed. She heard the sounds of determination.

"Charles," someone kept saying, "Charles! Wake up!" Orders were given and the sounds of white coats and white skirts rustling and people running to nearby cabinets and a cart coming. Then, "Clear!" And then a thump. And then silence. And then "Clear!" And thump.

Emily didn't know how long this went on. She couldn't look at her wristwatch, even if she'd had one on. It seemed as if that activity lasted a long time. Later she wanted to know if Charles had tried to signal anyone. Was it quick for him? Didn't he have some arm movement left? Why was his hand up near his throat? Trying to reconnect the tube, it was suggested. Emily wondered.

After some time that morning the orders and the bustling had ceased. Emily saw the workers begin slowly drifting back past her bed. Then she saw the emergency cart leave. And heard the curtains close nearby.

The next day a new patient was in Charles's bed.

■

March 17, 1983: I have been rereading my journal and shedding more tears. All that we have been through! Our attempts to fight the disease and make sense out of what was happening. This is no success story! It is incredibly sad.

I asked Bob if he thought I'd changed in any basic way. And he said, "No," I was the same. Ideas and feelings I thought were new I found written in my journal months ago. So I can't claim great personal growth.

Bob says the only good for him has been to learn to define himself more clearly.

Perhaps I feel more deeply now—such as my love for Bob, Alli, and Jenie. But it is an attached love—that I can't be with Bob and hear him express his needs, which he doesn't much anymore, and to feel how much I want to meet them and not to be able is excruciating. I have no answer for him in support of myself. I can wish he felt differently. I can say to myself with a desperate intensity that I must get better. I go through in my mind all the things I did in the past to try to get better, and how none of them worked, and I don't know what else to do. I pray a lot frequently—anguished pleas for rescue and queries, "Why such cruelty?" Probably that is not a proper way to pray.

March 19, 1983: There is more space here than at the other hospital, and while that lets me see the wonderful ways Alli and Jenie move, they are less often near me. This time I was in the wheelchair for the first time since being at home. It was hard. But they both stared!

They played on the floor with Bob, and I watched from a distance so I could see them over a wide space. Bob was absorbed and couldn't look at me as often as I needed, and I couldn't communicate with my nurse, Eleanor, to tell her to talk for me and move me as the children moved so I could still see them.

I explained to Bob why I needed two adults for these visits. I wasn't as clear then about it as I am now, and he thought it was because I thought he couldn't handle them alone. I think he's doing fine—but he doesn't. Also, he says, "We all struggle."

Jenie kept her distance, but right near the end Alli came up to me and said, "I think I'll sit on Mom's lap." But Bob and the nurse didn't hear her. And I couldn't get their attention in time. And, unencouraged, Alli moved away.

March 21, 1983: It is a gray day outside. And inside. The entire morning has been spent dealing with my secretions. I feel like I'm drowning in my own juices. I don't know where all the mucus comes from. But then I don't know where the illness comes from. My struggle to understand this all has not been fruitful.

March 26, 1983: Alli and Jenie did not want to visit this week. Maybe they feel pain—as I do—because we can't really interact. I can look and, I think, smile, but cannot talk with them as they usually seem afraid of lipreading. I guess because it's too hard.

I spend a lot of time on this journal, some days four to eight hours. I was reading from past passages that Jenie climbed up on me and said, "Mommy! Mommy!" Oh to have that now!

March 28, 1983: Bob visited. He brought new pictures of Alli and Jenie and a wonderful book Alli made on "My Family." I shed more tears over her expressiveness. She left me out of the family drawing. But she did say how she loved me hundreds. She told of all that she loved to do with Daddy, marvelous things at the playground I would love to see someday, and the pancake and bacon breakfasts that he fixes. Also of how she wished I was home, but I was "too sick." She drew a picture of me up on the North Pole where Santa Claus lives. Her home had a rainbow over it. What a delight!

■

Kite flying was a big deal for the Bauers in those days. Still is. Bob and his daughters would rise early on a Saturday and get the kites ready and after a big breakfast head off in the aging van for a large park or a field by a lake. There they would spend hours, each holding the end of a taut thin string that slanted up toward the heavens so high that it seemed to disappear, hanging there in the windy sky unconnected to anything but hope. Somewhere higher up there, which was far away from the here and now, their flimsy diamonds of paper and balsa wobbled wildly and sometimes soared. Alli, who could be so ridiculously demanding, and little Jenie with the big eyes, who was quiet but innately savvy in the ways of juvenile wiles, would silently stare up at the bright sky for the longest times, sometimes shielding their eyes, sometimes squinting, always with their little mouths open slightly in concentration or something.

Bob, who had sought solace in kites as a child, would look up there, too, and wonder how long that beautifully colored image could hang suspended against the deep blue sky. He figured it would hang there as long as he could stand up down here. He, too, was hanging, in a suspended grief.

The trio would have a picnic lunch then with lots of fruits, and then might rest a while on an old blanket. They'd go to the zoo or a movie in the afternoon, or to the playground, where Bob taught them all kinds of gymnastic moves on the equipment. Living around a dying body for such a long time, he wanted them to know how strong and active their own healthy bodies could be.

For dinner the girls usually clamored for Bob's Chinese diced chicken in a wok, which made him feel good.

Saturday evenings the father and daughters might do some drawings to take to Mom the next day. Bob tried to get them talking a little. Rather, Bob would end up talking as the two colored and exchanged crayons. Bob wasn't a psychologist, but he knew the girls must be hiding a maelstrom of feelings inside. He knew this because he sure did and because their feelings kept seeping out in various ways. A friend arriving to babysit one evening found Jenie sitting on the electric stove with a burner glowing red next to her leg. Jenie, who was going on three, said she had to cook dinner to help her daddy.

Sometimes it seemed that nothing was ever right for Alli. Bob would remember to pour the juice in her favorite cup at breakfast, but that day that cup was not her favorite; she wanted it in a different one, no, wait, in that blue one. "Get it yourself," one babysitting relative once said. "No one has a servant around here." But Bob could never say that. He would switch the cups and say, "You know, these cups are all the same."

Alli was often openly defiant of Bob, of anyone, which was noted by many but spoken by few, everyone being so eager not to add to the Bauers' burden. Perhaps Alli, who was nearly five, had climbed up on the couch to talk loudly right into an adult's ear, until Bob or the guest would gently push her away. She might try it again, with the same result, and sulk. Or Bob might find her in the bedroom taunting and pinching Jenie.

One day Alli announced that she hated school. Nothing was right. Her best friend was put with another teacher, so now they couldn't talk to each other during class. Once for a week there was a big deal about how all the other moms met their children at the school door

137

each afternoon and all Alli had was a warm, caring babysitter. It was really important, Alli seemed to be saying, to have a parent pick her up like the other kids. That seemed the kind of thing a kid would think. So Bob, who didn't want to add to the child's existing burden, added to his own; he took a few more afternoons off from work and appeared, all chipper, to pick up Alli. There weren't that many other parents on hand, after all, although there were a number of chauffeurs.

Emily said he should take Alli for emotional counseling, so Bob did. The counselor, a professional friend of Emily's, suggested Alli was constantly testing Bob to see if he, too, would go away like her mother. Sometimes Alli would ask right out. "Daddy, are you going to die, too?" Bob would laugh a nervous laugh and say, no, he wasn't going to die; they were stuck with him for a very long time.

Bob tried to conceal his displeasure with Alli's behavior. Once in a great while, he might blow up—"For Pete's sake, Alli, that's enough!"—and soon after, Alli would be climbing up into her father's lap to cuddle, followed almost instantly by Jenie. Alli tried to push her sister away then. Bob had two good arms, one on each side, one for each girl, and he could separate them and hold them both at the same time until it was time to brush their teeth for bed and hear a story. And another one. And another one. And another one. Anything to keep the light on and the darkness away a while longer.

■

March 31, 1983:

For Alli and Jenie,

Once upon a time there were two little girls, Lisa and Jill. They lived with their mother only, for their father was sick and had to be in the hospital. Sometimes they felt very sad and angry that they did not have a father like the other children, to take them places like the playground and the zoo. Sometimes they were so upset they did not want to think about it, so they wouldn't go to see him. Then the mad fairy would come and make them disobey their mother and not want to go to bed at night.

This concerned their mother very much. She didn't know what to do. The good fairy felt her worry and came to help. She told the mother that she would sprinkle some magic dust on the children so they would say what was troubling them. Jill said she didn't like to brush her teeth and she didn't like Lisa hitting her. Lisa did not like Jill bothering her and she missed her father, which made her feel sad, which she didn't like to feel. Their mother hugged them then and they cried and got mad together and felt much better.

That night they had a good sleep. The good fairy smiled down on them. And the mad fairy was far, far away. The End. Goodnight, darlings.

Love,

Mom

■

Sundays were not usually happy in those days, for those three healthy Bauers anyway. The coming of that dawn was grimly different from other days. It was Visiting Day. Sometimes on Saturday afternoons flying kites or Saturday nights drawing with Dad, they could all forget for a while what was happening to Emily, to Mommy, what a silent, haunting stranger she had become. They might try to pretend, privately and silently, that she was already a memory in the background. It was just the three of them now, which was sad and all but offered at least the hope of improvement over time.

Visiting Day was a painful reminder that this bad dream was not over yet—for Emily or them. For a long while Bob had visited every day. Then he cut that back to five times a week, eliminating Mondays and Saturdays, when she seemed to have other visitors. Emily had said he needn't come so often then. Maybe she was testing him again, like her suggestion that he find another woman, but he didn't care. He had taken her up on her offer and dropped Fridays and Wednesdays, too.

But waking up on Sundays, they could not duck the burden of the impending visit. It was actually worse in anticipation than in reality, because sometimes during the visit to Emily they almost forgot Emily was right there, so silent was her slumped presence in the bed or

139

wheelchair. Sundays meant they must get dressed in clothes that Mom liked and go and play in front of her as she liked and be reminded, once again, that she was not getting better, would not get better. "Is Mommy going to die?" Alli had asked again. Bob had paused. "Yes," he said softly, "I think so."

It was fun on those visits to see all their past drawings up on the wall and curtains all around Mom. It was an Alli and Jenie Art Gallery and Shrine for all the world to see and admire, and presumably for Mom's two eyes, too. But there really wasn't all that much to do there. Mom never said anything. Did they have to go today?

A few miles and several worlds away, Emily's eyes opened at dawn and became immediately bright and enthusiastic and excited. This was Visiting Day.

The nurse knew, too. There was much one-way chatter at Emily about the coming day's doings, the one in seven that shattered all routine. First, Emily had her temperature and blood pressure checked and got the medicine for whatever infection the doctors were fighting this time. Then came Emily's feeding, extra food this morning, since she wanted that ugly tube removed for the day for the children's visit. This extra load of liquid nutrition might easily upset Emily's stomach, but the staff acquiesced, knowing how important this day was.

Emily got a sponge bath, and some perfumed powder. Eleanor brushed Emily's hair, which had been cut some to make it easier for someone else to care for.

Emily insisted on getting dressed for these visits. So Eleanor went to the closet where Emily had kept a few favorite items of clothing, just in case she ever left or went out. The nurse held up a dress or perhaps two pairs of slacks for Emily to choose from.

"This one?"

Two blinks.

"This one?"

One blink.

"And how about a nice blouse. Let's see. How about this one?"

Pause. One blink. Then two blinks.

"Yes?"

Two blinks.

"No?"

One blink.

But when Eleanor got the blouse halfway on, Emily began blinking furiously.

"Something's wrong?"

One blink.

"Leg cramps?"

Two blinks.

"Cramps somewhere else?"

Two blinks.

"Suctioning? You need suctioning?"

Two blinks.

And Eleanor leaned down close to Emily to watch the pale lips. But they just opened and closed feebly and incoherently. And Eleanor made a silent mental note to brush Emily's teeth in a minute.

"I don't know, hon," the nurse said. "Oh, the blouse?"

One blink.

"You want the other blouse after all?"

One blink, very tight.

Eleanor fetched the other blouse, and a staff nurse helped put it on. Both healthy women pretended not to see the shrinking body. Then the slacks, which Emily preferred now since they hid what was left of her legs. Eleanor might wonder for an instant if she had taken the right clothes off the hangers. This blouse and slacks had obviously been bought for another woman. Or the same woman in an earlier life. But that was before Eleanor's time.

Then came the makeup. Eleanor, who was older, applied perhaps a bit more blush than Emily would have or than children think their mother should wear; Eleanor still called it rouge. The patient did look pale, and the nurse wanted some signs of life and color in those cheeks. Emily really couldn't object, even when Eleanor held the mirror up for her inspection. Emily could not say, "Too much on the right cheek" by blinks.

Emily also checked that her cubicle was in order, that all the children's drawings were up and straight, and that just as many of Jenie's crayon oeuvres were hung just as high and prominently as Alli's. During the long hours of writing that Emily did daily during the week, laboriously printing out letter after letter, three ticks of the head and three clicks of the machine for each character on the bedside tape, Emily likely had included instructions to orchestrate the visit: where the children should stand and play so she could see them and what she wanted Eleanor to ask them for her so she could hear and see them talk. It took so long to print out these orders and messages and the day's script that she had to do them in advance; there was no time to be wasted communicating during these precious visits.

Then the women, both of them prepared for the Visitors, settled down to wait. Perhaps to kill time they read the newspaper idly with Eleanor turning the page every few minutes.

"Are you through yet?"

Two blinks.

"Now?"

One blink.

More silence for reading and thinking. If Emily finished the page sooner, she would have to lie and wait until Eleanor turned from her book to check again.

Emily might print out a message then.

TIME?

"Nine-fifteen."

Reading. Thinking. Page turning.

TIME?

"Nine-thirty-five."

Reading. Thinking. Page turning.

TIME?

"Almost ten. Just another hour."

T?

"Ten-ten."

A hospital nurse might appear at the foot of the bed. "Eleanor," she said, "you have a phone call."

When Eleanor returned, she tried to look unconcerned. "Alli has a cold," she said. "Not a bad one, Bob says, but you know what the doctors said about visitors with colds. They'll come next Sunday." That's what Eleanor said. Emily said nothing, although the nurse had to dab her eyes and runny nose for a while.

"Well," Eleanor said, hopefully, knowing full well what lay ahead of her this day, "what shall we do instead for fun?"

■

April 3, 1983: I spent the day printing, reading the paper, and napping. I wanted to be with my family. I think of all the mothers I know who get to be with their children and take it for granted. And why can't I be one of them?

It is sunny and springlike out today. I want to get out and go, but I also know how I get uncomfortable in the wheelchair because I am so bony. Repositioning with pillows helps some. Last year I wanted to go someplace every Sunday, but it was a strain on Bob. I don't want that again.

I had the test done on my throat. The result is I have to have an operation to insert a feeding tube directly into my stomach. Why do I have it so bad? Where is my body's resistance? I feel so betrayed. Why? Why? Why must people suffer?

Charlie, the twenty-year-old who couldn't talk, died. His respirator tube became detached, and the alarm didn't go off. I had mixed reactions. I felt sad for him and for his family, and awe that he'd been released from the struggle. Right now, I want to live to write this journal and for my children—but release also appeals. I fear brain damage. That would be the ultimate blow. That is why I want "no code," no heroics in the event of oxygen deprivation.

■

Bob disliked confrontations, always had, especially with females. So on these Sundays if Jenie said she didn't want to go to the hospital, Bob said all right, you don't have to. It was unfair, he felt, to force them to face death so soon after they started learning about life. But, Bob always added, I'm going to visit Mommy. Jenie would decide to go along anyway, just to be with Daddy. Alli, however, was somewhat firmer. If she didn't want to go, she didn't want to go. She didn't want Bob to go either. Sometimes it was just easier to drop the whole subject, to phone the hospital, and say they were skipping this week's visit. Alli had a cold, which she did sometimes. The trio would have another quiet day together, although it wasn't so much fun for Bob because he was haunted by the guilt of thinking that he should be somewhere else.

Sometimes Bob visited Emily by himself, always bringing a colorful bunch of fresh flowers. Emily loved them. She loved hearing all about the children. Bob was careful, of course, to spice these descriptions with a few problems and some unpleasantness. Whatever he told her, though, prompted Emily to tap out by the next visit long lists of things she wanted the children to be doing and wearing and seeing and reading. Bob replied again, "I'll try to do some, but I can't do everything for everybody. I have to do it my way."

"I know," Emily tapped, which surprised Bob because, standing and sitting so close to this silent wife for so long, he hadn't thought she did. The gap had grown for him. The comfortable assumptions that bind a couple so intimately were melting.

Emily really didn't like Bob's attitude about the children's visits. This was an obligation to a parent, a sick parent, a parent who probably wouldn't always be around. Bob felt the obligation to visit was his, but the choice was the children's. He understood Emily's desperate feelings; this was the end of her life, and she wanted something done, for Christ's sake. He also knew that this was the beginning of the children's lives and he couldn't ruin those ideally innocent times with constant exposure to disease, decay, and death. They would do it his way, for once, though early in the mornings, lying awake, alone, he would silently wonder if his way was the right way.

Bob tried to have the girls visit, but he would not make them. As a sweetener, he planned a Sunday full of doing things that included a

two-hour stop at the hospital. Walking into that hospital was sand-
wiched between riding bikes and stopping at the park or zoo and
bringing home Chinese food from the family restaurant that always
gave the girls extra egg rolls.

Emily thought those outings were wonderful ideas. She'd go along,
too, which was not what Bob had in mind. It was expensive to hire a
fully-equipped medical van—with the driver, attendant, oxygen
tanks, and chairs—for the day. It was like moving an ancient poten-
tate, or a modern president, so cumbersome was the entourage required to assemble to ensure one person's safety. Queen Emily sitting
on a cushion in her wheeled throne with orbiting attendants watching
her every sign, serving her every need, performing for her, and point-
ing out the points of interest, though she never responded. The mon-
arch even had a machine that breathed for her.

The few expeditions that Bob did launch became not relaxing family outings to the zoo or an exciting family baseball game in the park
but exhausting, hollow scenarios produced for the benefit of one
spectator, who could never applaud.

It had all become more painful for the three healthy Bauers, this
constant scraping of a raw wound, week after week. Bob felt he had to
think of the future, their future for the rest of his daughters' childhood. For Emily, the future was next Sunday.

■

April 4, 1983: My God, why have you forsaken me? Even for Christ,
it was only three days. I feel such compassion now for all those suffering in the world, although I cannot do anything to alleviate it for
them, or me.

■

Emily was so depressed the day after these nonvisits that it was hard
to be around her, so wrong did everything seem—the pillows, the
bath, the TV channel, the book, the newspaper page, the sheets, the
weather, even the nurse. A number of her regular private nurses
moved on to other jobs, Emily refusing to do what a patient is supposed to do, namely, be patient. Eleanor, though, stayed on for week-

ends. When Emily really pushed hard, Eleanor turned to her and with a faint smile announced, "You're a psychologist, and I know what you're doing. You're taking out all your hostilities on me, and I just walked in here."

There was silence for a while. Emily tapped out, "The bounds of my life r this rm." Eleanor nodded and held Emily's hand for a while, two hands touching yet so far apart.

That nurse confronted Emily other times, too, which earned her a fond spot in the patient's heart because that reaction meant the friend truly cared about Emily. Once the nurse noted that Emily never said "Thank you" to her, as if paying someone negated the necessity of that courtesy. "I need 'thank yous' sometimes," Eleanor told her patient. At the end of that long night whose date was soon lost among the many others just like it, Emily's printer came alive for a moment. "Thk U," the message read.

Eleanor also approached Bob, thinking, "I can't imagine being married with all the responsibilities of a sick wife and two frightened children and a troubled job, all that giving, and no getting in return for all this time." That's what Eleanor thought. What she did was plead with him to sit on the bed more with Emily and hug her. "Can you imagine," Eleanor had said, "all these years alone in a bed and no one cuddling you?" Bob had complied, though like much of the activity in hospital visits, it seemed so contrived and stilted, sanitized of real feeling and spiced with the same forced small talk that presidents and visiting premiers exchange for the benefit of clicking cameras across the room.

Hospitals were full of formalities, enforced gaps that protected their populations from the dangers and pains of intimacy. And, always, important schedules to keep. Time for drugs. Time for hugs. Time for temperature. Time for blood pressure. Time to eat. Time to feed. Time to visit. Time for blood. Time to breathe. Time for doctor. Time to leave. Time to weep. Time to go. Time to sleep.

Until time was up.

But when was that, now that God's deadly decisions could be overturned on automatic appeal to the hospital staff? Now that humans controlled the clock. There was an established procedure for getting into the hospital, an established procedure for staying there and living there and visiting there. Bob wondered once if heaven required as many procedures and forms to get in and stay there. But short of an impossible cure or an unnoticed death like Charles's, there was no established procedure for getting out of the hospital. Or out of a life there deemed personally unbearable.

Bob didn't read much anymore. He wasn't seeing the stories that had started to crop up, isolated little news items about an elderly couple in Texas or Florida or Kansas or California. He was healthy. She was not. Alzheimer's maybe. Or coma. It varied. Poison, perhaps. Or the old man bought a gun, first one in his life. A cheap little thing not much good for anything beyond a few feet. The nurse heard a pop in the patient's room, like a steel oxygen bottle tipping over. She found instead a husband, the same one who had visited every day for all those months, standing there holding a smoking pistol while tears rolled down from his eyes and blood seeped out on the bedsheet. Sometimes the man shot himself, too. The anticipation of loneliness, no doubt. Or prison. Or having seen what could await him in this wonderful world of white.

The frustration was that the healthy people, who couldn't imagine wanting to die, didn't want to think about death. And some sick people, who couldn't imagine living on like this, couldn't do anything but think about death, if they could still think at all. However, these were obviously isolated incidents, scattered around the country. They showed up in the paper every few weeks, here and there. Sometimes there was a trial; sometimes not. Sometimes a sentence; sometimes not. Few outside the hospitals paid much notice to these freakish occurrences; the volume of other swift-flowing, seemingly important events was just too great to permit anyone's attention to linger long. Who's to say how anyone would act when they reached that brink? The victims were dead and gone over the edge and so, surely, were the private problems that had caused these continuing tragedies. So, on with life.

It was all deeply distressing to the individual hospital staffs, of course. They were there to help. They were trained to help. They had been asked to help. They had helped, as best they and the evolving machines could within the legal and moral limits that society seemed to have set for them long ago. The trouble was that "Do everything you can for the patient" meant one thing when not much could be done. Today doing everything meant a whole lot more. Because so much more could be done now, they had to do so much more. There could be no doubt about it. Ever. At least nothing could be said outside the quiet halls of private doubt.

Doctors and nurses, who acquired knowledge at such personal and financial cost, spent long hours and many months on a case, only to find themselves often praying, rooting, and mourning for the helpless patients who had asked for their help in the first place.

Eleanor was distressed over Emily's obvious distress over not seeing her children. The patient had taken her daughters' decision personally. Eleanor felt sure the girls were just bored, as her kids would be in this place, preferring to be out with their friends in the healthy world instead of with strange folks in uniforms and a mother who didn't move. Eleanor was a mother; she knew or tried to guess what all those afternoon tears meant, besides her having to wipe Emily's face and vacuum her runny nose.

"You're a psychologist," Eleanor said. "You're not going to let those kids get the best of you, are you?"

Emily's watery eyes settled on the nurse.

"I've been thinking," said the nurse. "Why don't we do something different for them each Sunday? You know, something special to lure them back, make them want to come, not have to. Kids hate 'have tos.'"

■

April 6, 1983: I have spent much of the morning printing notes to doctors. Communication is so tedious and difficult. I try to be direct, but even my written communications are responded to as selectively as if they were ambiguous Rorschach cards. This used to happen dramatically all the time when people tried to read my lips, with people revealing more about themselves in their interpretations of my lips than about what I was saying.

April 7, 1983: I have had a dream. It was about finding directions to a place I was going. I couldn't find this place, even on the map. The road was mountainous in a dry land. The place was a town in the valley, a green place.

April 8, 1983: I haven't been crying as much and sometimes I feel calm. Eleanor just told me my vital signs are too high, which shows how accurately I read myself. Eleanor says I get more picky when I'm nervous. Maybe I am bored.

I realize I haven't had any real dramatic spiritual experiences. They sure would be helpful now. I guess my talent there has yet to emerge. I wish it would hurry. What I want is a direct encounter with God where the meaning of my illness and life plan are revealed—small wish.

In the middle of the night I woke, legs and shoulders painfully cramped, needing to be turned. My buzzer did not work, and my nurse was asleep. The stillness in the room was complete and oppressive. I waited for some noise from another patient or nurse. Nothing. I cried and wondered again how this could be me, totally helpless, and what function this served in the order of the universe. Then I tried thought projection, which evolved into desperate mental pleading and then meditating and then sending out angry rays. I began grinding my teeth, hoping that sound would arouse someone. All ineffective.

Finally I decided to pray. I felt uneasy, but others have prayed in distress and been answered. What I hoped for was a definite sign, a loud noise or my nurse to simply open her eyes and look at me. Eventually, she did wake, after other nurses worked nearby endlessly.

But Sunday is coming.

■

Eleanor was right on time that Sunday morning, actually a few minutes early. She was carrying two bags full of toys dug from the closets of her grown children—blocks, statues, erector sets, Lincoln logs, things that were just old enough to seem new to two thoroughly mod-

149

ern children. After showing the toys to Emily with great fanfare, she put them in the hospital's solarium down the hall, a grim green place where rows of wheelchairs were stored like mothballed battleships anchored in forgotten agonies. In the afternoon sunlight, however, that circular room became almost pleasant, certainly a change from the wheezing machines and reclining residents of the ward.

The morning flew by for Emily. There was so much to do. They were the usual things—a bath, brushed teeth, makeup, combed and pinned hair, which she had decided to wear loose this day. No, wait, up in a bun. Or how about pulled back? What did Eleanor think? Slacks, of course. And the blue blouse. No uncertainty this time. She'd been planning everything for days. Emily, though motionless, seemed very excited. It must have been the eyes.

By late morning the mother was dressed and ready and reading and sprinkled with some of the perfume her aunt and uncle had given her. Above all, mothers must smell good.

"Eleanor," said a hospital nurse, "you have a phone call." Eleanor excused herself, hoping against hope, saying nothing.

Emily's eyes followed Eleanor out the door and stayed there for her return. After a few interminable minutes, Eleanor returned, looking pleased. It had been Bob on the phone, she said. They were about to leave home.

Emily began blinking furiously; she had to go to the bathroom.

What Eleanor didn't repeat was Bob's request; in fact, it was the purpose of his call. Could Eleanor have Emily in the wheelchair when they arrived and not put her back in bed until after their departure? Bob did not want the children to see Emily hanging limply in that crane-and-sling apparatus that lifted her out of bed and swung her over to the chair. Attendants had to stand by during the procedure because Emily's head and limbs flopped around.

After an extra-large breakfast was poured into that shrinking body of Emily's, now well under one hundred pounds, the feeding tubes were always removed for trips outside the hospital and for some special visitors. Eleanor also suctioned Emily again just before she figured the family was due; she thought Bob hated that raspy sucking sound too.

It took the Bauer trio somewhat longer than expected to leave home. Bob was getting better at tying bows and matching tights with skirts, but he was still slower than a mom. Emily noticed that once he figured out a set of little girl clothes that someone said looked right together, he tended to stick to that one. Eleanor oohed and aahed over how pretty the Misses Bauer looked on their arrival. She knew Emily liked to have another female at these visits as a kind of surrogate mother.

The girls were shy at first. Jenie stayed that way, much of the time clinging to Bob's trouser leg and keeping her distance from the woman in the wheelchair whom she couldn't ever remember seeing walk. Bob gave Jenie the flowers to carry over to her mother. But the little girl gave them instead to Eleanor, who said how thrilled she knew Jenie's mommy was. Which puzzled Jenie, who hadn't seen the nurse and her mother talk with each other. The nurse gave the preschooler a surrogate hug, which Jenie allowed.

Silently, the girls also presented that week's colorful drawings. Eleanor, holding them up before Emily's brown eyes, thought they were wonderful, just wonderful. Now where should they go? Maybe up here or over there? She'd hang them later for sure. There were getting to be so many beautiful drawings hanging all over Mommy's cubicle that pretty soon they'd have to build another wall. Eleanor and Bob, anyway, laughed.

Well, said Eleanor to the still-silent youngsters, why didn't they all go down to the solarium, that big round room down the hall? Mommy had a surprise for them there, which aroused only wary interest, since the girls did not immediately associate Mom with pleasant surprises.

But when they got there, the girls' attitudes changed. It was a more open space than the cubicle. The early spring sun was warmer than the fluorescent lights that bleached all the colors in the ward. There were some interesting colored bags waiting. The first of many, Eleanor said for Emily; each week there would be a different surprise.

Emily's chair was positioned off to the side; the respirator was checked. The bags were dumped out on the floor. The toys were a big hit. The girls immediately set to work assembling things, with Eleanor and Bob presiding and suggesting and helping, and the wheelchair watching and wheezing. Now and then, at Bob's suggestion, Alli would walk over to the wheelchair—she didn't run there anymore—and show her mother the latest instant masterpiece.

At one point even Jenie ventured over to the chair. First she looked at the plastic hose whooshing the air into a throat hole that other people did not seem to have. Bob momentarily feared Jenie would rip the hose out, the way Alli had snatched away the cane one day so long ago. But he held his own breath and said nothing.

Jenie then touched Emily's arm in several places, at one point mildly gritting her teeth while pinching the pale skin for a moment. There was no reaction from the slumped mother. Jenie stood there for the longest time, her face directly in front of Emily's, her little eyes peering into the big ones that stared out wide open. The big eyes blinked often and turned to follow every move of the little girl breathing by herself so gently so closely.

Then, with the big eyes continuing to follow her, the little girl walked with determination back to her father. Bob could tell that Jenie had a serious concern, even before the precocious mouth opened. But he was unprepared for Jenie's question.

"Is Mommy in there?" she asked.

Bob's expectant face froze for a few seconds while the full import of those four words sunk in. Then he closed his eyes briefly.

"Yes," he said. "Of course, she is." Then as much to warn the little girl as to inform her, he added, "And she can hear everything you say."

Alli had seen her father watching her sister and developed then a sudden need for assistance with those tiny pieces of macaroni she was slipping on a string.

■

April 12, 1983: The visit last Sunday seemed to go quite well. Eleanor's materials were well received, and both girls mastered nuts and bolts and strung macaroni on string.

It was Alli who asked why I was taking so long to be ready to join them. She made a necklace for me but kept her distance. It was Jenie who came close this time, staring at my face for the longest time and then going back to say something to Bob. A few minutes later she wanted to sit in my lap. She sat on my lap-board for quite a long time, patiently putting my fingers on the keys of a cash register and saying "Good" to me every time she made a finger depress a key. She showed no outward sign of distress at the flaccidity of my fingers. But I wonder what she felt inside to have a mother with such physical inability at a time when physical mastery is so central to her life. I felt horrible at the time and weep now as I write this.

Bob read aloud the tapes I had printed for them during the week. I think Jenie smiled a little and Alli showed no reaction then. Later Bob said she mourned not having a mother to take her to school like other children.

April 14, 1983:

For Jenie and Alli,

Lisa and Jill were talking and cuddling on the couch with their mom. Lisa felt so comfortable that she decided to ask her mom a question she had been wondering about a long time.

"Mom," she said, "at school we talk about God but at home we don't. Why?"

Mom hugged her and said that was a very good question and the answer was difficult but she would try to give a good one. Lisa took her mother's hand to encourage her.

"When I look at a flower like a daffodil," Mom said, "and can see its beauty and know no person can make something as marvelous, then I feel close to God. And when I see a tree, a rainbow, the stars, the ocean or desert at sunset, a baby being born or when I look at the beauty of you, my children, then also I feel close to God.

"But then when I think of your father in the hospital, and how we all deeply hurt in our hearts, as we are not physically together, and all the suffering people, I feel very angry at God."

"Why, Mommy?"

"I sometimes think," the mother replied, "that if God can make a flower, why can't She make sickness go away. Some people, like your dad, don't believe God has anything to do with sickness."

"Well," said Jill, wanting some attention, "I believe in the good fairy and bad fairy, not God."

"Okay," said the mother, holding the girl closely. Lisa reached over and hit Jill.

"Why did you call God she?" asked Lisa intently.

"Well," said the mother, "God is a Force which we don't understand—a mystery. We try to make God more understandable by giving human qualities to Him/Her. Most people think of God the Father, but God may also be Mother. We just don't know."

"This is boring," said Jill. "We all believe in Santa Claus. Why do we need God?"

"Many people today and throughout history have felt great love for God. From this love beautiful music has been written, wonderful paintings made, magnificent cathedrals built, fine books written. So it is important for you to know God. Your heart will tell you if you love and want to talk to Him/Her in what is called prayer."

Jill put her head on her mother's lap and fell asleep. Lisa knew it was her bedtime but thought maybe she could stay up later if she asked more interesting questions.

"Mom, what is prayer?"

Her mother hugged her and said, "You are smart. We will talk about it next time."

When the mother had tucked them both in bed, Lisa and Jill still wanted to talk. "It's time for me to go," said Mother. "Try being quiet with yourself and talking with God."

The next time Mother looked in on them, both children were peaceful and asleep.

Love,

Mom

April 16, 1983:

Memo to Steve

From E. Bauer

Subject: Nicole and Lewis

Nicole, who was in an auto accident at the age of three years, and Lewis, who had a poliolike virus at three months, both are handicapped by inadequate cognitive stimulation from their environment. The world they live in is very limited.

No trips to the grocery or elsewhere to provide a meaningful opportunity to learn with a teaching adult or child. No lessons in money or math. Due to the limited complexity of their lives, time is not very meaningful, and they have not asked nor have adults thought to provide a clock, which is very useful in teaching math concepts. There are no regular reading sessions. No discussions with peers.

Both children spend a lot of hours, especially on weekends, sleeping indiscriminately or watching TV. Depending on how much interest can be aroused in the nursing staff, given how they define their role and other demands on their time, the following could be done:

1) Check TV listing and post in the nursing station the schedule of the most educational programs, so staff can turn on the set at the right time.

2) Get them some kind of calculator, reading and math books to stimulate their minds. What about one of these printers?

You could leave a list of the learning goals with the nurses, so that every visitor would be aware and could contribute something. Even visiting school-age children have good teaching potential. Activities should have specific goals in mind, working with a clock, calculator, flash cards. A grocery game using coupons from the newspaper, or play money and clothing catalogues.

Nicole could easily count using her mouthstick. Visitors should be encouraged to read aloud as well as have both children read. You might even want to get a special tutor. I can help with getting and observing prospects, if you want. I used to run a children's tutoring group.

April 20, 1983: Four hours of work and details of my latest dream are lost due to bum printer, plus two half-days of lost working time. I'm here tapping away, letter after letter, hour after hour, and nothing is coming out, but I don't know it and nobody knows I'm tapping because nothing is coming out and I can't say anything. I always have to wait for people to notice something's wrong.

But the sun is shining in the window and lightly touching me with its warmth. I don't remember feeling the sun, and it feels wonderful.

I am looking forward to Spring and going outside. I want to see flowers and Alli and Jenie on the playground. I can see why Winter symbolizes death and Spring, rebirth and hope. But as T. S. Eliot says in my favorite poem (note my funeral plans and include), hope can be for the wrong things.

When Bob and I were together in seeking alternatives to the medical model, we shared a spirit and enthusiasm. But time passed and the burdens of coping with daily life with two preschoolers, a struggling business, and a sick partner (me) left little energy for dealing with much else. In the face of no results from the alternative methods and his own inner impasse with the philosophical assumptions behind these methods, Bob grew disillusioned. Since he is very bright and perceptive, he easily tuned into the faults of the alternative advocates. I feel he is like a betrayed lover in the intensity with which he criticizes, among other things, their naïveté and zeal.

I also feel that in his need to have some clarity in a life so full of ambiguity, he has polarized things so that the alternative healers are the bad guys and the medical personnel in whose hands my life is entrusted are the good guys. Bob feels I am unrealistic about the healers and paranoid about the doctors. When I told him of some limitations I saw in my doctor here, he was confused by my criticisms and thought I was looking for trouble by anticipating it. He saw no reason why my doctor here would object to an alternative doctor who wanted to treat me with herbs.

The confusion may have been due to my communication problem, which is great unless I print, which is too slow to do with a person waiting. Also opening the whole issue of the adequacy of this setting is opening up a conflict that takes energy to deal with, and he does not have energy to spare.

The conflict, as I see it, is between rehabilitation and treatment. This is a rehabilitation facility at best and chronic-care facility in large part, from what I've seen. Bob points to the printing machine as an example of what is being done for me. To me, this view is correct but incomplete. While Bob is pleased with this place, I am more ambivalent. I agree it is benevolent but find it, like most institutions, invested primarily with preserving the status quo and not very psychologically sophisticated. It is indeed ironic that I should be a physical prisoner in a place so incompatible with my own temperament. I would prefer a place more innovative and willing to take risks. Since such a place does not exist here (if anywhere), I'd prefer to be someplace where I could be in charge of myself and choose my doctors. Unfortunately, lack of money and backup help rule this out.

April 21, 1983: One thing to add: Bob has said he will do anything I want about the outside herb doctor.

April 25, 1983: Yesterday was a bright clear day in the high fifties— Harbinger of Spring. I was in lavender slacks and blouse, hair washed and curled, waiting for the children to visit. I was apprehensive, as Alli had been upset about me last week, so I thought I was prepared. When Bob called and said she had started crying and didn't want to come, I got upset but consoled myself that I understood and would see Bob.

157

I worked all afternoon on another story. Bob came, then Jenie, who gave me a twig with touching seriousness. Eventually Alli came with Bob's nephew. Alli kept her distance and watched me closely. When Bob read the tape to them, both girls touched it a lot. Which pleased me. When Bob's nephew said how hard it must be not to be able to talk and that he loved me, I started crying. Both Alli and Jenie looked at me intently with concern. Alli asked if I didn't feel well. Eleanor explained how I wanted to talk, tell stories, go home with them. Alli replied, "Maybe she'll get better." More tears.

Oh, God, please . . .

April 27, 1983: It is gray again outside and inside. Last night when Bob was visiting, I looked at his hands on mine and thought, "I want to be your helpmate." The tears flowed then and now. I make myself such a mess when I cry. My nose runs. It must be suctioned. It hurts.

Mag was here today and said she'd been coming a year. She gives me a wonderful massage with oil and meditates with me. When I was in the other hospital, she came five times a week. Now she comes once. Mikhail still comes once a week, too. And my old friend Vicky from the therapy group comes faithfully, too, every week. She helps a lot with talk and especially with this diary, which she organizes and transcribes. Thanks, Vicky.

Two things about Alli to be happy about. She was accepted at the private school. And three times she asked to hear the story I wrote. Jenie asked me to cut some paper for her, but with hesitation, so she is still struggling with my disability. Both children still ask why I can't talk. When they left, I cried, as I wanted to go with them from here. Eleanor says I snap back better than I used to. Mag says I look clear.

Bob may sell his antique rolltop desk to help pay for Alli's school. I must write more stories. We are very proud of her. Bob cried.

■

It was after one of the children's happy visits that it happened. Or almost happened, as Emily came to think. It was four P.M. A gray day. The children had just left. Emily was slumped in the wheelchair by her bed. Her face was moist, as usual at that time; Eleanor would have to suction the patient's nose and throat, as soon as she got her settled.

Eleanor stepped away for a minute, a moment really, just to get some help with the crane and sling by the bed; somebody had to hold Emily's head while the device lifted her back into bed.

"Be with you in a sec," said the hospital nurse. Eleanor, who had four more hours to go on her shift, walked slowly back to Emily's side and patted her shoulder, while they waited. The bag of hair ribbons had gone over well with the girls that day. They spent the entire visit braiding them and trying them all on in their hair and then showing them off to Bob and Eleanor, who expressed delight at their beauty, and sometimes to Emily, who said nothing.

"I think the girls had a good time," Eleanor said, thinking nothing of it when no response came. But Emily was sitting a little funny, more slumped over than usual, perhaps. And there was something different about the slump. Eleanor squatted down urgently. She lifted Emily's head. The eyes were closed. And the respirator hose was . . . loose!

"Oh, God!" Eleanor thought, instinctively shouting, "Code Blue! Code Blue!"

■

May 2, 1983: Last weekend while I was in the wheelchair, the machine stopped working and I could not call for help because my bell was not working. I tried to call for help, but there was nothing I could do. I felt like I was suffocating. I passed out. When I woke up, there were a lot of people standing around me, staring and doing things.

I felt that passing out was not so bad. The time before I passed out was awful, but it did not last long. I think now, after what happened, I am not afraid to die. I had been afraid of the suffocating feeling. But now that doesn't seem so bad.

I felt very happy that now I have a way out. I felt I had the courage to go through the bad part, that awful feeling of not being able to breathe when the respirator is off. But this afternoon the machine malfunctioned again, and I called for help. I was very disappointed that I did not have the courage I thought.

■

"Oh, thank God," Eleanor said when Emily regained consciousness. "No," she told a terrified Emily, "we're not angels and you're not in heaven." The nurse was smiling. Emily was not.

■

May 3, 1983: I am very upset. My weekday night nurse quit. She got into a fight with the hospital staff and authorities over her playing tapes for the children and she said the nurses here were cold to her. She also had a cold and was tired.

Now I am disoriented by lack of sleep. My new night nurse repositioned the call bell, so it didn't work very well, which made me tense. We didn't communicate very well. She has been with me before. It would be worse with someone new.

I am so tired of the immense effort.

May 5, 1983: I have gotten back to my old, good sleep, now that my nurse knows my routine, where the call bell goes, and my turning preferences. If the night hospital staff knew these, I would consider stopping my night nurse. A brief orientation for that staff is all that is needed. But how? I am anxious about it and need help. My intent is to save insurance.

What would make me less anxious would be if the staff nurses knew the basics in my life: my Spelling Card, my Call Bell, my Eye Blink Code Card. Day shift should also know about my printer and other shifts how I like to be turned. If I could talk, none of this would be needed. I require extra effort, for I am helpless and more prone to anxiety. I have been grateful for the patience of the staff under most frustrating circumstances. I have had notes explaining all these things posted behind my bed if people would take a little time to read them. Maybe this would reduce the frustration.

It's so hard.

May 7, 1983:
For Alli and Jenie,

Lisa and Jill are going to different schools. Jill will continue where they have both been going, the Cozy Rabbit Hole School. Next year she will go there more days, for she is getting older. She plays with her friends the rabbits and the teddy bears. Because she is strong and brave, Jill is not afraid to do what Teacher Deer asks the class to do when they are dancing and singing. The school is a comfortable, busy place, and Jill likes it very much.

Since it is located in a rabbit hole, it has many rooms: Room 1, the red room, is full of big beds for jumping on. Room 2 is the green room with trees to climb. At the top your favorite bottle is filled with juice. Room 3, the orange room, is full of ways to stop your big brother or sister from hitting or biting you. Room 4, the pink room, has the magic dust that lets you become bigger or smaller or a kangaroo or whatever you want to be. Room 5, the blue room, is full of books and supplies of magic dust that let you go into any story in the books that you want—Hansel and Gretel or any story. Room 6 is the brown room, the music room, where with magic dust you can play any instrument you want without practicing much, and you learn lots of songs. In the gold room you can bake all the cookies you want.

Now that you know about these rooms, you can see why Jill is proud of her school, and why Lisa is sad to leave it, even though her new school will be an exciting, grown-up place.

ANDREW H. MALCOLM

May 8, 1983:
For Alli,

Lisa was going to leave her school in the rabbit hole and go to a new school. She would miss her old school friends, especially Kandy the zebra, although, of course, she could still see him after school. But that would not be as often as seeing him every day. So Lisa felt sad about Kandy. She would miss her teacher too. And all the other animal grown-ups who knew her. Also, she would miss knowing where to go and what to do each day.

The new school would be exciting, though, as it had marvelous rooms to explore. There is the French room where students learn to speak French so well that their parents must take lessons to keep up. The turquoise room has secret treasures, but you can find them only if you know how to read, which I think you will soon. The lavender room is for ballet, as I know how much you like it. The scarlet room is full of things to hit when you feel mad and want to hit your little brother or sister. And then, of course, some of Lisa's favorite rooms from her old school—the bed-jumping room, the climbing room, and the magic-dust room.

Then Lisa got a wonderful surprise. Her dear friend Jerry is going to the new school, too.
Love,
Mom
The End

∎

Bob and Marjory were going to make one more try at their secret relationship, an affair as doomed as their previous marriage. Their basic relationship had not changed, nor had their basic behavior patterns. Marjory, who had grown and developed her own career, saw and understood Bob's emotional hunger for intimacy. The hunger was nothing new to him, but its desperate intensity made him seem like a starving man ravenously wolfing down his first meal in days, knowing

162

full well that he would vomit it all back up again. In one of his lives, Bob was giving everything and getting back nothing. In his other life, he was taking everything and giving virtually nothing. And he knew it.

Emily could feel everything and move nothing. Bob could move easily, but he was going numb. The situation left Marjory feeling unsatisfied and used. It left Bob feeling more guilty and alone, a feeling that had once been the most terrifying thing in the world. Now it seemed just normal.

He and Marjory had agreed to spend a spring weekend in Washington together, visiting museums. But what they were trying to get away from they took with them. So it wasn't exactly relaxing, although the long Saturday dinner with some good wine was not unpleasant. But they ended up walking the aisles of the museums separately, drifting off into their own worlds there, too. Outdoors on the sidewalk on the way to the next relaxing array of art, their feelings erupted into angry words and angry silences.

There was a moonlight stroll across a bridge over the Potomac when the colorful, moving lights from the cars and the stationary, soothing lights from the sky almost brought them back together. But everywhere they turned in that city of stone stood a statue of someone dead. And at the end of the bridge was a mammoth cemetery.

They slept on opposite sides of the same bed that night, vowing silently, together, not to do this anymore.

Back in the hospital that night Emily was silent, too, and sleepless. Eleanor remembered that weekend as the most difficult in all her time with this patient. The tears were nonstop. Eleanor had always seen something exciting about Emily, even when she was motionless. She had radiated enthusiasm, ideas, sadness, eagerness, even without speaking. Now Emily was radiating anger—no, rage. Her temperature shot up to 102°. She wanted to be turned every minute. And if Eleanor anticipated this desire, Emily was annoyed; "2 soon," she would tap out. The pillows were wrong. So was the TV channel—every TV channel. The pages of the book couldn't be turned fast enough. Or slow enough. She needed suctioning; she didn't. It was too cold. Or too hot. Too noisy. Or too quiet. The hospital nurses called Eleanor out of the room many times during those two days. Eleanor sighed and sat on a hall bench to muster her patience. The hospital nurses smiled sympathetically, nodded at her, and looked up at the ceiling, too, feeling glad inside that they had a whole ward to care for and not one woman, that woman.

Mikhail knew something was very wrong the moment he touched Emily that Saturday afternoon. She was very, very tense and stiff. The knots in the muscles wouldn't come out, no matter how firmly he rubbed and told Emily to think of good things.

Mikhail brought along his girlfriend. He had talked about her with Emily and he thought another face and voice might liven up the visit a bit. It certainly would ease the strain on Mikhail, who had personally dedicated himself to easing this woman's passage. Before each visit he normally sat outside Emily's cubicle for ten or fifteen minutes. Just to compose himself, so strongly was his mind taken by the emotions and fears of dying, or living like this. Once, Saturday had been his favorite day of the week.

Mikhail had heard from Eleanor that Bob was going away again this weekend. Maybe that was causing all this tension. Sure. Or maybe bringing the girlfriend wasn't such a good idea after all. Because she could answer, Mikhail found himself talking to her instead of Emily. Did the girl know that Emily was, uh, is a psychologist? Had her own practice. And her daughters—the photos there on the table—had done all these drawings up here. Mikhail thought they were good, too. He also thought he saw jealousy in Emily's silent eyes.

After two hours—actually a little less that day—Mikhail said, well, he and his girlfriend really had to be going. They had an engagement. The girl, who didn't know Emily and never would, said there really wasn't any rush. Their engagement wasn't until 5:30, she was saying when Mikhail stepped behind the bed, shook his head, and made some hand motions. But, of course, the girl added, she did have to go home to change first, so maybe it was better that they be on their way. It had really been very nice to meet Emily. She hoped that Emily would, uh, was feeling better and she hoped to see her again sometime.

According to Eleanor, the massage accomplished nothing that Smithsonian Weekend.

■

May 10, 1983: Bob went to Washington for the weekend to go to museums. It was gorgeous weather, the kind that makes one want to do things. I'll bet the stars were out. Eleanor took me out in the afternoon. I was the only one in the ward out. No one came to see Lewis or Nicole. I have a very hard time accepting that I can't go and be with Bob. I love to go and do.

A year or two ago I flew to Washington, was met by a friend and an aide, and we went to a museum. I am glad I did it when I could. I am glad Bob went. I wish I could have gone, too. I had only a few visitors this week—Amy, of course, Bob before he left, a former student, and the wife of a former colleague. I was touched by their concern, but the visits were hard for me. I know how uncomfortable I make people feel.

May 10, 1983:
Dear Lacey,

I was watching the Donahue show, a panel of working and non-working mothers. Many of the tears I shed are over not being with Alli and Jenie. Happiness would be to be home with my family.

I think less about work. I miss certain patients and exercising certain skills and the status.

Your letter aroused memories and questions. I remember those grueling Saturdays interviewing potential Ph.D. students and the power implicit. I wonder if you have mixed feelings about working and mothering.

How is Becky? Alli is copying printed words, learning some French, telling Jenie stories, artistic, aggressive to Jenie, hurting about me, and difficult. Jenie knows about ten letters and numbers, is self-confident, and a leader at school and playground, is easy and fun but often negative and a strong personality.

We all hate the situation. Sometimes I still think this is a bad dream and I am going to wake up any day.

165

How is the clinic? What are you teaching? Who is teaching my courses, and how? Please write again soon.

Love,

Emily

■

Emily did wake up from one bad dream. Or was it good? Emily knew the importance of dreams as windows into the unconscious. But she also knew there could be as many interpretations as there were interpreters. Letter by letter she tapped out the recollected details on tape for Steve's next visit: She was up in the mountains—Italy?—on a narrow winding road along the edge of a steep cliff. It was overcast, like her life. She was trying to get down the road. To the valley? Or a town? But the road was strewn with big boulders. It was treacherous. Around one bend she came upon Steve, waiting to help her through. They didn't get to the bottom, not in this chapter anyway.

Emily thought the dream meant she was starting to accept death. At least, she said, that's what one of the day nurses had suggested. Emily didn't know. What did Steve think?

Emily watched her confidant closely, as he ran the narrow tapes through his fingers slowly reading the endless thoughts of Emily's that seeped out onto paper each week. This was their routine. Emily tapping during the week. Steve reading right after lunch on Wednesday. Emily watching Steve read and then listening. It was frustrating for Steve because there could be no spontaneous give and take between patient and social worker. Steve would stand by the bed and say something to the reclining woman there and, if the reply was any more complicated than "Yes" or "No," he would have to wait seven days to get a reply. It was worse than the mail, and they were in the same room. Although Emily's physical condition had deteriorated steadily since entering the second hospital, her thoughts hopped back and forth between despair and hopelessness.

It was impossible to explore these thoughts and dreams in depth to check on the personal associations. The recent one about gardens, for instance. She was planting new growth in that one but also cleaning out old debris. This mountain-road dream was obviously important, if only because she thought it was.

Steve took somewhat longer to read the tape that day. He was actually thinking while pretending to read. He thought Emily was drifting more toward an acceptance of reality. This could be a crucial one. He'd make it a test.

Interesting dream, he said. It could be death, he supposed, but he had a somewhat different interpretation. Steve thought maybe the dream showed instead that Emily was becoming more interested in life, in living. After all, she wasn't going up the road to heaven or to be alone on the mountaintop. No, she was going along the road (he almost said downhill but caught himself) back toward town and the green valley and other people, healthy people. She ought to think about that, he said, rejoining the living. They'd talk some more next week. Okay?

One blink.

Otherwise, everything else okay?

Pause.

Is everything else all right?

One blink.

■

May 12, 1983: Alli and Jenie don't want to go to sleep at night. Bob said they fell asleep last night at ten and twelve. They say they are scared of the rats biting them. We know it is anger and a need to be with Bob more. But it is very upsetting. Also, I found out Alli had Mothers' Visiting Day at the school. Alli was very upset and begged the babysitter to go with her and pretend to be her mother.

Alli also began not wanting to go to school. She got sick and was out a week, including the Visiting Day. I feel badly we didn't tune in sooner to give her the support she needs. Last week she bit Jenie. I am glad she has a sensitive teacher Bob can talk to. He feels the need for family therapy, but so far none is available through any of my associations. We have eighteen months of insurance left.

167

I am learning personally what I knew professionally: the need for family-oriented help in crises such as sickness. I'd like to see an outcome study comparing families that did receive such help and those that did not.

Raising children is stressful and under conditions of chronic severe illness, extremely so. My family has plenty of strength. I would predict the best outcome would be strong families that got help.

May 13, 1983: I haven't mentioned the outcome of my memo on suggestions for Lewis and Nicole. Not one idea was implemented. Lack of nursing time is the reason given. But a lot of my ideas were not that hard to do. My ideas didn't fit people's ideas of what is necessary and possible.

May 14, 1983:
For Alli,

Lisa was at school when she heard the teacher say there was going to be a Visiting Day for fathers. All the other children began to talk, excited about how important their daddy was, and what they were going to show him when he came to school. Only Lisa was very quiet, because her father couldn't come from the hospital. She was very upset and didn't want to go to school. She didn't like being different from the other children. Their dads could come and hers could not.

She wished she had some magic dust so she could disappear until after Visiting Day was over. She felt very angry about her father and she didn't know what to do with these angry feelings, which were like rats!!! They seemed to bite at her. She didn't know what to do to make the feelings go away. She asked her mother to buy her things. But that didn't help. She kicked the dog. But that didn't help. She bit her sister. But that didn't help either.

Finally, she broke down and cried. Her fairy godmother heard her and came to help.

168

Lisa explained she was angry and doing strange things because her father couldn't go to Visiting Day. Fairy godmother put her arms around the girl and wiped her tears. "My dear child," she said, "I will help you."

"What will you do?" asked Lisa, still sniffling some.

"I will make your father well for Visiting Day," she said. "On that day he will be able to talk, breathe, eat, write, and walk. In return, you must promise not to do these strange things anymore."

"Oh," said Lisa, "I promise." And she kept her promise.

Visiting Day came, and Lisa walked to school holding hands and talking with her dad. They had a wonderful time. That day Lisa felt so happy and she remembered it a long, long time.

The End

Love,

Mom

Story for Jenie,

Once upon a time there was a little bear. Now this little bear was a good little bear most of the time, except for one thing: She didn't like to go to bed. Late at night when it was way past her bedtime, she would be wide awake. All the other children animals in the forest would be snug in their beds. Little Bear would be up.

And why do you think Little Bear liked to stay up so late? Was it because she wanted more pizza? More ice cream? Is it because she wants to do something without her sister being there? Is it because she is waiting for Santa Claus? Or maybe the Easter Bunny? Is it because she wants to sit on Papa Bear's lap? Is it because she wants to talk to her fairy godmother? Is it because she is afraid of the shadows in her room? Is it because she wants to watch TV? Is it because she wants to cuddle with Papa Bear? Is it because she wants to play with her toys? Is it because she wants to talk with Papa Bear?

Little Bear was so tired from answering all the questions that she fell asleep!

The End

Love,

Mom

May 15, 1983: I have started to drool.

May 16, 1983: I was going to write more on my feelings about getting worse and my depression over two other things, one with Lucy and the other with Vicky.

Lucy was hurt by something I said in my journal last year. I have not represented an accurate picture of her. Lucy is an excellent nurse with thirty-five years' experience, who makes me feel very secure in the knowledge that I am well taken care of. She has turned many book pages for me. She does a wonderful job helping transcribe my journal from the tapes. She has stayed with me, a difficult case, for a long time. She is always on time, has interesting things to say, and is very concerned with my welfare. I am lucky to have her.

Then Vicky, who comes faithfully every week. We tried to communicate this week. I wanted her to include a letter in the journal. She couldn't understand, and I intensified my efforts to make her understand, which made things worse. She thought I was lecturing her. She told me to limit what I said to "yes" and "no." This was very frustrating for both of us. We have never had things not go smoothly between us before. It is so awful to be unable to express myself. Oh, to be able to talk with Vicky!

Why must things be so hard? Sometimes I wonder how long we all can go on. Among other things, it will be a relief when it's over. I hate my dependence and being so limited.

But I have decided I can't prepare for getting worse. It's too much like willing it to happen. I have a desperate yearning to do something to stop the disease, but what? I don't know. I will do what I can as long as I can, and curse and try to hope and cope with any new losses. At this rate, I'm not going to be here that long anyway, nor do I want to be.

I guess I really haven't faced that I am still getting worse and the ultimate implication of all this. Along with excruciating sadness there is a sense of relief at the possibility of relief for all of us. Fate would, in a way, be kind to bring death.

There has been no kindness so far, except for absence of physical pain and the presence of people around me. Cruelest would be if the disease stopped after taking everything but my life. There are people like that. My relief night nurse was caring for a twenty-nine-year-old stroke victim—totally paralyzed with no facial movement at all. And I used to think this was a beneficent universe, never giving much thought to those aspects of the dark side out of our control.

May 17, 1983: I slept fairly well, despite the fact my relief night nurse called in sick. I missed the use of the TV because the hospital nurses were too busy to turn it on.

I have decided to give myself a visit home. Bob and my weekday nurse Lucy, who will work Sunday as a special favor, felt strongly about backup help. So it was arranged for a man who maintains respirators to go with us, and a special van with extra batteries and another respirator. Other good things these days: I got a wonderful letter from my brother Bryan. Some friends sent a bouquet of roses. My nurses recently brought in lovely cards. And the hospital nurses sang to me.

■

Emily's expedition home was arranged with military precision. At eight that Sunday morning, Lucy relieved the night nurse and began the journey's preparations on Emily—bedpan, bath, powder, slacks, blouse, hair, food, medicine, nose tubes out, bedpan, makeup, suction.

At eleven, Earl arrived with the respirator-equipped van. Bob followed minutes later. The children stayed at home with several relatives who had come over. Bob and Lucy rode in the back with Emily in a wheelchair with the respirator by her side, wheezing away. The ride along the bumpy streets seemed endless to Bob and Lucy, who watched the patient like a hawk. Away from the bed, the call bell, and the printer, there was no way to communicate with Emily, except through her eyes. Emily had become most fluent in that language. Her eyes were wide open then, taking in everything, when someone remembered to hold her head up in the moving vehicle.

It was a bit awkward getting her out of the van in front of the apartment building. Bob wasn't sure where he should stand or what he should hold. Earl handled everything; he did this work every day. Quite a few strollers on the way to a fashionable brunch or a movie interrupted their animated sidewalk chatter as they passed by this struggling trio helping the little girl in the wheelchair, probably retarded. Then the people began talking again, eagerly. They did not look back.

"They're here!" someone said high overhead from behind the apartment's dirty window.

The doorman was new, well, he'd been new nearly a year now. He didn't remember ever seeing Emily before, in or out of a wheelchair, though like most others in the building, he knew something of the family's ongoing problems. The doorman was uncertain what to do or if this person could still hear. So to avoid any embarrassment, his own mainly, he played it safe.

"Good morning, Mr. Bauer," he said, holding the door open and smiling at everyone as they passed.

The elevator took forever to reach the lobby for its next load; some things never change. On their floor, the doors slid open and immediately began to close again, until Lucy pushed the "Door Open" button. Then after a moment as the group struggled to roll the entire load off, the impatient buzzer sounded.

Soon they were all in the familiar dark hallway. It was a little hard pushing the rubber wheels over the carpeting. Bob was puffing slightly. They eased wordlessly down the hall past the plastic plants, the pay phone, and the big mirror over the tiny table that was never used as a table toward the end of the hall where one door stood open, leaking light.

The nurse came through the narrow doorway first, backward, holding the respirator tube away from the doorknob. Once through, she stepped to the side. And there was the chair with little Emily slumped in it. Her eyes peered out at the eight or nine pairs of eyes peering in at her. The family crowd then erupted into applause and hellos and welcomes. There were some timid hugs—mustn't hurt the fragile patient or the machinery, whatever it does. The girls were there, too, all dressed up in outfits that Emily hadn't seen before. As usual, Alli gave her mother a big kiss. Jenie was more hesitant.

Everyone stood back then, uncertain of what came next, what the social protocol was for such affairs. Everyone agreed, though, that Emily looked good, real good—nice color. The fresh air certainly agreed with her. Wasn't it a perfect day for the visit? There was a brief pause in the forced festivities when tears began cascading down Emily's cheeks. No one knew how to respond because no one knew whether they were happy tears or sad tears. Lucy needed several tissues, and Earl set up the suctioning machine right away, before leaving until pickup time. One or two of the women quietly slipped from the throng then and for some reason went into the bedroom or bathroom, Emily couldn't turn to see which.

As Bob wheeled the chair farther into the room and maneuvered it around the furniture with the glasses and plates of snacks he had prepared earlier that morning, Emily's eyes could scan the room. It was the shape of her old apartment, all right. But it certainly didn't look like her old apartment. Could her memory be going, too, after all these months away?

No, there was the couch where she used to lie with the air hose in her left hand. The medical bed was gone, and the floor-to-ceiling doors that had set it off by the windows were gone, too, no more privacy at that end of the room. The place was so much bigger than she remembered and a different color. Bob, or someone, had painted

the whole place. White! Why blah white? Where were all her hang-
ings? And the photographs? And the rugs? Someone—and not Bob,
obviously—had redone the whole place; it was so much lighter. The
books were rearranged, too; where had all the ALS books gone? The
chairs were moved. Not that it mattered; Emily had brought her own.

"No, put her over here where she can see everything. That's it.
How's that, Emily?"

One blink.

Everyone smiled.

There was pretty much one-dimensional chatter in the apartment
for a while, until everyone got used to the idea of standing and talking
and eating, having a good time, in front of someone who couldn't.
Then separate chats erupted around the room with all eyes occasionally turning back to the body in the chair. Some guests reported to
Emily on relatives who couldn't come to the party, though they had
wanted to. Or on their own doings and how nice the apartment looked
with the balloons hung around. What a good idea that was! Who blew
up the balloons? Did you, Alli? Bob or Vicky, who was always nearby,
would translate Emily's responses.

At one point Alli climbed up in her mother's lap and sat there a
while, her head on her mother's breast, just below and to the side of
the respirator hose. Lucy lifted Emily's limp arm around the little
girl's shoulders. No one said a word.

There was an unseen episode of suctioning in the other room,
which had also been repainted. Later, just before it was time for Emily to leave her former home, Jenie walked purposefully across the
room and leaned up close to her mother's face. It looked as if she
were saying something to Emily. But in a few moments she walked
away again.

Everyone agreed it was good to see Emily outside that hospital.
More important, it was good to be outside that hospital, seeing her.
Many of the friends and relatives, who were there that first inspiring
Thanksgiving nearly one thousand very long days and an equal number of equally long nights before, found it impossible to visit Emily in
the hospital as much as they said they would like. Everything was just
so busy in their lives, you know. Some sent flowers to the hospital with
a card the nurse could read out loud, or they wrote letters to Emily

and mailed them a day or two later. They were thinking of her, praying for her. Bob was handling things so beautifully. They had to be very careful not to send a card that mentioned recovery, another item on the growing list of topics that must be censored during dealings with Emily.

The friends still felt they should visit Emily, but when they got there, they felt they would rather be anyplace else but the hospital, a grim place that reeked of the future. They didn't stay as long as they once did, or they went with another friend, or when they knew the girls would be visiting and they could help tend to the living, too. Anything to have someone else there, someone they could chat with, someone to fill the long pauses. An hour was an eternity in that wheezing ward. How could Emily stand it twenty-four hours a day, 10,080 minutes every week, week after week, season after season? But, of course, they never really asked her, and they knew the answer anyway. Emily had no choice—yet.

■

May 23, 1983: The visit home went very well. Bob and Lucy were very pleased with the respirator man. Jenie looked at me a lot, gave me her balloon, and signed a card. Alli was very attentive, made two beautiful cards, and cuddled me, which made my heart soar!

Bob's sister remarked on how Alli looked cuddling me. Bob's nephew's girlfriend cried for me and with me, and I was touched. I got flowers from Mother and Judy, and Alli's flower drawings and streamers were hung about.

Alli talked to me. She was talking about Bob picking her up at school just like the other children. Then she paused. I wanted to say something to keep the conversation going. But, of course, I couldn't. The others didn't notice. And Alli drifted away.

When Jenie was saying good-bye, she put her face close to mine and said, "I know you don't want to be in the hospital. I wish you could be home very day. I know you are sad. I am sad, too."

The apartment looks nice. But it's not mine anymore.

May 25, 1983: Steve, you asked me to write on my reactions to therapy and my goals for spiritual development. Steve, I am satisfied with our format—I write, and you read and comment. I benefit from your knowledge of the adaptations which must be made, such as in my relationship with Bob and the children. I guess maybe I can't be the wife and mother I want to be—I just do what I can.

I have been thinking of Bob's anger because he gives so much and gets back so little. I think this is very hard on him, and he has few people who ask how he is. Nor is it easy for him to reach out. He just told me that he had considered suicide.

I know it would be better if Bob had a functioning partner, for him and for Alli and Jenie. It is so hard to give up my plans. One thing, maybe with all he has to do I shouldn't ask him to take all those pictures for the albums and scrapbooks I am making. The books mean so much to me. I want him to take the pictures I want to take, and that can't ever fully happen. How I wish I could take my own; I'm a journalist in my approach, while Bob is an artist. I feel conflict between his needs and my own.

For my spiritual goals: They are to pray and meditate well, to have a strong faith, to achieve inner peace in the face of death or handle increasingly limited life, to understand why this happened to our family from the perspective of reincarnation, and to know and follow my dreams. My psychological goals are to know and balance my needs with those of my loved ones and live as fully as I can.

May 27, 1983: Alli has been telling some lies of late, but she likes the stories; Bob says she asked to hear the magic-dust story two times. Jenie shows little or no interest, he says, preferring attention-seeking negative behavior. At story time she loudly says, "No!" and runs away. Bob told the story about Jenie being asked to brush her teeth and how she said, "No way, Jose," and ran away. There was another big scene on the street, too.

I talked to Bob some more last night about the picture taking. He feels that taking pictures excludes him from the event, and he says he doesn't care about posterity. He feels very strongly about it, and I will have to change the format of the scrapbooks. I have to adapt.

I feel like a burden on Bob and I find that hard to deal with. Also he has more trouble now understanding me. I have been wanting to die. I have been trying to meditate. But it can be very noisy here. I have a long way to go, I fear.

May 28, 1983: Throughout the process of my physical decline, I never totally believed it could happen to me, that it would keep progressing. I keep thinking I've had so many losses, surely now mercy will be forthcoming. But now I don't know.

For Alli and Jenie,

Lisa and Jill sprinkled magic dust to make themselves small. They went in their dollhouse to borrow some dolls' clothes, though the dolls were not eager to share. Everything was small in there. The tables were the size of spools of thread. The plates were smaller than pennies. The brooms had toothpicks for handles. Jill and Lisa and the dolls jumped on the beds and then slid down the bannister. Jill and Lisa climbed on Marigold the butterfly and flew off to explore the kitchen. They climbed on the cans. They put the plug in the sink and filled it with water. They undressed and went swimming. Then they got small paper cups and made a sail from paper and a toothpick, turned the fan on, and went sailing.

When they got tired, the little girls curled up in teacups and took a nap. Later they climbed on Marigold and flew out over the garden and above the trees, all the way to the top of the rainbow. Then the butterfly brought the girls home safely, where they sprinkled magic dust to make themselves bigger, and joined their mother for dinner.

May 29, 1983: Bob says the children are asking more now if they have to visit every Sunday. Bob said no, they didn't. I said it was very complicated. I need to see them. They need to see me but are ambivalent or testing or both.

This could be their wish to do what Dad did when he went to Washington—not visit. Maybe they are testing rules to get adult status, like not going to bed. Or it could be retaliation and an attention-getting device. I don't know how they should feel about Bob going. Certainly they have evoked a reaction in him, and because he gives such thought to matters concerning the children, he was put on the spot. I wish he felt that visiting was just something that is done—that is not negotiable. That's my gut feeling about it. It's a very primitive, basic feeling and feels right.

Bob feels as strongly that the children are expressing something legitimate that has to be recognized. He talks about the deprivation and loss he feels, and they feel, and how the visits are stark reminders of all this.

When I asked how he felt about the visits, he said he felt good, that he tried to make them special, that they do something, not just visit Mom. He thinks they'd feel guilty if they didn't come. He sees his task as balancing their needs and mine. And he has decided not to respond anymore to Alli's negative behavior, which he has done in the past. Instead, he'll respond to the good things she does.

Maybe he could praise her for her conversation with me and not respond to the visits question. Bob and I may both err by being concerned with the children's feelings too much, creating anxiety by giving too much choice.

May 31, 1983: I spent a long time today imagining being able to eat a huge California-style hamburger. Then I imagined talking about it.

Lucy has been taking me outside sometimes, now that the weather is nice. The feel of the sun and the wind on my skin is delicious. Two hospital nurses and a woman who visits Lewis and Nicole told me I look pretty. I don't show on my face what I am going through. My nurses comment on frowns that I don't know I'm making.

■

Emily wanted to be outside everything—outside the hospital, outside this situation, outside herself. The family's Sunday visits had always been something to look forward to, intensely. Now they had acquired a taste of pain. Eleanor, who was also a mother, remembered one incident when Jenie fell down and badly scraped her knee. Eleanor, who was watching Emily closely every moment now since the respirator failure, saw the body twitch slightly in the wheelchair. The eyes on the front of Emily's drooping head strained to see, and Eleanor imagined the internal ache, an ache that did not subside when the little girl ran to her father for comforting.

Now the visits had a sense of routine and desperation. Emily's tiring preparations each Sunday morning. The regular fear of cancellation. The family's arrival. They would all go outside where the children would perform—maybe ride a bicycle by in front of the wheelchair or hang upside down on the jungle gym. Despite all Bob's coaxing, Jenie would end up playing behind the chair, out of one stranger's sight. Emily would need suctioning. The children would eat a picnic lunch in front of the chair. They might play with that week's surprise, perhaps a pair of craft kits, then walk back toward the big brick building, a walk that was so short and quick for the person in the chair and so far and long for the others, who left the cubicle as soon as the nurse swung the lift-sling out near the wheelchair.

The worst part about the visits for Emily was that while they sometimes didn't happen, when they did, they always ended. For her the visits became a drug, eagerly, even desperately awaited, the moments mentally counted one after the other until the next visit. Then the event was ravenously consumed, and its end instantly lamented. The post-visit sadnesses came to last longer, much longer, than the visits.

Emily's depressions spread like an oozing river of mud from Sunday evening, into Monday morning and then the afternoon and on into Tuesday, and beyond. Emily's enthusiasms waned then—she had less interest in the news and reading, more frequent desires just to listen passively to music on her headphones, fewer visitors, less excitement when they did come, no more ideas for treating the nearby children, or dreams of going to relatives' weddings in a few months.

■

June 5, 1983: Steve has helped me see my tendency to respond to my difficulties with self-hatred, hurt, and some withdrawal. I need to be more self-respecting, but it's hard in my position. I wish I knew how deprived the children really are.

Bob visited and said he had heard from the insurance company; I have money for seventeen more months of nursing care. I have thought of going to court to turn off the respirator, if I don't get any better—but how much better to want to live on indefinitely, I don't know. I think about not living in the hospital and I could be more of a wife and mother and work. I can't go on like this indefinitely. Watching TV all day is not my idea of living.

For Alli,

Lisa sprinkled magic dust on herself, making her small, and climbed on Marigold's back and flew away. It had been raining and Lisa and the butterfly came upon a rainbow. They rode each color of the rainbow—red, yellow, and blue.

Up there, they met Lisa's fairy godmother. She had something special for Lisa—magic ribbons for her hair. When she touched the ribbons, she would feel better and not grouchy. She didn't thank her fairy godmother because she didn't like to think about when she got grouchy or mad. She rode off on Marigold, feeling angry at the fairy godmother.

While brushing the hair out of her eyes as they flew along, Lisa accidentally touched her magic ribbon and was no longer mad at the fairy godmother. Lisa decided she would wear the ribbons in her hair every school day so she wouldn't be mad and grouchy about going to school. She and Marigold flew off to Lollipop Land and Lisa picked her favorite candies. She flew home on Marigold, sprinkled magic dust to make herself bigger, and gave one of her lollipops to her sister Jill.

The End

Love,

Mom

June 8, 1983: I've had some dreams. Two were sexual. In one I was making love with Bob, the other with my cousin. They were very explicit and pleasurable.

Last night I dreamed that I was making plans for what I needed to do in my garden. Someone was with me, a vague figure, a woman, I think. We looked at the land all around my house. There were weeds that needed to be removed and extensive, very specific transplanting to regroup some plants together. I wanted each side of the house to have different kinds of plants, depending on sun and water. One side was to be succulent, and another roses. Then I was concerned whether the hose was long enough to reach the long strip of land in the front.

I am particularly interested in this dream, as I had it when I was having strong death wishes. What does it mean now? If I want to die, I have to be sure it is the right thing for me and I am ready. No one can answer that for me. And dreams can tell me, if I interpret them correctly.

I have such deep sadness—it's not that I am depressed. That's too facile. I have some inner work to do to get my garden in order. There were no new plants in my dream, but many were already there. I think the four-sided house is an image of wholeness, completion.

I was most focused on the shady side of my house. The kinds of plants were everlasting and green. This all has to do with inner order. When this is achieved, then maybe I can go.

June 10, 1983: How am I? I am committed to doing things right: I continue to feel I want my struggle time limited. Bob says if I feel that way, it will happen that way, I won't need to go to court. Lucy says that's suicide. Steve said it was illogical. I will follow my dreams. Bob said he had contemplated suicide to get out of this situation. It is so hard.

For Alli and Jenie,

Soon summer would be there. The weather would get hot. It is a good time to do new things. But Lisa did not want to go to camp, even though the camp has grass and trees and swimming and lots of fun things. She didn't want to leave her friends.

"The only way the camps might agree to take you part-time," Mother said, "is if they don't fill up full-time. And if we wait, you might not get in at all."

"That's all right, Mom," said Lisa. "You could hire a student teacher to paint, read, do projects with us at home on the days we would have gone to camp. And Jill can have friends over. It would be fun. I like to be home sometimes with my friends. There is a student teacher at Dad's hospital who works with the girl across the hall from him. They have a good time together."

"You'd help her clean up, wouldn't you?" Mom said, laughing.

"Oh, yes, I will," said Lisa.

"Well," said Mom, "there is a lot to think about. How will you feel if you don't learn how to swim?"

"I can learn when I'm older," said Lisa, "or you could teach me."

"Won't you miss the grass and trees?"

"Yes," replied Lisa, "but being with people I love is more important to me. Anyway, you said you would take us to a pretty place with

182

lots of trees and rocks to climb on. That would be fun, Mom."

"It sure would," said Mom. "We could go on Friday and come back in time to visit Dad on Sunday. It's going to be a good summer."
The End
Love,
Mom

June 14, 1983:
Dear Alli,

A card arrived from you. It has hearts and sparkles on it. I look at it lots and think of you. Then you also made me a wonderful bean collage. Both are hanging above me. Thank you very much. You looked so pretty in your new dress. You did a terrific job on the hard puzzle. I'm very proud of you. I want you to help Dad with plans for this summer. Wear your magic ribbons and don't be grouchy. He really wants you to go to camp, so if you don't want to go, tell Dad why and what you do want to do. This is important. Please help.
Love,
Mom

Dear Jenie,

Today I opened the blue tissue-paper package you gave me. Inside was a beautiful picture you made. I wonder how you made it. I like the colors—greens and purples. Thank you very much. You looked very pretty in your pink and white dress. I loved looking at you doing puzzles. I wish I could give you a ride on my back. I love you very much.
Love,
Mom

June 14, 1983: The visit began with Bob arriving with a big bouquet of lilacs. Then the girls arrived to present their gifts. Jenie really came close and looked at me.

For the day, we went to the botanical gardens with the van and all. The tulips, lilacs, wisteria, and azaleas were blooming. The cherry blossoms had fallen, of course, and Alli and Jenie played in the petals, throwing them in the air like snow. I looked at everything as if I were seeing them for the last time.

Bob got exhausted from pushing the wheelchair up the hills and carrying all the emergency equipment. I held up very well in the sitting department, which I regard as a gift from God, as I usually have big problems after two hours. Then we went home where the girls worked on puzzles for several hours. Both of them like to be helped a lot. They got piggyback rides from friends who stopped by.

I returned to the hospital happy for the outing but sad about all my limitations.

June 15, 1983: I have been sleeping a lot. It's too easy to attribute it to tiredness from the outing. It is the wish to withdraw. It feels so good to sleep, like a drug. I try to meditate but end up sleeping, the one thing that feels good.

June 17, 1983: Today is my brother's birthday. I have been thinking about him a lot. Maybe I'll hear from him soon. Things are not so bright for me physically. I have lost almost all movement in my left thumb, which I use to ring my call button. It is a particular problem at night, as my nurse sleeps lightly and when my bell doesn't work, I have to wait until she wakes when I want something, which is extremely upsetting. I will have to ask her not to sleep. She is a good soul.

Two doctors have advised against having the feeding tube surgically inserted in my stomach. So unless I insist, I'm stuck with a tube in my nose. I had to have a very unpleasant test because blood showed in one suction. It involved taking my trach out many times. I can be off the respirator only one minute, while others can go as long as ten minutes.

I have been praying for help. My meditation taught me only that I chose all this for spiritual growth, which leaves too many unanswered questions. Why should I put my family through this unless we all chose it together? It's very hard to understand.

Bob visited. I asked him how he felt about Sunday's visit. He said it was difficult and was surprised that I wasn't sure what he meant and had asked for elaboration. He said he hadn't been sleeping because of worry. He said nothing was going right, but that he didn't want to talk about it because my troubles were so much greater and he had to solve things alone, not talk about them. I, of course, wanted sharing of troubles to be reciprocal, that if he said nothing, then I couldn't help. And I said I need to be needed.

I guess I had an impact about Alli's camp. He says she feels she's being shipped off and he's not going to send her. Another problem with Alli is her feelings about my illness. She used to talk to Bob about the possibility of my dying. Since I've been coming home for visits, she has told her best friend that I'm going to get better and that I'm coming home to stay. Children her age with divorcing parents also use a lot of denial and fantasy.

June 21, 1983: There was no Sunday visit with the children because Alli was sick. Too bad. It was a beautiful day and there was a carnival down the street, which would have been fun to go to. My life is so limited, so characterized by sameness, which is increasingly unbearable for me, who is used to such a rich and varied time.

These nice days are for bike rides, trips to the zoo, picnics, boat rides. I don't know how anyone with access to a normal life can expect me to accept such a limited one. That others have accepted a drastically limited life does not mean that is the right course of action for me.

Steve, how do I do a "Living Will" requesting that the respirator be turned off? For those who say this is suicide and playing God, I believe it is merciful and just. My life has been prolonged by non-God means, so it can be terminated. My God-death was last summer, which would have had harmony. I should have gone then. It was so peaceful.

June 22, 1983:
For Alli and Jenie,

Lisa and Jill climbed on the magic white horse and flew away. First they came to Lollipop Land, which was full of trees that talked and had lollipops on their branches. Jill and Lisa reached up to pick some of their favorite colors. Suddenly the tree said, "Stop! No lollipops until you tell me something important."

"What must we tell?" asked Jill.

The tree replied, "You must tell me something you do that upsets your parents."

"Oh," said Lisa. "We don't do anything that upsets our parents."

"All children do things that upset their parents," said the tree.

"Oh, all right," said Lisa. "I'll tell you. I upset my parents by not wanting to go to school." Then she picked her lollipops and got back on the horse.

"What about you, Jill?" asked the tree.

"I don't like to go to bed," the little girl said and picked her candies. Later they had a delicious lunch at the house of the good witch.

"I know what you said to the lollipop tree," said the good witch. "I know children don't like to upset their parents. So I am giving each of you a magic stone. When you, Lisa, don't feel like going to school, and you, Jill, don't want to go to bed, take out your magic stone and rub it and think of me. I will come and put my arms around you and we will talk. The stone will help you talk about what is bothering you.

It will make you strong and unafraid and happy. Remember, I will always be there to help and I will always be thinking about you."

Lisa and Jill thanked the good witch and promised to use the stones. Then they asked her for help getting home. The good witch said she would, but first they had to tell her something that made their parents happy.

"I brush my teeth real well," said Lisa.

"I got my sister something to draw on," said Jill. "That made my Mom and Dad very happy." The good witch said she was very proud of them. She kissed them good-bye. "I will always be thinking of you," she said.

The girls got back on their white horse. The good witch waved her magic cane and wished them home. When they got there, their mother was waiting for them, smiling.

The End

Love,

Mom

June 25, 1983: Sunday's visit was very unsatisfactory. Alli and Jenie did not want to come inside to see me. I went outside where they were. Alli gave me a leaf. Neither wanted to listen to the story I wrote for them. I was very upset at my immobility. I can't do anything to interact with them.

Jenie wouldn't kiss me good-bye.

Monday I did not have a nurse. Imagine staying in one position without moving, except to go on the bedpan, for twelve hours! Imagine lying for twelve hours with nothing to do but sleep or watch TV— and the same channel all the time! I don't plan to be here when I have to live like that all the time. Only some of the nurses will take the time to figure out what I need. Others just walk away.

I must have said "bedpan" fifty times to each nurse, but they couldn't understand. Oh, the relief when a nurse comes who understands.

How am I? Some of the things I think about are the feel of Bob's body beside mine in bed, what it's like to go antiquing, out to dinner, to a play. And what it would be like to have gone to the circus the other day with Bob and Alli. It deeply pains me to see my children indifferent to me, for it wouldn't be that way if I was more active.

I keep thinking how more right it would have been to die a natural death last July. But we are programmed to take sick people to the hospital without thinking of the quality of life the sick person will have after. I wonder if Bob would have the courage not to take me to the hospital today, knowing what we know now. I have never known such unhappiness. To have to go through further decline and have my children witness it is cruel.

June 27, 1983: I keep thinking about Alli and Jenie and how things have grown less involved between us with the passing of time, especially with Jenie. I remember their responsiveness the first few visits last fall. It has been a gradual process, I think because I don't put out enough to sustain interest. I guess for Jenie it is easier to reject me totally than to have to relate so incompletely. It's harder for Alli, but she tries to extricate herself, too. I see no solution to this problem. I don't understand the way Alli changed in one week. Maybe they were mad about something else.

June 28, 1983: I have been spending more time meditating and praying, trying to overcome my inner misery. My night nurse reads the Bible to me. I pretend I'm in a monastery. Maybe that will help me accept all my restrictions. I have been sleeping more, too. I have to get more at peace with myself so I can die, which I want to do as soon as possible.

Here I am, me, wanting death rather than a severely limited life.

No, death is my second choice—my first being to make myself better. I have not been able to make myself better. So I have no reason to believe I can bring about my death. I must ask for help.

I've had enough. Steve, tell me the procedure. Please.

■

Steve saw, or rather, sensed the changes in Emily's thinking. There were no more requests to admit new healers, less concern for the details of living—she hardly ever asked to have her hair washed anymore—no more talk about cures, hesitant mentions of death, and frequent fears about comas. That was a legitimate fear, in his mind. Six or eight minutes of another unnoticed respirator failure, with no oxygen getting to the brain, and the body's defenses would take over, shutting off brain function, leaving Emily to drift unconscious somewhere for a very long while. They could restart the heart in the hospital, reinflate the lungs, cleanse the blood, all by machine. They had nothing—yet—to reawaken the brain.

Emily could fall into such a coma at any time. Steve knew the risks. After Emily's desires seemed genuine and permanent, she had been listed as DNR. But that required a heart failure. If someone slipped up on the respirator alarm or the machine itself failed, they would have to do everything to bring her back. They couldn't risk a massive lawsuit by a grieving family suggesting hospital sloppiness or complicity in a mercy killing; modern Americans always seek to blame someone for any pain.

Steve had heard rumblings about negotiated deaths. Doctors, patients, and families in terminal cases quietly discussing the future, or lack of one, and then, if agreed, acquiescing to the inevitable by removing some machines or withholding some medicines. The unwritten rule of these open secrets, however, was that none of the parties ever mention that dark subject again, which meant that the awful and awfully painful lessons of technology and death had to be learned anew by each individual family that arrived at that station, alone and frightened. Painful pioneers in an uncharted land.

The only ones who knew for sure that it was going on all day every day everywhere were the doctors. And they weren't talking openly, not if they wanted to keep their reputations and malpractice insurance intact. Of course, the doctors or hospitals couldn't intentionally cause a patient's demise. There had been charges of that in a few isolated cases around the country, though nothing that stuck in the end except the memory of those headlines, DOCTORS INDICTED IN "MERCY KILLING."

The growing chapters of the Hemlock Society based in Los Angeles were openly advocating legalization of voluntary euthanasia for the terminally ill. Two other national groups, Concern for Dying and the Society for the Right to Die, both based in New York, were working quietly on the local level, educating citizens, legislators, administrators, and prosecutors on the rapidly developing issues and lobbying for laws to let people go when they wanted. None of the groups regarded this as helping to kill people.

Actively causing death would violate the doctors' Hippocratic Oath to do no harm, though some of them knew, and fewer acknowledged, that such a step might also meet another professed medical goal, to relieve suffering. But what could one doctor or one family do? And the patient who had been dying wasn't around anymore to pass on any lessons, observations, or regrets. Certainly no one in that condition or position had kept a diary to recount what it was like to be kept alive involuntarily, a paralyzed captive of the best-trained best intentions, no one who ever let that document get out, anyway.

Steve's friends remember him seeming more serious in those early summer days. Instead of talking about what medicine could do, he talked about the inadequacies of a technological society that had raised several generations to believe that anything was possible—indeed, it was expected—if just given enough money, machines, and determination. Today's generations of parents and children lived apart and died apart. When someone was hurt, they went to the hospital. When someone was sick, they went to the hospital. When someone was dying, they went to the hospital. When someone was uncertain, they went to the hospital. Can't go wrong that way. The hospitals care, at least they have the equipment to care. And there's no one at home anymore to really care for the sick anyway.

People in this society, it seemed to Steve, were much more prepared now to fight death, black and white. Therefore, they were much less prepared to accept death when it came, all foggy and gray.

He believed strongly that a hospital could never help a patient to die, to put them out of a misery defined by others. That was something man did for animals. For humans it was obviously out of the question, morally and ethically. But was it always necessary to stand in the way of a dying patient? Couldn't medical miracles sometimes become medical manacles? Wasn't there a difference between treating a human's illness and an ill human? There must be a humane way to handle these needs in a pluralistic society. Now that death often could be thwarted by the advanced society of the United States in the 1980s, there were no social or legal guidelines on when not to. The designers of miracles had assumed everyone would want to cling to life as long as possible, no matter what, although no one ever bothered to research all the differing definitions of "life." The feuding American interests and groups couldn't even decide when life began, let alone when it could be allowed to end. There was no protective process where someone could say, "I want to die," and a panel could say, "No, you don't really," or "That seems reasonable under your circumstances." No one who wasn't involved in such a painful case wanted to think about those things. No one who was involved had the time to do anything about them.

Steve certainly didn't. But he figured time was running out.

Bob was running a little late that morning. He was trying to invest more time in work, so he was cutting a few more minutes off his one-way visits to Emily. When he stepped around the cubicle's curtain, he looked rushed, which he was supposed to.

"Good morning," he said with a kind of forced optimism, as if, deep inside, he doubted it would turn out to be good. This day didn't seem any different from any other weekday. He kissed Emily on the forehead and took the same limp hand that had squeezed his so tightly during Jenie's birth. He couldn't remember that. He couldn't even remember if the sun was out when he came in the hospital; he forgot to notice, or forgot he had noticed.

"The girls are fine," he began. "One of Alli's drawings was chosen to—" Bob was a little annoyed at the staccato sound of Emily's printer interrupting his edited news report on life a few miles away. He waited a moment, starting to sigh and then catching himself; sometimes it was hard to remember Emily was in there. That machine took so long to print anything out; the conversations ended up like two semaphoremen signaling each other from opposing hills miles apart, in the same room. This message came out single letter by single letter, in a slow, thin, continuous stream of yellow.

I WANT TO DIE

Bob didn't move for a few seconds. He was stunned. And frightened. The way he was when his dad would talk so circumspectly about his ailing wife's health. The way he was way back in Dr. Berghoff's office years ago when the doctor said, "I need to talk to you." Bob didn't know what was frightening him now, or then. But something was out there. Something was coming. And it had to be bad. Good things didn't sneak up on Bob; he could see them coming for days, like a thirsty man squinting across the sand hopefully and fearfully at a distant oasis that could, probably would, evaporate as it got closer.

Now, Bob's wife was saying that she wanted to die. He knew she was going to die. Of course, she was going to die. At times he had wished she would die; at others he considered her dead already. But going to die and wanting to die are two different things. In one, you can't do anything about it. In the other, you must. He must.

Bob chose to misinterpret those four words for his own sake. He was just trying to get along here, to get through another day. He nodded and patted Emily's hands and finished his report on the family. It was a little more detailed than he had planned during his long walk down the hospital hall. Then he had to go to work; they had an order, and he couldn't let that one go. He couldn't make it Friday either, but he'd bring the kids on Sunday. They sent their love and said they missed her.

When the nurse returned, she noticed that Emily's heart rate was considerably higher than normal. But it calmed down after a while.

■

June 30, 1983:
Message to Dr. D. and Steve
From Emily Bauer

I wish to request that my respirator be turned off after giving me a shot to put me to sleep.

July 1, 1983: Holidays are not to be looked forward to. Bob and the girls are going away for July 4th. How long must I wait?

My regular night nurse couldn't come last night. The relief nurse didn't care about communication, including my call bell. Frequently, she would say it was working when it wasn't, leaving me with no way to get her attention except opening and closing my mouth a little. She would look at me doing this and say, "I'm right here. Try to get some more sleep." Totally ignoring me. The feelings of helplessness and rage I feel are indescribable.

July 3, 1983: Irene read in my chart that I wanted the respirator turned off and with tears in her eyes, she told me how much that upset her. She told me my journal was beautiful. She said the hospital needed me because someone wanted to give money to the hospital through muscular dystrophy and I was the only patient here who qualified, since ALS is related.

My friend Vicky visited as always. She got tearful, too, saying she felt today that I was different somehow, as if I'd started to leave. And she didn't know if she could handle the separation.

Mikhail came and gave me a massage. That I do look forward to.

July 6, 1983: Lucy has read my letter to Dr. D. about turning off the respirator. He replied, "Who will do that for you? That's murder."

He suggested I pray and keep working on my journal.

At least he agreed to DNR.

July 7, 1983: Dr. D. stopped by and talked to me about why he couldn't turn off the respirator. He is Jewish and he spoke from a thoughtful religious viewpoint. He told me to write a book to teach doctors and nurses.

I had another frequently ignoring nurse last night. One more grim time. I think of how I was, and to be so helpless and treated with such disrespect is unbearable.

Memo to the Nursing Staff
From Emily Bauer

Since I can't talk to you and you take care of me when I don't have private nurses, I'd like to tell you about me.

I need the bedpan and suction about every three hours.

I need my nose suctioned. Often my trach leaks, and my mouth drools. I like to use my printing machine from nine to one and two to five. The machine is put letters facing me. The switch is put under the right side of my head. Move my head and the switch until the switch clicks. When you pass by, look at me to see if I need the switch adjusted or something else, as I cannot use my call button when I'm printing.

The button is kept on the respirator. Please set it up when I'm not using the printer. I like to watch NBC weekdays from one to two and 5 to eight.

Further information is on the wall behind my bed. Please read how to communicate.

Thanks so much for your attention and time.
Emily Bauer

July 9, 1983: None of the basic factors causing me to want to die have changed. What could make me feel differently? On the negative side are the vast deprivations and limitations, the exclusion from a normal rich and varied life. Then there are the consequences of profound disability, the frustration, anxiety, discomfort, and helplessness. On the positive side are moments with people like Irene and Vicky and also Alli and all the others who give me love. Whether or not I'm here, that makes a difference. Related to this is feeling needed. When Irene said she needed me for a hospital project, my mind soared.

But I feel uncertain about how useful I am to Bob, Alli, and Jenie. I think Bob is coming into his own with the girls, and they are settling in. Mother, Bryan, and Barbara each spoke of how much happier they seemed. Bob says Alli is more peaceful and cooperative recently. At the most I'm needed by Alli as an image. My influence will come from what I have written and what people tell them about me. I have decided to become less emotionally dependent on them.

July 12, 1983: I am not yet consoled by the monastery image, but I will keep trying. I am so tired of being uncomfortable. My neck, shoulders, and legs hurt now. I wake up in the morning and have nothing I look forward to except more of the same. Even with visitors it's harder because I am not happy and not enjoyable to be with, and I keep falling asleep. There is nothing I can do to make my life richer and more varied. And I don't know how I'm going to get myself dead, as I don't like to feel bad.

July 14, 1983: I had another garden dream. This time I had a rather small, rectangular garden patch in the middle of the lawn and perhaps the corners of the walkway. I was concerned about selecting plants and seeds which were easy to grow. I was going to plant cosmos at the back of the patch. I was worried if there was enough room, as cosmos are big plants. Then I would plant dahlias and different sizes of marigolds. The earth was prepared in the garden patch, and I just had to add some fertilizer. The ground in the walkway corners was not prepared, and I wondered if marigolds would grow there. These were all flowers I grew by process of elimination; these were the ones that always worked and were known to be hardy.

I had a garden when we had our house in the country, which we had to sell when I got sick. In her description of me in her book on "Our Family" at school, Alli described my love of gardening and identified me as a good gardener. She was two when I last had a garden. Of course, my teaching, doing therapy with my patients, and having babies is like gardening—making things grow.

This dream may be a wish to be involved in such activities, as, consciously, one reason I want to die is because I have such an impoverished life—no gardening in the larger sense. I was concerned in the dream with things that grow easily—I want an easy death. All the flowers that I was planting were annuals, dying at the end of the season. As I want to.

■

Bob had thought, had hoped, that Emily's ticker-tape desire for death was part of a passing depression. It wasn't. It was part of a coming depression, one that would hang over her motionless bed through that summer season and into the fall. It would be broken at times by bouts of happiness, brief moments of joy, like when her children kissed her, ordinary moments for ordinary folks that seemed all the sweeter for Emily because they were surrounded by sour grays.

Bob had hoped Emily would forget her ten-letter plea for death. But Bob had forgotten that this was Emily. The original Emily. The ALS might have ravaged her body, killed the nerves, atrophied the muscles, confined her world, but it couldn't touch her determined mind. If Emily's husband thought his active wife was determined when she devoted an entire afternoon to shopping all over the city for just the right gift for a friend, he hadn't seen anything yet, not until he witnessed this now inactive woman's determination to get herself a gift, some relief.

I WANT TO DIE

He knew what she wasn't saying, too, as husbands sometimes do. There was only one way that a completely paralyzed Emily could

die—with someone's help. And he knew instantly who had been nom-
inated as helper. Bob's reaction was anger, a real, full-blooded rage
that rose rapidly like a flash flood consuming everything in its path
and frightening those who weren't. Bob had been coping with the
larger picture—the destruction of his wife, his life, his family, his
dreams, and the echoes of it all—by focusing on the snapshots of
his daily existence. What does Alli need for lunch? What should
Jenie wear to nursery school? What was the weather forecast? Which
bills could be paid today; which ones could be ignored a while longer?
When to leave for the office? Where to get gas? Was there change in
his pocket for the tollbooth? Where would he find a replacement secretary by Monday? Where would tomorrow's work come from? What
was in the refrigerator for dinner? What should he give Alli for the
sniffles? Which story should he read to Jenie? Which paragraphs
could he skip tonight? What calls needed to be returned? Where did
this colossal headache come from? "You couldn't dream up a horror
story like this," he told one friend.

Bob had been angry that Emily had suffered, was suffering. He
loved her, he really had—he really did. He was angry that he had
suffered, that the children had suffered. And all in this hopeful and
then hopeless, grinding struggle to prolong mechanically a life he
considered over, as if the actor in an admirable play kept coming back
out for more bows as the last members of the audience donned their
coats and walked up the aisle.

Bob was angry, too, that Emily had not yet died. Please, God, get
this agony over for her, for him, for everyone. He was angry he felt
that way. He knew he shouldn't; no one had ever told him anger was
allowed. On one level, he admired and accepted Emily's tenacious
hold on life. It was something he cherished too. On another level, he
despised that tenacity. For as long as Emily lived—or rather, as long
as they kept her living—she held the same tenacious grip on his life
and Alli's and Jenie's.

He had always thought of life as a long unit, with parts being cut off
as the years and decades passed. And one kept going, kept trying to go
forward, hopefully in some kind of graceful way. But here they were,
the four Bauers, milling around blindly in the forest, bumping into
each other, knocking each other down, stepping on each other, hurt-

ing each other, forgetting the good times. An exhausted husband who wakes up wide-eyed at four A.M. and doesn't know why. Kids who cry at night for their mother and then won't touch her the next day.

With few exceptions, other friends and some relatives were steadily drifting away, speaking of sympathy but earnestly consumed by the continuing joys and passing problems of their own lives. There was nowhere for Bob to drift. And now, knowing that, Emily had decided she wanted out and she had decided she wanted Bob to help her. The nerve! The pain! The relief!

One of his first thoughts was genuine hope: Could the real end really be in sight? He had had dreams, before four A.M., of striding into Emily's cubicle and pulling the respirator off and holding her while she died. But he knew he could never do that; anyway, all the alarms would go off. And all alarms, like all telephones, must be answered.

The next thought was, "Wait just one fucking minute! What are you asking me to do? Kill you? Your husband? I didn't agree to kill you when I married you! You want me indicted for murder? Who'd take care of the kids? You made the decision to live. You lived. You've made the decision to die now. You die. You get the doctors to do it. Why do I have to do everything from removing your diapers to removing your respirator?" No! Absolutely not! Impossible, he told her.

Bob wondered at times how this ordeal could get worse. Now he knew. Emily's manipulation again. Her living in limbo and his visiting the same place were very painful, but they were familiar. He had gotten used to that pain. It had become so much a part of him and his daily life that it was the one thing he could always count on. When you wake up—and you will wake up—nothing will have changed; everything will hurt just as before, maybe worse.

But killing Emily was something new, something threatening. She'd be gone and he'd be left, living with that act. "I grew up in a loving family," he thought, "I went to high school, graduated from college. My life has not been sheltered. Why wasn't I prepared for these decisions? No one ever said, 'Get ready, practice, start thinking because as you get older, you're going to face some life-and-death decisions about your loved ones.' Why is this all a secret until it's too late? Since when must everyone be a god unto himself?"

Bob was also frightened because, deep down inside, he knew he would eventually agree to help Emily die. He knew what that meant for her, unless you believed in all that reincarnation business, which Bob didn't. But he didn't know what her death that way meant for him, the one left behind who could still move and feel. Was it the beginning of a new life or the beginning of jail or his own emotional decline? He didn't blame the doctors for not letting her die; they were just humans, well-intentioned and earnest, incredibly prepared to deal with science but many incredibly unprepared to deal with humanity. They were just earning a living, building a career, protecting themselves while facing decisions once reserved to celestial authorities. The doctors had their own lives to lead, their own fears to feed. He didn't blame them for doing their job, stalling the inevitable, hoping something would happen in the meantime to save them from real involvement. Bob was about to do exactly the same thing.

■

July 23, 1983: Doreen, a former patient of mine, came to visit. She told me how much inner strength she had developed working with me. I cried and still do. (M, suction plse) I was a good therapist, and now look at me. How can I use those abilities now? She also had many valuable things to say about her father's dying and death, which I now know are two very different things. It was a very demanding yet enriching experience for her. That's probably why she's not afraid to visit me. She talked about his going back and forth to the other side and how he said either place wasn't so bad, before he went to the other side. She said they never had a concept of Heaven before or a religious feeling of purpose, but now they did. She said her father had feelings and dreams like mine. Again, my sleepiness interfered with a visit. I want to know more.

I've had a fever the last two nights. My relief night nurse says it's pneumonia and I'll die in six months if I don't turn to move the phlegm in my lungs. Do I have a choice—about dying or turning?

The way she turns is very uncomfortable, so I didn't sleep. Sometimes now I sleep most of the day and lie awake all night, thinking.

Bob visited, and it was a very good visit. He has been thinking about his mother's illness and our relationship. I feel increasingly secure in our love, which makes leaving easier, but so sad, for I love and want to be with him so much.

Bob asked me questions. He wanted to know if I'd live another life after learning what I have from this one. I appreciated what I had and was happy. I never thought I could be sick and I didn't realize fully how precious what I had was. Just to walk in the grass would be a miracle which most take for granted. To hold and talk to one's children would be a gift. To work alongside one's husband, another.

I pray for a painless death. I'm getting antibiotics for my pneumonia, which is awful. The fever felt like I was suffocating. There must be another way.

July 24, 1983: Bob, I think we need a lawyer for my decision. Maybe we should go to court? I want out of this.

July 26, 1983: I have lost a tape again due to printer not working for several hours. I was describing my father's visit and my mother's arrival. Now my brother and his wife are here. Seeing my closest family is both wonderful and sad. For we all have so many memories of how I was before. Communication was very difficult, but holding my hand easy and appreciated. They all came such a distance that it's too bad they couldn't stay longer. I thought Mother was going to stay longer than two days. She went to visit Bryan. Maybe she'll come back.

Sunday's visit with the children was like the last one. Alli gave me good kisses and Jenie didn't. Alli asked me if I liked tuna and fruit salad and later commented, "Mom doesn't ever eat."

Alli also made some wonderful pictures, which Bob hung up for me. She drew some family figures. The figures have good vitality except in one the drawing of me has well-formed, appropriately sized arms. Bob, this and Jenie's nonresponsiveness to me make me wish you'd call the institute for help.

July 27, 1983:
For Alli,

Lisa was asleep in her bed. She had a dream. In her dream she was a princess. She had the most beautiful clothes and whenever she wanted something new, she would snap her fingers and someone would buy her what she wanted. She never had to share with her sister. She never had to clean up at school, for her teacher came to the palace and there were many servants. Because she was a princess, her friends did whatever she wanted and never disagreed with her.

When she awoke, Lisa decided she wanted to be a princess like in the dream. So she summoned her fairy godmother, who hugged her and waved her magic wand.

Suddenly Princess Lisa lived in a beautiful palace with a bedroom as big as her old apartment. She could even ride her bike in her bedroom! There was another room just for her clothes, and shoes to match. She went shopping whenever she wanted, or rather, the merchants came to her at the palace.

At first Lisa liked being a princess. But after a while (and it was hard for her to admit this) she began to get a little bored. She missed wanting to buy things and asking her mother for them. She missed being bothered by her little sister. She missed her real friends.

Princess Lisa called her fairy godmother with another wish. She waved her magic wand and lo and behold, there was just Lisa. Her sister Jill was there to welcome her back, and so was her mom, who was smiling.
The End
Love,
Mom

July 28, 1983: Before my mother left she told me of how she asked God for help so she wouldn't cry around me and if you ask God for help, He will give it! Barbara told me of a man who had ALS who died in his sleep before going on the respirator. I have been asking God to let me die in my sleep. That is the kind of death I want and it is possible.

Of course, I don't know if I have any control over my own death. Some people like Bob believe one does. They believe if I really want to die, including at a deep unconscious level, then I will die. I have heard of people where this seems true. I don't know if it is always true. But I do know the world of immobility and intense discomfort is a very lonely one.

July 30, 1983: I've had two dreams. In the first I was going someplace. I was to go and return and meet Bob. And we were to go to a friend's house on a hill. At first, I was walking in the countryside and in a small town. Then I got worried I wouldn't be back on time, so I decided to take a cab. The teller at a small, white old post office said he'd get a cab. But it would be expensive. He asked how much I had and I said twenty-two dollars. The cab came, and I met Bob on time.

In the second dream I was at my friend Janice's house getting ready to go to a party. I was wearing an orange ruffled dress. The dream felt just like when Janice and I used to do things together and had a good time.

The first dream is a recurrent one in that I'm going someplace and I'm afraid I'll not be on time. Unlike the others, in this dream I got where I wanted on time.

I am ready to go now.

August 2, 1983: I think of Jenie, Alli, and Bob all the time. How sad I am it has to end this way. I have always looked forward to a good marriage and raising my children. Thank God I have complete trust in Bob and how he will raise them. I feel they will have a good life. My writings should let them know how much I love them. Hopefully, Bob will marry again. I will live on through them.

Bob, could you please hang the quilts I made Alli and Jenie back up on a wall at home where I could see them next visit. The girls came here on Saturday. Alli kissed me. They had picked flowers for me. Sunday I went to chapel.

Bob, did you talk to an attorney? Please!

■

Bob had not talked to an attorney. He had not talked to anyone—"Hi, you know Emily is still alive. The hospital won't let her die. So she wants me to help her kill herself somehow. What do you think I should do?" Although after a while he indicated to Emily, or rather to her eyes, that he was discussing her desires with someone. For more than a month he stalled her with "I forgot," "Too busy," and "Don't know." Long before, he had contacted some hospices, those new caring institutions designed as halfway homes for the terminally ill to free them from the hospital without going all the way home. The hospices preferred cancer patients and wanted nothing to do with Emily's elaborate medical maintenance apparatus.

Bob seemed battered and struggling, so much so that his sisters feared that he might commit suicide, so consumed was he with guilt, duty, and fatigue. That thought crossed Steve's mind, too. "Stretched to brk pt," Steve wrote in the notes all psychiatric social workers keep as reminders and for possible protection someday.

Steve had been stretched himself in recent times. Passing his mid-thirties, the young man had amassed considerable experience in the workaday world of medical wonders and bureaucracy, enough to know some fresh changes were badly needed, yet lacking the power to do anything about them. He was still building a career and had to be careful. Steve's developing concerns focused on death and the American abhorrence of talking about it. Some of the country's most prominent citizens could sit before a television camera on the nation's electronic front porch of an evening now, and there discuss for the benefit of millions of eavesdroppers the most intimate details of their personal lives, complete with titters and tears, innuendo and slurs. But let that ugly five-letter word—death—slip out and silence falls. Everyone is reminded. It isn't funny. It doesn't sell. No jokes. No smiles. Time for these important messages and we'll be right back. Now smile.

"We are not focusing on the whole sociology of dying in this country," Steve would think to himself. There was a time, which he barely remembered, when dying was done at home in the bosom of loved ones as a normal part of living.

"There is nothing dignified about dying," one of his teachers had said. "You just try to go in the least worst way possible." Now in an age of specialization, Steve thought, the ill and dying were often going in the most worst way possible. And loved ones, specially dressed for the special visit, acted stilted and stuffed. The body was removed to a funeral home and then to a cemetery and that person entered the family memory bank. The rubber gloves were disposable, too.

Steve wondered how the natural process could be made more natural and humane.

During one of his regular chats with Bob the idea slipped out, unformed, just a thought for Bob to pursue or drop. Had he contacted any of the developing right-to-die groups? Steve asked. The one he knew about was called Concern for Dying. Up in New York City.

"Bob showed up here in great turmoil," said one officer in the group's office. "We see them all the time, more than a hundred a year in person and maybe fifteen a day by mail. They are all different, but they have some common points. They all are facing death somehow and the agonizing decisions that come with that. These are new predicaments for our society. These people want to discuss it openly. But who can they talk to and say, 'I'm thinking of turning off my wife's respirator'? Others will dodge it, or judge it, and maybe call it murder. These folks—husbands and wives, sons and daughters—want to know if their thoughts are permissible—I mean, 'My God, I'm her husband, the father of her children, can I even allow myself to consider this? Am I participating in a suicide? Will I go to jail? Has anyone else ever had such thoughts? What's right anymore?'

"They are so desperate that they'll talk with strangers like us. We give them an open ear. We want to make sure that the end is a real desire of the patient's and not just a spouse trying to get out of a tough situation."

There were several visits, several long talks. A representative of the group discussed the situation with other family members, and one visited Emily, who was still going through the same long days and cherishing the long nights of sleep. Emily looked elated at the visitor's news. Progress!

Then they gave Bob the news. In their experience, the Bauers had two basic choices: A long court fight with the hospital, which would entail lots of publicity and videotape of the girls, especially if the lens caught them crying. Or somehow getting Emily back home again where humane arrangements could be made to let nature take its course, just like in the old days.

Bob had neither the stomach for even a short legal fight, nor the finances, having fallen more than $30,000 into debt to a bank and his sisters. What would that second choice involve?

The group put Bob in touch with a sympathetic attorney in a prestigious law firm in the Bauers' hometown. A short, precise veteran of many legal wars, the attorney not only worked cautiously, he lived cautiously. He was the kind of man who, stepping through a door, would pause there to survey everything and everyone before committing himself to enter fully. The attorney would take no money for the case and give no guarantees, just expertise as part of the developing underground to facilitate such matters in the least illegal manner possible. A new Underground Railroad to a different sort of freedom.

He was impressed with Bob—a big man, sincere, warm. And he had kind eyes; the attorney relied on legal books as much as his colleagues, but he always drew his first impression from those blinking windows into the soul of a client. Bob was obviously troubled, too, which was very good. The attorney's suspicions flourished when clients saw everything as black and white, cut and dried.

Bob explained the situation, and the attorney listened carefully. Bob was obviously deeply tormented, he noted, but the attorney tried to ignore that, like a doctor seeming to ignore an injured patient's shrieks while he sews up the wound. The attorney had never met his hospital counterpart, but he knew immediately from long experience what that lawyer would argue. He would interpret Emily's two-year-old permission for initial treatment as valid over time and from one institution to another. That was the easiest defense strategy: The patient agreed to the treatment a long time ago. We're just following her wishes. We can't stop simply because for a brief period she claims she wants to die. Besides, withdrawing treatment violates our professional ethics.

The attorney explained to Bob his two basic legal concerns. They were called criminal and civil. Assisting a suicide could be manslaughter or second-degree homicide, intentional murder, against either one of them, or both, and anyone else who helped them. This was serious stuff, and Bob paled. In addition, the hospital would be afraid of civil liability, which would leave it, the doctors, and the nurses vulnerable to being sued by someone—maybe even Bob if he felt guilty enough later—for not taking proper care of Emily. Or someone could bring a suit against Bob for wrongful death on behalf of his own children.

But, Bob said, she wanted to die. She was determined. You wouldn't believe how determined this woman can be. The attorney nodded. This was not his first such case in nearly a decade of work for the right-to-die movement. Nor would it be his last. But it would be the most moving and open. The attorney would later liken the power of this experience to that of having a child. For years afterward every time he went near a hospital, his mind would flash back to that afternoon when he walked around the corner of the hospital curtain with Bob, and saw Emily for the first time.

It was not a pretty sight. Of course, the lawyer had never seen that vital woman with the lovely legs pumping on the bicycle in the park sunshine, or the well-dressed psychologist probing the problems of her patients, or the energetic mother orchestrating a huge family Thanksgiving. What he saw was a puny, pale pile of bones. The muscles long since withered from disuse. The arms arrayed any way the nurse wanted them. That day the withered hands were resting on a little satin pillow, the long fingers slightly bent. Clear plastic tubing the diameter of a pencil ran into both nostrils for feeding. A thicker tube ran to the front of the throat and tensed with each rhythmic rush of air from the bedside respirator. The woman's chest rose, then the machine clicked. The tube relaxed, and the chest fell. He felt that the sounds contributed to a kind of ward-wide low thunder of whooshes, clicks, and then short silences.

The "conversation" was awkward for an attorney accustomed to verbal responses. It was interrupted at one point by a nurse who stuck what looked like a little vacuum inside Emily's throat to noisily suck something out, but the conversation was necessary. The attorney knew Emily was angry at her plight in this invisible straitjacket of disease and good intentions, but it was important for her to sort out these angers. If the attorney was going to help someone enforce her last rights, he had to be convinced this was an unequivocal desire and not some passing angry reaction. There would be no appeal to a higher court for Emily.

A courtroom veteran, the attorney showed no emotion, save for a touch of his hand on hers. He was struck by two things: how well the husband and wife communicated without speaking and how full of expression a motionless face could be. The eyes, he figured. She could look right through someone or cause goose bumps with the warmth of a glance. Bob would lean down by his wife's mouth and read her lips, the slightest movement being full of import. That's all that was left now, the slightest movement. The attorney tried lipreading, too, with modest success. Emily could still nod her head slightly and move it a little sideways, so some progress could be made, though the woman often reverted to eye blinks—one for yes, two for no.

The lawyer had to make certain of the woman's mind in his own mind. He came away believing she was very determined and angry with delays. She had already been waiting a very long time, according to her schedule. The attorney told her that for practical as well as legal reasons there could be no rush. She would have to demonstrate over a period of time her determination to die both to convince him now and anyone else who might inquire later. He wanted to place as much of the ultimate responsibility as possible on her bony shoulders. If everything went well, according to the attorney's slowly forming plans, by the time any curious stranger could make any trouble, she would be way beyond the reach of any prosecutor.

Did she understand?

Blink.

Did she want him to be her lawyer?

Blink. Nod. Nod. Nod.

He could make no promises.

Blink.

But just because Emily was paralyzed did not mean she lost her right to control her own life. The lawyer thought they could do something.

Silent tears.

They would have to be very careful.

Blink.

This would take some time.

Blink. Blink.

Well, he was sorry, but it would.

Blink. Blink.

These things take time for a number of reasons. And she wouldn't want to leave behind any serious legal problems for her husband, would she?

Blink. Blink. Blink. Blink.

Bob dabbed her eyes with a tissue.

What does that mean?

Blink. Blink.

All right. He promised he wouldn't take any more time than necessary. He had to talk to some people and draw up some strategy. Meanwhile—Is this the printing machine? How well can she write on this thing? Meanwhile, he wanted her to write out for him a detailed statement of her wishes. He'd be back later, maybe in a week or so. He had to go out of town. He left her some samples of statements in legal form, then he touched her hands again. He tried to smile.

■

August 4, 1983: Bob had a long talk with my brother, which I think brought out Bob's concerns with his involvement both emotionally and legally in my death plans. He said I was putting all the responsibility on him and not assuming any myself. He mentioned refusing treatment for pneumonia and having the alarm taken off my respirator. I couldn't bear the feeling of suffocation with a fever, but I guess I can bear the feeling of suffocation from respirator disconnect. I never dreamed I'd be faced with such decisions. We were not prepared.

August 4, 1983:
To Dr. D. and Mrs. K.
From Emily Bauer.
Please take the alarm off my respirator and inform the nursing staff not to revive me in the event of a disconnect.

August 6, 1983: It has been beautiful weather recently. I wake up responding to the weather and wanting to be active and happy. I still can't believe this is me—so limited. Bob has taken the girls swimming and sailing. I want to go with them. I want something to look forward to—to hope for. All I have to look forward to is my death.

August 9, 1983: Denise came to visit. A nice change from long hours of TV. She thought she might be able to edit my diary into a book, but wondered if I'd stick around long enough to help. It would be a constructive thing to do. She said she thought I had important things to say and my writing had a special honesty. I was worried that readers would be alienated by my wish to die and the developing plans to accomplish this.

She also said that when she was picking raspberries with Jenie, several times Jenie said that I was at her birthday party. Denise said I am a real presence for both Jenie and Alli.

What she said about a book and the children deeply affected me. And I asked myself if I was sure I wanted to die, maybe next month. I thought about it a lot and with great sadness I decided I still wanted to die.

August 12, 1983: We had a meeting with a lawyer Bob found. A nice man. From a well-known firm. We must make the responsibility for the end my own as much as possible. Looks like I will try to discharge myself from the hospital and dismiss my nurse. I'm so tired of it all.

August 15, 1983: I had a dream where I was warming up some food for Bob's supper. It was Thanksgiving supper. I think the dream expresses my wish to be a wife to Bob, to nourish him. It also recognizes the limits in my ability to do so, as I didn't cook the food. I just warmed it up. I feel like giving thanks to Bob.

More muscles in my mouth are not working. Bob and the nurses have an increasingly hard time reading my lips. They seldom can understand whole words anymore. I bite my tongue a lot. Sometimes my mouth and tongue won't move. This disease is so cruel.

Lewis and Nicole lie in bed or sit in their wheelchairs, watching TV all day. They don't have much fun and they are children. They don't complain or act depressed. I guess they don't know all they are missing. Maybe if I had a more limited life before, I could adjust to limitations now.

The staff has so little concern with the quality of life for a person as disabled as myself. Only private nurses like mine concern themselves with this issue to any depth. Doctors and nurses should think about this. Patients should routinely get attention to their most complex needs, not just food and water and the toilet. Those patients like myself who choose death rather than their present life should be helped to die when the quality of life is judged intolerable by the patient.

August 19, 1983: I, Emily Bauer, say I am a fully competent adult. My doctors inform me I am terminally ill and there is no hope for my recovery, but with the aid of a respirator I may live for some time. I know removal of the respirator will speed the natural course of my fatal illness. I voluntarily make this statement now because as my paralysis worsens it may become impossible for me to express my wish to be relieved from the physical discomfort and mental anguish of my condition.

I want to let nature take its course and to die in peace with dignity. I know my husband, Robert, will take good care of our daughters. It is better for them not to prolong the agony of my death. I hereby withdraw my consent to any further medical treatment other than palliative care and demand that the hospital or any doctor disconnect the respirator and medicate me to relieve my suffering as my disease runs its natural course.

I release Robert and all other persons and institutions from any liability whatsoever for carrying out my wishes. I hereby appoint my husband, Robert Bauer, my attorney in fact to act in my place with respect to all matters, including all decisions regarding my medical affairs and the use or discontinuance of all treatments and the withdrawal of my consent to any treatment. This power of attorney shall not be affected by my present illness or my subsequent disability or incompetence.

Emily R. Bauer

■

The attorney was firmly convinced that Emily's wishes were genuine. Of course, it would have been a whole lot easier if before her illness, Emily had written a living will and a durable power of attorney, stating what kind of medical care she wanted or did not want and appointing someone as surrogate decision maker if she ever became incompetent. But the attorney knew how much Americans dislike thinking about death, let alone planning for it. And this trait did keep a lot of lawyers and court clerks employed.

The attorney saw Emily's case as a pure civil rights matter. Emily was an adult. The hospital couldn't touch her without legal consent. If she could give legal consent, she could also revoke and modify it. Those basic civil rights weren't annulled by a terminal illness and they weren't changed because the person standing by the bed had a medical license hanging on the wall.

Emily's competence could be an issue. That's what Emily's attorney would argue anyway if he represented the hospital. It could be drawn as a clash between her competence to make this decision and the doctor's overriding medical competence. In that legal no-man's-land lay a lot of the difficulty. Which came first? Which took precedence in a litigious society that relished showdowns with million-dollar stakes?

"When to struggle privately and when to go to court," the attorney told Bob, "is very hard to figure out sometimes. Litigation is a clumsy, cumbersome, expensive, and risky way to resolve disputes. And often delays and screwups can make it impossible to achieve the patient's wishes. In these cases you must do three times the usual number of cartwheels to avoid going to court. But sometimes it's necessary when the hospital, for its own protection, insists."

He said so much of it depended too on chance. The attorney recalled a case where a client suffered a heart attack on Saturday. Friends instinctively called an ambulance. His family doctor was on the golf course. The man's brain went without oxygen for at least twenty minutes. But the emergency room got this stranger going again—at least the heart was beating; that was their job. But the mind that made the patient a human would never function again.

If the attack had come on Friday, the wife could have reached the family doctor. Knowing the man's wishes, he would have simply signed the death certificate. Instead, the patient languished for many weeks in a permanent vegetative state. It could have been years, but the wife brought in a lawyer. He quietly told the hospital something surely could be worked out, but, if not, there would have to be a court fight. This woman had the financial resources to do it. Somehow, the attorney said, the patient developed pneumonia about ten days later. Antibiotics were not administered. The patient died again, this time officially.

Emily's attorney knew, though, that the appearance of a patient's lawyer usually stiffened resistance and, like a nuclear arms race, led inexorably to a steadily escalating series of confrontations with each side building up its legal weaponry and stockpiling expert testimony by the megaton. This time, however, his instincts told him that court was avoidable. There just might be a narrow path through to a mutu-ally protective compromise. By the way, he asked Bob, how did you come to contact Concern for Dying?

Well, said Bob, Steve suggested it. You know, Emily's psychiatric social worker.

Within an hour the attorney had arranged a meeting with Steve at the hospital, Steve's home turf. The attorney took no briefcase that day, no yellow pads or stacks of imposing documents. He was just a friend of the Bauer family, an attorney, as it happened, one of those men schooled never to ask a question without knowing the answer. Today, he said, he was mainly just a friend interested in Emily's wel-fare. Was there any hope for recovery at all?

None.

You know, the attorney said, Emily wants to live. But not like this. She wants out and she has been pretty explicit about it. A determined lady. He had talked with her now, oh, two or three times and the woman had laboriously printed out this statement here, which seemed pretty definitive to the attorney. She wanted the respirator turned off. There could be worse ways to go.

Yes, said Steve, there certainly were. He was thinking coma. He was also convinced from her dreams and diary that Emily was ready. It didn't seem like she would ever accept the disease, but death she had come to grips with. The burden of continued existence like this on Emily and her family seemed the deciding factor. Steve didn't think what they were proposing was right. They wanted the hospital, which is devoted to preserving life and restoring health, to simply switch off the respirator. Just like that.

Why not? asked the attorney. The hospital had switched it on just like that. You could argue that Emily had consented then, but that was way back—what?—over two years ago. At another hospital. There could be no argument now over her wishes. She was withdrawing consent.

Well, said Steve, he wasn't a lawyer.

Good thing, the attorney interrupted, there are probably too many of us as it is. They both chuckled.

Well, Steve continued, what they were asking was just not a very humane thing to do, not in this place anyway. Who would the lawyer or Emily select to turn off the switch? Could the doctor or a nurse or Steve or even the attorney be forced to do this, standing beside this woman who silently stared out with those big eyes? Ordered to stand there and watch the chest go down one last time and the eyes maybe open wider and wider as the suffocation takes hold. And then see them close slowly, almost all the way. Who do you nominate to throw the switch? Steve asked the attorney. There must be a better way to find a humane solution.

The attorney said nothing. Steve said nothing. So the meeting seemed over, but not the business. As the lawyer donned his raincoat, Steve made an observation. You know, he said, Emily used to visit her apartment regularly, even with the respirator. She had enjoyed those outings away from the hospital. There was no reason why she couldn't resume them. They might do her good.

The lawyer showed no excitement. He just nodded and said thank you.

"We are gathered here in the hospital room of Emily Bauer," said her attorney, gathered like the others standing silently but alert to every detail, as if they were already in a funeral parlor. "Mrs. Bauer is present. And her husband, Robert. So is Dr. D., her nurse, Steve N., a social worker here at the hospital, and a secretary–notary public from my office, who will transcribe and notarize these proceedings.

"Doctor, has there been any change in Mrs. Bauer's condition?"

"No."

"Is she mentally competent to understand these proceedings?"

"Yes."

"Is she on any medication that would affect her thinking or understanding of these proceedings?"

"No."

"We are here essentially to witness this tape that Mrs. Bauer has printed once again on her machine. This is the third time Mrs. Bauer has printed out the same tape expressing her wishes for treatment or, rather, nontreatment. Mrs. Bauer wishes the respirator, which is maintaining her life, be turned off.

"Now, Mrs. Bauer, I'm going to unroll this tape in front of your face so that you may read it word for word and be very sure that it ex-

presses your wishes, that it is correct, and that you haven't left anything out or included anything in it that you want to change.

"Have you read this statement?"

Blink.

"Mrs. Bauer, I'd like you to print out your reply, yes or no, if you
would. I know it takes some effort. But we will wait."

YES.

"Thank you. Now have you made this tape on your machine voluntarily and without any interference from anybody?"

YES.

"Having just now read this tape, is it a correct and complete expression of your wishes?"

YES.

"Do you swear under penalties of perjury that this statement is true
and accurate and that you made it?"

YES.

"Now, I'm going to ask all the witnesses present to sign and date
this tape."

The attorney's plan was a dual one—to lay the documentary
groundwork for a court suit if necessary to force compliance with
Emily's wishes and simultaneously to show everyone at the hospital
how serious and firm the patient was. There should be no doubt in
anyone's mind about Emily's wishes. To make doubly sure, every few
days the attorney had Emily reprint a short message for her diary,
chart, and relatives to have: "I, Emily Bauer, hereby republish my
sworn statement and power of attorney dated August 19, 1983."

Meanwhile, he set up a meeting with the hospital's lawyers. Some
hospitals had begun organizing ethics committees of doctors, nurses,

and laymen to develop policy and mediate life-and-death disputes. Emily's hospital was not one of these institutions.

Emily's attorney did not want to create a sense of confrontation, not yet anyway. An atmosphere of purposeful discussion would do for now. He would make the usual request to turn off the respirator. He knew the reply and he was much intrigued by Steve's remarks about home visits. He knew of many visits home by terminally ill hospital patients, visits that became one-way trips, one way or another.

At the meeting Emily's attorney reviewed the case briefly and went over the accumulating pile of witnessed documents. They all agreed on what Emily wanted. No problem understanding that. The hospital lawyers' responses did not surprise Emily's attorney at first.

The doctor had informed them, they said, that he went along with a Do Not Resuscitate order in case Mrs. Bauer died naturally. The doctor also said he could not in good conscience participate in or approve of the removal of Mrs. Bauer's respirator, for ethical, moral, and religious reasons, because this would result inevitably and virtually instantaneously in her death from suffocation. In addition, they said, it was hospital policy never to allow this on its premises. They would not provide a private room for Mrs. Bauer where something like this might happen.

Emily's attorney allowed a pause to sprout then. He was thinking and waiting. And so were they.

The chief hospital lawyer said he had the highest respect for Emily's attorney and his distinguished firm. They all knew what was certain to come to Emily at one time or another. He hoped the attorney understood their side, too. The institution had to protect itself from liability in court and, worse, in public, where a reputation as Terminator could jeopardize the hospital's future. As Emily's attorney no doubt knew, the hospital representatives said, the laws and court decisions had not provided clear general guidelines yet. Sincere people could make strong arguments both ways. The hospital simply didn't want any trouble afterward.

Emily's attorney assured them there would be no trouble from the family.

Well, the hospital lawyer said, they were sorry they couldn't help. Of course, the institution would allow Emily to sign out for visits.

What happened outside the hospital's walls was out of its control and none of its business. If Emily died during one of these visits, the lawyer said very carefully, the hospital would ask no questions, provided the death certificate was signed by a licensed physician.

Emily's attorney nodded. And they shook hands, initialing their open secret.

■

August 24, 1983: The attorney has met with the hospital lawyers, and they still don't want to do anything, but Bob and the attorney are working on how to make the responsibility my own and not jeopardize anyone else involved. Progress at last. Maybe I can bear up better now.

I did not write for a few days, but instead watched TV and slept. A part of me enjoyed this doing nothing, and another part felt uneasy. I am thinking about things like funeral arrangements. I want all my friends and relatives to gather somewhere happy and sing songs and get up and speak about me. But writing about all this is difficult. I will write more when I've gotten clear in my thoughts.

They have moved our whole ward, and I am no longer near the children. I have asked to be put near them again several times, but the head nurse hasn't done anything about it.

August 29, 1983: A lot of people have talked to me about all the suffering caused by expectations—and that is true. I have suffered from my expectations of physical comfort and full functioning. A lot have talked about acceptance too. I've given it considerable thought. I feel acceptance of my present state would violate something basic in me. Death is preferable to me. I've lived a full life here and believe there is some kind of comparable life after death.

I welcome a state different than my present one. Until my release I will continue my mourning, my grief, my work. I know my abundant tears upset some people and make them interpret I must not really want to die. To me, my tears express my recognition of the implications of my present state, and my death. I feel my loss is great and my crying necessary. Grief has a deep influence. It should not be given up too quickly, as it reflects a confrontation with how things really are. I am at peace with myself and don't wish I felt any differently.

I know you, my loved ones, don't want me to die, but I don't want to live this way.

September 1, 1983: I want to write about something happy. I went home for both girls' birthdays. Everyone said I should get out more for myself and to help with the arrangements.

Both girls did just what they wanted all day. Jenie even took a bath to try out a new toy. Bob spoke of what a superb child she is and how I should be very proud of her. I took it in part as his way of saying thank you.

After their naps the girls played a lot with Bob's sister and she does all the things I would do. She gave Jenie a magic wand and lots of ideas for using it. Jenie likes playing a baby, and Bob's sister cuddled her like a baby, as I would have done and wanted to do. Jenie enjoyed telling Alli she couldn't play with her new toys. On the playground, they were both very self-assured.

Alli showed off her skills on the jungle gym. And she impressed everyone with her knowledge of nursery rhymes. She cried some when Jenie wouldn't share the toys. When asked what she wanted to be when she grew up, Alli said she wanted to have her own children and be a babysitter. That shows how fond she is of the lady down the hall who's taken care of them so much.

I look at the girls and feel very mixed emotions. I love to look at them and watch what they do. For their sakes I am glad they are so comfortable and complete with Bob and all the other families. For me, I wish they needed me for something I could give. I am always the observer and then only if someone places my wheelchair so I can see. We were outside and a mother from Alli's play group came up to say hello. We used to have good talks. But that's all she did this time, say hello. She didn't talk to me. There is no talking with me. I find this exclusion unbearable.

When I left, Jenie kissed me good-bye!

■

The silence forced Janice almost to tiptoe down the hospital hall. It must be nap time or something because there wasn't a sound, except the respirators, of course. No one was stirring in the new ward. They had moved Emily, and those two paralyzed children were nowhere to be seen. It was dark in the ward today and maybe she had just overlooked their little bodies in one of the beds. They all looked alike. Janice had flown in for the day just to visit Emily. There would be no trip to Puerto Rico this time. The visit would likely be their last, it seemed from the allusions everyone was making. Janice thought she had prepared herself.

Janice crept up to the curtain partially closed around Emily's bed. She peered around the edge of the drape and squinted toward the bed in the dimness. It looked like a child's room, with the little stuffed good-luck bear and all the drawings and cards hanging about. Except for the green lights of the respirator, monitoring the rhythmic whooshes flowing toward that bed.

"Emily," said Janice, "it's me. I'm here."

Janice paused. There was no answer from the bed. No movement of that shrunken body. No sound. "I'm here," Janice repeated, moving closer to the bed. Then the visitor heard a strange, slow clicking sound, as if a message was being received on a printing machine from somewhere very far away.

Janice moved toward the clicking on Emily's bedside table. The broad yellow tape was creeping out of the device, letter by letter:

I'M HERE TOO.

Janice patted her friend's hand and looked for a fabric pillow. None was in sight. Janice hadn't planned this visit. She had gotten a letter from Emily. Actually, it was an envelope full of paper tape. The tone of the words on that paper had prompted the immediate airplane reservation:

DEAR JANICE,
   IN MY DREAM LAST NIGHT YOU AND I WERE
GETTING READY TO GO TO A PARTY THE DREAM
FELT JUST LIKE WHEN WE USED TO DO THINGS
TOGETHER I FEEL THE LOSS OF THE WAY THINGS
WERE BETWEEN US AS YOU DO YOUR LETTER WAS
SATISFYING IN ITS HONESTY AND DETAIL AND
PAINFUL IN ITS RECOGNITION OF MY SITUATION
LIFE IS INDEED ROTTEN AND I'M TRYING TO
ARRANGE TO END IT VERY SOON I WAITED TOO
LONG AND NOW I NEED HELP BOB WILL CALL IF
ANYTHING EMERGES SOON I AM VERY SAD BUT AT
PEACE ABOUT IT I AM VERY JEALOUS OF YOUR TRIP
TO EUROPE BUT VERRSI XXX VERY GLAD YOU GOT
TO GO DESPITE WHERE I AM IM STILL
INTERESTED IN THE DETAILS OF YOUR LIFE. I
LOVED HEARING ABOUT YOUR FAMILY WHAT
ABOUT YOU? MY FAMILY IS HOLDING ITS OWN BOB
IS STRUGGLING BUT VERY THERE PLEASE WRITE
SOON I LOVE YOU
EMILY

But there was silence in this cubicle of Emily's now. So Janice be-gan talking, as many do when faced with silence, a powerful tool at times for those who are not prisoner to it. Janice talked about mutual friends back home, her sister, her husband, and her memories of the expedition to Puerto Rico the two women shared. Emily had seemed so sick way back then, but that Emily looked healthy compared to this one.

HOW YOU?

Janice talked about her health. The cancer had not returned. She asked about Emily's health.

ALWAYS FEEL PAIN

Janice talked about some redecorating she was finally doing at home. Emily would remember that awful room, well—

TRYING ARRAGE DEATH HOME

So that's what was in the works.

BOB AFRAID.

She didn't blame him. Well, Bob was a strong man. Janice had always said that. So honest.

HONET

Yes, indeed. Yes, indeed. Are you comfortable? Do you need anything?

HOSP NO HELP

You mean, about the business at home?

YES

Are you sure you want this, hon?

YES YES THIS IS NO LIFE

Janice kissed her friend's cheek then. It was wet and salty. Janice dabbed Emily's eyes. And her own.

T R UG EOH XXX

Janice didn't understand that message.

KEEP IN TOUCH WITH ALLI, JENIE   AFTER

Janice nodded. She cleared her throat. She had brought belated birthday gifts for the girls. Cute little gym suits. She'd leave the boxes on the table for the Sunday visit. Okay?

But Emily seemed to be sleeping. Janice stood there for several moments, looking at the remains of her friend and thinking of the past and that prayer she heard Emily make in the sun: "This far and no more."

A few minutes later the clicking resumed in Emily's dark cubicle.

THIS IS NO LIFE

But Janice had gone.

The number of Emily's visitors picked up early that fall as word of the plans seeped through the family and network of friends. They came down the long, cracked sidewalk strewn with crisp, bright leaves that had fallen as part of the natural cycle, and they entered Emily's cubicle saying the same thing—how good it was to see Emily again she looked good today we brought you some flowers, purple did you notice?

Emily seemed further away on those visits. She was getting outside some still. Bob had taken her home several Sundays, for some reason. Emily seemed alert then. Her eyes were riveted to the girls, and only Eleanor saw her cry, back in the hospital afterward. They were deep silent sobs.

When Emily was alert, she radiated warmth to her visitors, even without talking. She'd always ask, right off, how the visitors were. But more often now when visitors came, Emily seemed to drift off. Either her eyes would stare off in the distance for a moment, or she'd seem to fall asleep. But few visitors left before she woke up. They wanted to say good-bye this time. Emily loved their loving her. Sometimes her eyes still showed that brightness.

The regulars still came to visit, of course—Mikhail once a week and Vicky at least every Wednesday, to get that week's tapes for typing and to sit with her friend. For a while Vicky had hired a lip reader for these visits, to give them more give and take, since one short tape could take Emily hours to do. Vicky might massage her friend or just sit and hold her hand as she drifted back and forth. Sometimes Emily wanted Vicky to reminisce about delicious meals they had shared, always ending with a description of the taste of Emily's favorite dessert, chocolate chip ice cream.

Vicky had been highly praised by everyone for her devotion to Emily. Vicky actually felt a little guilty, and as a psychiatrist, she knew why. She had not endured this routine; she had enjoyed it. She had never really felt so good about life, about herself, about her friendship with Emily as when she was in that depressing dying place. She appreciated her family more in those days, her health, her ability to walk and talk. She left the hospital every time feeling energized somehow. Everything in life then became the special brightly colored gift that it is. And Vicky felt intensely good about making Emily feel good.

Vicky knew how deeply Emily loved Bob and how worried Emily was over her family's financial future. She also knew right from the start about Emily's desire to die. Initially, Vicky tried to dissuade her. "Who are we to decide when a life should end?" she would say. "If God wanted you to be dead, you'd be dead. There is some reason for all of this—we may not know it, ever—but there is some reason. You can't take matters into your own hands." The two women had some gentle arguments over that. And besides, Vicky had to admit to herself, she didn't want to lose Emily, whose illness had become a constant in her life too.

One weekend Vicky was in Emily's cubicle when Bob and the girls visited. The friend felt the strains immediately—the mother who couldn't speak, the children who could get no response from their mother, the husband hung in between in suspended grief, unable to mourn.

And then one day at home, soon after, Vicky got to thinking: "I would never think of telling Emily how to live. What right do I have to tell her how to die?"

We are trained as doctors, not gods, she thought. To us, death is a defeat. Accepting death raises such deep moral issues, but it isn't a part of medical school. It was, "Don't worry about the ethics of it, just save everybody." Well, she thought, that's logical up to a point. But we are unprepared to be gods and make these decisions.

So Vicky told her friend she supported whatever Emily decided. She thought Emily smiled.

Vicky did not know about the series of meetings that Emily's attorney was having. After the session with the hospital's lawyers, he made voluminous notes for his files, deleting the names, just in case. Then he arranged through Steve for a meeting with Emily's hospital doctor and the nurses on her wing.

The attorney generally reviewed Emily's case and her repeated requests to remove the respirator. The doctor repeated that he could not agree to that unless her heart stopped first. The attorney said he understood and respected the man's concern. The attorney wanted no confrontation here. This meeting, and a later one with the night nurses, had two purposes. One, to continue to build a careful record of purpose and deliberation for Emily's decision and an upcoming event that looked like it could come in early October.

And, second, the attorney wanted to smoke out any potentially troublesome whistle-blowers before that event. It would take only one person to feel outraged or suspicious over Emily's death if it occurred outside the hospital's control. One phone call to a district attorney or a newspaper . . . The attorney made some deliberately provocative comments, but there were no outbursts. As usual, the nursing staff seemed more empathetic. One or two of the nurses had not seen Emily's sworn statement. The attorney happened to have copies. They were passed around the group gathered in the hospital's sun room, with the friendly attorney noting that the statement was probably very familiar to some there, like the doctor, who had witnessed Emily's questioning and signed it there at the bottom.

No one outwardly supported Emily's desires that day. But no one denounced them either. A good sign, he thought.

Next, the attorney just happened to stop by the office of an old pal, a lawyer who had gone into government as a criminal prosecutor. It seemed a spur-of-the-moment thing, nothing that would show up on any appointment book. They talked about their wives and their children and their golf games, which were no better in the fall than they had been in early summer. They also talked about an imaginary case, hypothetical, the attorney called it.

This case concerned, say, a middle-class woman in her forties, college educated, two little kids, a loving husband. A good family. This woman, though, had a deadly disease like ALS. You know, Lou Gehrig's disease. A terrible disease. It buries people alive within themselves. The prosecutor knew. Well, this disease can go on three, four years or more because of medical technology like respirators and such.

The prosecutor nodded. His father's cancerous life had been prolonged by machines, but whether that was the right thing, the prosecutor would never know. The old man had fallen into a coma before dying. The question hadn't come up again, and the prosecutor did not cherish the memory of his father's death, so he wasn't fond of returning to the subject.

Well, the attorney said, coma might also be a legitimate concern in this case, this hypothetical case. Now, originally the woman wanted every treatment, the full-court press. But, let's say, that was some time ago. Now she can't do anything herself except blink. Her mind's real sharp, though. She wants out. She executes a durable power of attorney, and husband and wife request the respirator be turned off. The hospital refuses.

Now, that woman can still visit her home or apartment or whatever it might be, using a portable respirator. If the woman died during one of those visits, say her lungs finally fail, and the husband or someone turns off the respirator, what did the prosecutor suppose might happen legally, if anything?

The prosecutor looked closely at his friend. He had respected him and his judgment ever since law school. The prosecutor paused. He said he couldn't imagine anyone making a fuss over something like that. It seemed very humane. Same kind of death as in the old days, really, with the family.

That's what he thought, too, said the attorney, who had to be going.

■

September 8, 1983: Alli did a project at school on what makes her sad and happy. "Mom being in the hospital," was what makes her sad, and "seeing Mom in the hospital" and "when Dad hugs me" are what make her happy. I know she is going to miss me, and I think a lot about that. I can't bear what I would have to bear to live for my children. I hope the suffering my children experience due to my illness and death will cultivate compassion in them.

September 10, 1983: One of the nurse practitioners got to talking with me. She said the staff has difficulty understanding my wish and plans to die, perhaps because they are trained to prolong life and they perceive me as rejecting their care. She said she felt I had ambivalence about dying. I asked her what I did to make her think I want to live. She thought about it and decided I had done nothing; rather it was her own feeling of wanting me to live that she had attributed to me. She will explain this to others, so with her considerable help maybe I am still a teacher.

I don't know which staff know about my feelings and plans, or how they feel. Some will respond (generally the nurses) and some avoid me (largely the aides). I know my wanting to die can arouse strong reactions in people who take care of me. One relief night nurse was so upset that she left. Lucy, my day nurse who's on vacation, feels very strongly out of her religious beliefs that it is suicide and wrong and sometimes she feels angry at me. Eleanor talks with me about it whenever I want. Others are nonjudgmental. All these diverse reactions are okay with me because I know there is caring for me underlying them.

What is not okay with me is being ignored.

September 13, 1983: Well, no word on The End. Maybe we'll have to go to court and that will take months. I struggle on, not with any happiness or joy.

I have had another grim night with a relief nurse who ignored my communications and didn't set up my call button. I got a mucus plug, passed out, and was found blue by a staff nurse and revived. If not found, I would have died. It would have been a fairly easy death, and I wish it had happened. All I experienced before passing out was a feeling of not being able to breathe.

I had to weather another weekend without my regular nurses. The staff nurses are not careful about repositioning me after putting me on the bedpan. One day I chose to wet the bed and stay in a comfortable position. I can't believe these are the concerns of my life. So primitive!

September 18, 1983: The last four mornings I spent writing out two copies of my sworn statement. The attorney says I must repeat this now and then. Afternoons I listen to tapes, have visitors, watch TV, and sleep or read. I am tired (or maybe it's boredom) a lot of the time and sleep more than I thought possible.

When the lawyer came to notarize the statements and we had finished, Bob had tears in his eyes. It has been a long time since I've seen Bob cry. I love him so and hope we are gaining something from all this sadness.

Joan stopped by and asked if after seeing Bob and my children, I ever weakened in my decision. I cry, but I do not.

September 19, 1983: I've had some short dreams. I was tentatively roller-skating on uneven cement. In the second dream I was traveling very fast by rows of tomato plants. I remarked on how many ripe tomatoes there were so late in the season. In the third dream I was kissing Bob and feeling his body next to mine. It felt strange because it has been so long, yet also very familiar. I loved the smell and feel of him. I will think about these dreams.

September 22, 1983: I am ready to go and thought I would be gone by now. I have no zest for life, although most days I still look forward to outings and visitors. In the last week Vicky visited, and my cousin and two friends, Bob, Alli, and Aunt Ethel and Uncle Richard from California. It was wonderful to see them all. It is the other hours in the day, the majority, that are so difficult.

On Sunday we went to a fair for the disabled. Surrounded by people in wheelchairs, I asked myself if I felt a part of this group. I have wondered what the purpose is of being severely disabled. I envy most people in wheelchairs because they can use their arms and talk. I have met only two other people who couldn't talk. I felt for them, but couldn't get to know them because we couldn't communicate. I can't see how my condition has prepared me to do great things in another life. I have gained some ideas on how to train nurses and run a ward. I don't know if I'd want to work with people like me, as there is so little one can do except help the person to die with dignity. I, who believed so strongly in change through effort, have been faced with massive contradictions to that view. I don't know the value of this profound learning except to sensitize me to the diseased and dying. I don't understand a lot. I don't know how great my spiritual growth has been. I do believe in God now, although I've had no profound personal experience of Him/Her.

I also believe in an afterlife and reincarnation, so I feel I will be well taken care of after I die. But, of course, what I know best is this earthly existence, which I loved so before my incapacity. I have looked at other realms of being because I was so unhappy and sought understanding. I still feel very tied to this existence, although I can participate only minimally in it. I look forward to death and release and an existence allowing more full participation. I will miss my loving and loved family and friends.

■

The attorney gave the go-ahead on a Tuesday. Everything was in place, he told Concern for Dying. Final arrangements could be made.

That same day the group telephoned two doctors active with the organization. The talk was necessarily circumspect. They had another interesting case, the group's officer told the doctors, a family facing inevitable death from ALS, the hospital wouldn't unplug, the same things as usual. The woman did get home on visits regularly. Would the men be willing to see the family and help?

Dr. L. was about forty then, religious, the father of one, and experienced enough in the ways of life and death to have a few firm opinions. "We have some fundamental misconceptions in our society," he would say. "We think we're going to live forever. We don't teach death. We don't talk about death. Death is invariably a tragedy. At a funeral for a 105-year-old woman everyone is saying, 'It's so sad.' What they should be saying is, 'Isn't it wonderful? She lived so long and led such a full life, with great-grandchildren.' Our society doesn't recognize that the death rate is one per person. That's a fundamental statistic that's unlikely ever to change."

He had been involved with negotiated deaths—maybe a half-dozen a year directly and many others indirectly—for about eight of his fifteen years in medicine, ever since he watched a group of very professional colleagues study, poke, and test a dying man virtually oblivious to the person. Dr. L. realized that day they were doing exactly what they had been taught in medical school, to try to heal. But they were treating a disease, not the human being suffering from that disease. The question, Should we be treating this man at all, was a second-tier consideration, just like the ethics course in school, an elective. He knew there were other good reasons for this—the legal system, for one. "I've seen doctors who have known patients for twenty-five years," he would say. "The man is in a permanent coma. The doctor tells the wife, 'My dear, I'd love to remove your husband's respirator, but the law doesn't permit it.' That doctor was using the law as a straw man, a way to beg off his responsibilities to relieve suffering. And the wife accepts the doctor's advice. He's the doctor, right? Her husband's final agonies are prolonged needlessly. And society picks up the bill." So Dr. L., who specializes in infectious diseases, including AIDS, tells his terminally ill patients, "If you ever feel you've had enough, don't hesitate to talk to me and we'll call it quits."

"They know at the outset if they ever want to go home with an overdose of Demerol, they won't get a hard time from me. Of maybe two hundred patients, only one or two have done that. But it seems to make them all more comfortable, knowing they have a way out."

Dr. L. said he has had many sleepless nights. "I've never had a case where I thought I did the wrong thing. I don't see myself as Dr. Death here. I don't earn my living terminating people. But I have had many thoughts about whether I should be doing this kind of thing in general. These deaths are far more common than anyone realizes. I'm a nice Jewish boy and I put people to sleep. It's heavy duty. I regard what I do as very ethical, compassionate, sensible, and moral. On the other hand, Hitler put people to sleep, too, and he thought what he was doing was right."

Dr. L. is also very careful in evaluating which cases he helps. They must have a very grim prognosis with tremendous suffering, no hope for return of any degree of normal functions, and the patient cannot be merely depressed but must seem to be acting from a logical consideration based on his or her quality of life. "Somebody calls me up Thursday night and says, 'Doctor, I can't stand it anymore. I want to die.' I say, 'Fine. Come see me next Tuesday.' I do this purposely. The patient's initial reacton is, 'How can you do this to me? I'm suffering.' The reason I do it is very simple. A decision like this is a one-way street and it should never be taken in a pained context. I need to be convinced that the decision and its reasons are long-term and broader than a bad day. I once had dysentery in Calcutta and if someone had come to me with ten milligrams of morphine, I'd have been ready to check out.

"My feeling is that helping someone to die with dignity is perfectly ethical and moral. But the law is not helpful in this. And the fact of the matter is that you cannot accomplish these objectives without a certain amount of surreptitious behavior. If you made a public announcement of your decision, you'd be arrested. My compromise is that nothing is surreptitious within the family. I have a ninety-five-year-old lady, totally incapacitated with Parkinson's disease. She wanted to terminate her life. It was perfectly reasonable. She'd had a long, productive life. She felt she had no life to speak of, a bed-chair existence. She didn't participate in society. She wasn't depressed. But she wanted total secrecy so as not to injure her housekeeper, children, et cetera. I said, 'Nothing doing!' Keep it a secret from society, okay. But if the patient wants to keep it a secret from the family, then the patient perceives something is wrong. And if the patient perceives something is wrong, there is something wrong. The patient should feel that what they want is logical, understandable, and supportable in view of their life and its circumstances. And if so, then there's nothing to be secret about. That old lady is still with us. I see her regularly. She screams at me."

Dr. L. talked with Emily's attorney and Bob. He regarded Emily's case as a clear-cut one. Her wishes were easily documented over time. She wasn't like many, in a coma having left no living will instructions on their wishes. "I remember all the cases," says Dr. L., "but, quite honestly, her case hasn't haunted me. Her bravery, like that of many others including the parents of Baby Doe, their bravery to me is not in the decision. The bravery of Emily and many others is to buck the fears of the system. For every Emily with the courage and determination to pursue this matter, there are dozens of others who are told by some hospital administrator, 'No way, my dear, we won't let you die.' So they give up and their torments, not their lives, are prolonged."

Dr. L. was to be the number-two man on that coming day. His assignment would be to minimize any chance of a medical examiner's involvement. An inquiry might find telltale signs of a suspicious sedative. Emily's death must seem very natural. The point man was another doctor, Dr. Y., in his fifties, who was also concerned about the technological directions of modern medicine. "The current crop of doctors," he said, "has grown up in the malpractice atmosphere of medicine terribly, terribly concerned about going strictly by the book and not sticking their necks out. They are technicians, someone who cares for bodies, as opposed to physicians, who care for people."

Over many years his thinking has changed about assisting deaths. He is more concerned about the so-called "slippery slope" argument now, the fear that allowing some merciful deaths will inexorably lead society to slide, Nazi-like, into ever widening circles of homicidal permissiveness. "Absolutely, I'm worried," he said. "I've met more unscrupulous doctors than I care to think about. I would just as soon not legislate permission for euthanasia. That's a shift from my position in earlier years. I'd prefer to keep it difficult and to force each physician to think through his own personal philosophy and then run the risks, putting himself on the line due to his commitment. I'd leave it as a difficult, ad hoc system. That also forces every patient, family, and the physician to band together and consider all the risks and advantages very carefully and then, because it is the right thing, to take their chances together, all of which I have done many times."

Dr. Y. has developed his own standards for assisting a death. "I have been asked to help people die to a greater degree than I feel comfortable with," he said, "and also by people whose judgment and exploration of this issue I question. If I don't understand their motivation, I don't become involved. I must have a real sense of trust in the family. I must believe deeply in them and the patient, that they have done their homework well, that it is not a momentary impulse or a depression, that they made this decision a long time ago and have been living with it and examining it back and forth over time. And the degree of suffering must also be very real. Emily Bauer met all those criteria."

Dr. Y. would have to travel some miles from his office to visit Emily's old apartment at the appointed time. Scheduling Emily's appointment with death was the lone remaining hurdle for the developing team. There were many considerations. Both doctors and the attorney had their own busy work and family lives. Their brief absences would have to be well coordinated and easily explained. Dr. Y. did not want the day anytime around a Bauer family birthday or anniversary; he had seen happy family memories forever soured by such juxtaposition. He also did not want the children anywhere around; if they were ever to learn what really happened, he wanted it to be from their father, not from unexpectedly walking into a room. The ambulance, respirator, and a cooperative nurse would be required, too. That ruled out Lucy. But Eleanor was a real possibility.

■

September 28, 1983: I am hanging in, although not by choice. The doctor who was going to turn off the respirator won't return Bob's phone calls. Bob could only visit early this week and hadn't found out if the attorney talked to the prosecutor. I am afraid this is going to stretch into months, which I dread. I don't want to live through another holiday season. I am trying to see some good in this delay.

I try to read the New Testament most afternoons. I fall asleep a lot, so it goes slowly. Vicky says sleepiness is a side effect of my stomach medication.

I no longer can observe and hear Nicole and Lewis, which is a great loss. I enjoyed listening to them talk and seeing them with their visitors. A new child is in my old space, and I can see her and her visitors but not hear them. The little girl is very pretty and as far as I can see totally unresponsive. Her parents are young and very handsome. They are also very devoted, visiting every day, talking to and fussing over her. I am awed and pained by how much they give, getting back so little. The girl's name is Cassie, spelled out in big letters on the wall behind her bed, alongside brightly colored posters. So much love expressed. So sad. I don't think they have any other children. I wonder why. There are other children, all very unresponsive. The parents visit three or four times a week, which I think is very dedicated.

I wonder what motivates these parents to be so attentive with so little feedback.

September 30, 1983: This past Sunday, like most Sundays recently, Bob, Alli, and Jenie visited. Alli always greets me enthusiastically and climbs up on the bed and interacts with me in some way. Those first moments are the best part of the visit. The rest of the time I helplessly watch them play or interact with an adult I wish was me. While Alli will do things to thwart Jenie, Jenie seldom reciprocates. Bob says Jenie is as direct as Alli is indirect. Jenie does not interact with me at all but is so straightforward with others.

Bob put up some paintings around my bed, and Jenie proudly and accurately exclaimed that five were hers. Bob said the attorney's talk with the prosecutor was positive for me. Now he must talk with the specific doctor involved.

October 6, 1983: Well, another week has gone by and I'm still here. I don't cry as much, perhaps because I anticipate an end. I somewhat cut off thoughts of all I'm missing by saying it will all be over soon. I am weary of dealing with my body and want to leave it. I drool on myself and can't control my tongue—the latest indignities. This is not how I want my children to know me. Bob wrote Dr. Y. a letter asking him to respond. If he doesn't answer, then we'll have to find someone else. I wake up at night worrying about it.

I went home this week for the visit. My brother and his wife were there. The best possible visit under the circumstances. They told me of their support of my wish to die and how they would communicate to my children about me after I'm gone. Both meant a lot to me. I enjoyed seeing them with Alli and Jenie. Bryan plays an airplane game with them where he lifts them in the air and swoops them around the room to their great delight.

October 12, 1983: Still no word from Dr. Y. I feel in limbo, neither here nor there. How can I be this way? Oh, God!

I have pneumonia, and Bob said why didn't I do something for myself and refuse the antibiotic. If he had experienced how awful I feel, the catastrophic nature of that feeling of not being able to breathe that comes with a fever, I'm sure he wouldn't have said that. There is only one thing in normal experience remotely like it: When one runs out of air when swimming underwater. That feeling, prolonged and intensified, is what it's like. I am terrified of that feeling. I could bear it for minutes, but not hours or days.

I have been very upset going over in my head what Bob said. It's obvious we are in disagreement, which distresses me very much. I know he has a tremendous burden to bear. Nothing is easy for him. Not only does he have me to worry about and the children, but also his business. He hasn't received a salary for months, and now that some work is coming in, he says his partners are considering asking him to leave the company because he can't put in the hours they do. He is optimistic things will work out and has good spirit, but it must be another strain on him. He is so fine, and I love him so much. I wish I could make things easier for him by dying of pneumonia. But just as he can't turn off the respirator for me, I can't do that for him. How awful.

October 14, 1983: Yesterday I had another one-position, one-TV-channel day, which I loathe. It was a beautiful fall day outside. I was awake from thinking about Dr. Y.

What is taking so long?

October 15, 1983: Bob, my maternity clothes and baby clothes are with Janice's niece. Get back baby clothes for Holly. Loan Jenie's too-small clothes to Becky, then Holly.

Funeral arrangements: Chapel here. People sitting in circle. Mikhail officiating. Read first part of T. S. Eliot's "East Coker." Ask people to write about me, and they or Mikhail read it. Ask Holly to write of me as a teacher. Ask Bob's sister to talk of me as a mother and artist. Ask Larry to sing, "She's Got the Whole World in Her Hands." Have them speak, too, of my relationship with you and how much it has meant to me. Then everyone light a candle and let Mikhail lead a meditation wishing me well on my journey.

October 16, 1983: I, Emily Bauer, hereby on October 16, 1983, re-publish my sworn statement and power of attorney dated August 19, 1983.

I look back now on those years with Bob and Alli and Jenie and being able to do things with all of them, and cherish them. I only wish that it would continue. I am with the three of you always—even though I am physically separate.

■

The Day dawned clear and brisk. A chill wind from the north had cleared the leaves from the sidewalk as Eleanor hustled along the cracked pavement in her soft white shoes. This Saturday in late October was about to become etched in her mind forever. She had stayed with Emily every night that final week; so many nurses had quit over the months. Eleanor did not want Emily to be alone. She didn't want to be alone herself. The nurse had cuddled the woman. She held her hand and she even found herself humming a soothing song to this frail body, as she had years before to her own ailing child.

Eleanor had anticipated some difficult times that last week. But those days Emily had really been very easy to care for. She was remarkably calm, almost serene, ever since Bob's visit the previous weekend. That was when Bob had asked Eleanor if she could please work the next Saturday. It was special. They were going to take Emily home for a visit. Eleanor agreed, knowing what that meant. So did Lucy, who had been so impressed with Emily's sudden peacefulness that she seemed reconciled to the inevitable, too, even if it was scheduled. "Emily has been a long time suffering," she told Eleanor. And Eleanor had agreed.

As Emily grew increasingly calm, listening to classical musical tapes for hours on end instead of watching TV or writing, those around her who knew about Saturday grew more tense. Eleanor considered herself a professional. She had lost patients before. Anyone sick is sad. But the nurse nearly lost control of herself that previous weekend when the children made their last visit, unknowing. They had played around as usual, doing puzzles and drawings, and Eleanor had turned Emily's wheelchair wherever the children's activities took them. Bob

236

had looked absolutely drained. Emily was in remarkable control of her tears, even after her husband whispered something in her ear. But as the girls were leaving, Emily grew very agitated. Bob had insisted they both kiss Mom this time and he had, too. They were walking away when Emily's fingers moved faintly to ring her bell time after time and she blinked constantly until Eleanor leaned down by her mouth.

"What is it, hon?"

Emily's lips barely moved. It was impossible to decipher, although she was repeating the same word or phrase over and over. Bob came back to the bed while the girls waited by the curtain opening. Both adults stared at Emily's mouth for agonizing moments guessing sounds and looking for the confirming blink. But every time they were wrong. Then, it came to Eleanor, who froze with the realization. She hadn't read the lips. But she knew. Eleanor straightened up and turned to Alli and Jenie.

"Your mom says, 'Good-bye.'"

Now, early on this chilly Saturday morning, after a few hours of sleep at home, Eleanor was making her way back to Emily's bedside. Nervous and tense, the nurse found it hard to look hospital colleagues in the face. She seemed unusually consumed by busywork, gathering all the papers of instructions and doctors' phone numbers for any emergency, straightening things several times, and talking with another nurse about what Emily should be fed that afternoon when she returned, as if she would. Eleanor also laid out Emily's clothes hours before the van and respirator were due to arrive.

Eleanor dressed Emily in a burgundy jacket and slacks outfit with a white blouse and matching shoes, stuffed with tissue because it seemed the shoes had become too big. Eleanor combed the woman's long hair out to soften her gaunt look, gathering some of it in the back with a clip. And, once more, she made up Emily's face, adding a little color for an outing.

When Emily, Eleanor, and Bill, the van driver, arrived at the Bauer family's home not long after eleven, the apartment was as tidy as a man would think to make it. Bob had placed numerous candles about the cramped room, which he was lighting as Eleanor came through the apartment door, backward, followed by Bill pushing the wheel-chair. Bill lifted Emily from the wheelchair onto the familiar couch with the overstuffed pillows. Eleanor maneuvered the respirator and hose next to Emily. Bill left then, to return at four for Mrs. Bauer's trip back to the hospital. The children had left for relatives' the night before.

After the big wooden dining table, the couch was probably Emily's favorite piece of furniture, a gift for herself years before, as carefully chosen as any gifts for her friends. She and Bob had made love there a few times, when the wine and the hour and their brand-new intimacy had suggested it. They had sat there, too, with Emily's lithe legs curled up under her, that rainy night after she had first stumbled in the street, way back at the other end of that long road.

Almost immediately, there was a knock on the door. It must be one of the handful of friends expected soon. It wasn't. It was a stranger, a tall, handsome man in an overcoat, well dressed, very serious, but warm. He introduced himself as Dr. L. and said he had just stopped by to see how Emily was, which was a little surprising because he was one of the few doctors in that city that Emily had not seen at one time or another.

Bob didn't seem to know him well either, but he was nice and only stayed a couple of minutes. Before he left, the man handed Bob a slip of paper with his phone number on it, just in case Bob needed to call him later. Or had he said, when Bob called him later? Anyway, Emily couldn't ask any questions because she was a long way from her print-ing machine. Soon she was occupied motionlessly monitoring other arrivals to that tiny apartment.

They came just as she had asked—three of Emily's friends, Bob's son and sister, his best friend from theater days, and then Mikhail. Vicky wasn't there. She had gone to the country that day to stroll through the woods with her family, thinking about someone who could no longer do that. Vicky had not checked her answering ma-chine the previous night—perhaps it was an oversight—so she had not heard Bob's voice inviting her to the Bauers' apartment Saturday noon—Emily was coming home for a visit. Judging by the tone of his voice, it was not to be a party.

When Mikhail entered the room he went straight to the couch. He had met Bob a couple of times before. He liked him but detected some jealousy, which Mikhail understood. But Emily was the only one there he really knew. A few weeks before, when he sensed the end was near and felt the depth of Emily's loneliness, the young man had told Emily during one of their meditation sessions that in a way he thought of the two of them as lovers. She had cried then, as now, her eyes once more expressing what her throat could not. Long after that Saturday morning on the couch, rubbing her shoulders and legs through the blanket, Mikhail would remember Emily as the best conversationalist he had ever known, even though he never heard her utter a word.

The small amount of food Bob had laid out was left by the kitchen, untouched. Bob was struck by Emily's calmness. He had not seen her eyes so bright and happy in three years. But he also seemed worried, preoccupied, unusually attentive to his guests. He had awakened very early that morning or, rather, very late the previous night, a nervous habit that was to continue for a long while. At the first instant of wakefulness, this Saturday had seemed like any other long, painful day. But immediately it struck him: Was this really the end of something bad or the start of something bad? Or both?

The friends and family hovered self-consciously around the couch, around Emily, speaking softly but not listening hard. The respirator's whoosh seemed to cow people. There was a sense of travel, a sense that Emily was not just leaving them but was journeying on somewhere. But they were afraid, too, for Emily, for Bob, for themselves, and for anticipating a sense of relief for their friend on the couch and each other. They had been through a lot together and separately, much more than any of them would be able to remember later. The mind has a way of doing that. They did not know exactly what was to happen next. But they knew someone else was expected—and soon. It was after twelve.

The phone rang once. Bob's son answered. It was Emily's brother and his wife. They were at the airport, en route. Bob's son told them everything was going smoothly.

Emily's favorite music was playing on the stereo, Bach's "Passion According to St. Matthew." Its somber strains were interrupted briefly by the harsh rasp of the intercom. The doorman was calling

Bob. A Dr. Y. was on his way up. Bob made no announcement to the group. A few minutes later the knock came.

The two men greeted each other as if they'd met before, but there were no introductions around the room. The doctor went into the bedroom alone. That was the signal.

One by one, each guest broke from the others and sat down next to Emily for a private moment. The friend spoke. Emily stared. The others pretended not to look. Some took her right hand and stroked it. One or two kissed it, the others put their lips to her face. Eleanor said nothing; it had all been said already. In a few months, for many months, the private nurse would go back to the same hospital to the same ward on another assignment, as medical escort for Lewis and Nicole, who were starting a special school. Every morning Eleanor would walk by all those cubicles, looking straight ahead, until she passed Emily's old bed. The nurse always looked at that one. But she recognized no one; the patients came and went continuously. Eleanor's kiss that last Saturday lasted longer than usual.

Bob's bachelor friend took Emily's hand tightly. He'd found himself experiencing more intense feelings in recent months and now he was near tears. He and Emily had not been good friends at first. He didn't like her bossiness, and she saw him as a link to her husband's past life, as second wives often do. But they had grown closer over time. While he wasn't much for hospital visits—too confining, he said—Emily knew that he had lavished countless hours on her daughters; this "uncle" had shown up in some of their drawings. The friend tried to think of something significant to say to Emily, something that would be sympathetic and kind and maybe a little droll; she had liked to laugh. What came out of his mouth was, "Have a good trip."

A few told Emily how much they loved her and what she had meant to them. The eyes of their friend said she reciprocated. "See you soon," said one who thought the determined and orchestrated manner of Emily's passing suited her personality perfectly, as did her refusal to do it sooner. For long minutes one friend cried uncontrollably over the loss of Emily, then stopped, suddenly feeling a tremendous relief with the realization that she had lost Emily a long time before. "I love you," Mikhail told her, "and I'll be thinking of you."

Bob's other sister was not there; her son was being married that same hour. The previous week, when the sister heard about the approaching Saturday, she had written Emily a long letter and taken it out to the mailbox late that same night. The letter was waiting for Emily back at the hospital then. It would be returned to sender in a few weeks with the purple notation "Patient Deceased" stamped boldly on the front. The letters on that rubber hospital stamp were badly worn.

The friends then drifted from the apartment, talking softly. Virtually all found themselves savoring life more. For days, their hugs were more enthusiastic. For weeks, their appreciation of walking and talking was deeper. For months, their thankfulness for health was intense. For ever, their belief that quick death is a mercy would be unshakable. Each carried their own personal memories, carefully packed and preserved. For years, one would think of Emily whenever she saw the color purple, which for her carried a depth and sense of rejoicing. For one, the trigger was the word "motherhood." For another who would receive Jenie's old baby books, it was one volume about butterflies. It was inscribed, "To Jenie, on her Second Birthday, With All My Love, Mommy." But it wasn't Emily's handwriting.

The friends would go to a nearby restaurant that Saturday, where their orders indicated little hunger. For some, whatever dish they ordered that day would become associated with Emily's memory.

Left behind in the apartment, each alone, were Bob and Emily and Dr. Y. The doctor had been struck by the sight of Emily—her gaunt body, bony and so shrunken that the head now seemed far too large for the frame. He was, of course, intimately familiar with the physical ravages of disease, but from the stories he had heard about Emily, he had anticipated a more powerful physical presence. The only powerful thing about this person on the couch was her eyes, big, bulging, and, he thought, most expressive.

He then explained to Emily what would happen—a long, slow injection of Thorazine. She would feel a little prick from the needle, then a tingle in her arm and, almost immediately, a warm sleepiness that would grow deeper and deeper. She would become essentially unconscious. Only then would the respirator be removed. She shouldn't worry. There would be no feelings of suffocation. Did she understand?

Blink.

Did she still want to proceed?

Blink.

Would the two of them like a few moments together, alone?

Bob said yes, and Emily blinked.

Her husband sat down on the couch and took her little hand.

"I love you," he said. In his mounting agitation of recent days, Bob had not formally practiced what he wanted to say. But now the words just flowed forth anyway. He recalled, through tears, their meeting on the bikes and how beautiful he thought she was but how frightened he, a grown man, was. He talked about their daughters and what fine women they would be and what kind of people he and she wanted them to be. Bob told his wife that he couldn't raise them her way, but he would try to do it their way and they would all climb that same mountain together. He never mentioned the disease. He said it was the end of one path they had started together. She just wouldn't be there for the rest of the journey.

Emily had seen her husband pick up her old T. S. Eliot collection from the table. He opened it now and turned to read from a marked page titled "East Coker."

In my beginning is my end. In succession
Houses rise and fall, crumble, are extended,
Are removed, destroyed, restored, or in their place
Is an open field, or a factory, or a by-pass.
Old stone to new building, old timber to new fires,
Old fires to ashes, and ashes to earth
Which is already flesh, fur and faeces,
Bone of man and beast, cornstalk and leaf.
Houses live and die: there is a time for building
And a time for living and for generation
And a time for the wind to break the loosened pane
And to shake the wainscot where the field-mouse trots
And to shake the tattered arras woven with a silent motto.

In my beginning is my end. Now the light falls
Across the open field, leaving the deep lane
Shuttered with branches, dark in the afternoon.

Bob would read out loud like that many more times before his family would leave that apartment and move out of the city into an old country house where the floors creaked and the leaves seemed to bury everything each fall when the rains pattered on the roof. But his readings then of those private writings were for the girls and they dealt, not with shuttered lanes, but with two butterflies who travel through the sky on rainbows and moonbeams.

The doctor returned then, to sit by the couch. He didn't know their religion, but he asked the couple if he could read a psalm, Psalm 15, his favorite? And the Bauers said yes. It began:

O Lord, who shall sojourn in your tent?
 Who shall dwell on your holy mountain?
He who walks blamelessly and does justice;
 who thinks the truth in his heart
 and slanders not with his tongue;
Who harms not his fellow man,
 nor takes up a reproach against his neighbor;
By whom the reprobate is despised,
 while he honors those who fear the Lord;
Who, though it be to his loss,
 changes not his pledged word;
 who lends not his money at usury
 and accepts no bribe against the innocent.
He who does these things
 shall never be disturbed.

There was a silence then.

"Mr. Bauer," said Dr. Y., "would you please step out of the room for a moment?" There might be an argument someday in a different kind of room before a crowd of spectators with one person in a black robe presiding. There could be disagreement then over the cause of death or the moment of death or the sequence of events. But for everyone's protection Dr. Y. wanted no witnesses present at this moment, especially no family members, who have a way of attracting guilt whether or not they actually unplug the machine.

Bob knelt down and leaned over his wife's face. She actually looked happy. Bob kissed her, on the mouth. "Good-bye," he said and went into the bedroom.

Dr. Y. spoke softly. "Are you ready, Emily?"

Blink.

He turned her right arm over, looking for a vein. But the skin, draped around the bones without muscles now, hid these conduits and it was one or two minutes before the doctor could find a vein. Just before he stuck the needle in, Emily seemed to want to say something. And Dr. Y. halted immediately, He looked at her eyes; yes, there was something there, something trying to get out.

"I can't read lips," he said. But she tried anyway.

"You," the doctor said, "something you?"

Blink.

"You. Something you," he repeated. "Oh. 'Thank you'?"

Blink.

"You're welcome," he said, touching her cheek.

Slowly, little by little, the doctor pushed the syringe's plunger further and further down that clear plastic tube. Emily's eyes closed slowly. Two minutes. Five minutes. Seven minutes. Ten minutes.

"Emily," said the doctor, "Emily, can you hear me?"

The eyes stayed closed. The pulse was slow.

"Emily. Emily! Open your eyes!"

Nothing.

The doctor reached over then to the faithful respirator and switched off first the alarm and then the power. The sudden silence was deafening.

Bob would be frantically busy again soon, phoning the undertaker, the crematorium, the hospital, and absent family and friends. "It's over," he said. Vicky, who strangely, had fainted about one P.M. that Saturday, would not get this second message until Sunday night. She would miss the informal Sunday memorial service in a neighborhood church basement. Several friends stood up there to recall Emily and her kindnesses and determination. Holding Jenie in his arms with Alli clutching his leg, Bob would read from T. S. Eliot again. He would thank everyone for their support. During one quiet moment he would ask Eleanor, fearfully, "What will I do on Sundays now?"

The girls were somewhat intimidated by the crowd gathered beneath the peeling ceiling paint. But the girls were calm, as they had been late the previous afternoon upon returning home to the apartment and finding a few friends huddled around their father. The girls would have curious questions later about cemeteries and gravestones and why some diseases make people die but others don't. Bob would answer them all, or try to. He would mention, seemingly in passing, how sometimes Mommy and Daddy did have arguments, even fights. He vowed to himself to tell them, someday—perhaps, when they became teenagers, negotiated deaths might be more openly accepted by society—the true story of their mother's wish and her death. "I must," he said. "It's part of me too." But that Saturday in the apartment Jenie was quiet and clutching and Alli, looking at Bob's red eyes, had only one question:

"Mommy's dead, isn't she?"

Steve heard the news Monday morning during his regular rounds at the hospital. He was not surprised. "I was happy for her," he would say later, "but sad for society that we focus so little on medical technology that we force people to such lengths to die." Most everyone who knew Emily at the hospital could guess how she died. There were a few whispers, but no one said anything out loud. Emily's bed was prepared for the next patient.

The attorney, who had bid farewell to Emily the previous day, the first time he ever wept with a client, happened to be visiting friends only three blocks away from the Bauers' apartment at the moment Bob's call came for him. The attorney was in the neighborhood, he had told his friends, and had been meaning to drop by to see their little newcomer ever since his birth a few weeks before. The couple was so pleased that they hadn't thought to ask how, then, the man on the phone had known where to reach the attorney, who seemed very relaxed after the call.

245

Immediately after Dr. Y.'s departure, Bob phoned the number on that little slip of paper. Dr. L. answered.

"This is Bob Bauer," the husband said. His voice was tense and flat. "Emily has died."

Twenty minutes later the doctor arrived. He was businesslike but sympathetic. He went straight to the couch and sought a pulse. He listened for the heart. He checked the pupils. Then he signed the official document certifying that he had seen her alive and examined her dead and as far as he knew, death did not occur in any unusual manner and was due entirely to natural causes.

"Are you all right?" the doctor asked Bob.

"Yes," he replied, "I think so." But he was growing numb.

When the apartment door closed behind the departing doctor, Bob sat on the couch one more time with his wife. He couldn't believe it was over. He couldn't believe it had happened. He couldn't believe he had done this. So he thought back, as he would so often in the distant future, to those last two minutes. She had been sleeping when he returned from the bedroom. She looked very peaceful. Dr. Y. was standing by her with his coat off. The room was deathly silent.

"Emily," Bob said, "Emily, can you hear me?" He looked up at the doctor, who nodded.

Bob reached out then. He took off the respirator hose and flung it away without looking. At last, she was free of this tether. He pulled up the blanket—the one they'd bought together in Italy—and tucked it under her chin, hiding the hole in her neck. Bob began to sob, deep wracking convulsions of grief. He thought it was all over.

But then, as the husband watched in wonder, Emily's eyes opened. They were so beautiful. Her mouth opened slightly. Her lips moved.

"Thank you," they said, faintly, and then she was gone.

Bob's jaw fell. He turned to the doctor and started to speak. But the man was packing his gear and donning his coat; it had grown chilly. Bob looked back at Emily. Her jaw was slack. Her eyes half-closed. And very empty. What was happening?

Quickly, Bob knew. He knew a dying Emily had just given him the greatest gift, a new sense of life. Hers. His. Theirs. For countless hours, days, weeks, and months he had thought of Emily as all but dead already, an immobile shell of a person filled only with determination, anger, and sadness. But now, seeing her so starkly empty of spirit, he finally knew how full of life she had been, even lying there skinny and motionless in all those beds of white. He came to regard that incident as her moment of death and his moment of rebirth.

The friends found him there later, staring silently at Emily, remembering.

It ended with a sigh.

ABOUT THE AUTHOR

Andrew H. Malcolm is the Chicago bureau chief of *The New York Times* and has covered the issue of death and dying in America—the medical, legal and ethical ramifications—in depth for that newspaper. An award-winning correspondent, Mr. Malcolm, author of *Final Harvest: An American Tragedy* and *The Canadians*, has also reported from San Francisco, New York, Ottawa, Japan, Korea, and Indochina. He and his wife, Connie, have three children.

KALAMAZOO VALLEY
COMMUNITY COLLEGE

Presented By

Rick Konieczka